MIDDLE EAST DRUGS BAZAAR

PHILIP ROBINS

Middle East Drugs Bazaar

Production, Prevention and Consumption

OXFORD
UNIVERSITY PRESS

OXFORD
UNIVERSITY PRESS

Oxford University Press is a department of the
University of Oxford. It furthers the University's objective
of excellence in research, scholarship, and education
by publishing worldwide.

Oxford   New York
Auckland   Cape Town   Dar es Salaam   Hong Kong   Karachi
Kuala Lumpur   Madrid   Melbourne   Mexico City   Nairobi
New Delhi   Shanghai   Taipei   Toronto

With offices in
Argentina   Austria   Brazil   Chile   Czech Republic   France   Greece
Guatemala   Hungary   Italy   Japan   Poland   Portugal   Singapore
South Korea   Switzerland   Thailand   Turkey   Ukraine   Vietnam

Oxford is a registered trade mark of Oxford University Press
in the UK and certain other countries.

Published in the United States of America by
Oxford University Press
198 Madison Avenue, New York, NY 10016

Library of Congress Cataloging-in-Publication Data is available
Philip Robins.
Middle East Drugs Bazaar: Production, Prevention and Consumption.
ISBN: 9780190462451

Printed in India on acid-free paper

For my family

CONTENTS

A NOTE ON TERMINOLOGY

This book is concerned with the origins, evolution and impact of drugs on the states and societies of the Middle East. A conventional definition of the Middle East is used for no other reason than that it might be familiar with a general readership: the Arab world, together with Iran, Israel and Turkey. The adoption of too precise a geography in the study of drugs may be disadvantageous. It may result in the loss of a sense of the distances and disparate terrains that can characterise aspects of the supply and distribution of drugs. It can lose an empathy for drugs that are trafficked by sea and by land, and those that are distributed by insurgents concerned with other matters.

The primary focus of the book is ten countries, chosen because of their substantive yet contrasting experiences with different aspects of drugs, from cultivation, through consumption and trafficking, to state responses and the final incorporation of drugs into the cultures of the different societies. Case selection decisions were taken on the basis of the author's judgement, based on fifteen or more years of working in this broad area, and more than thirty-five years working on the wider Middle East. They were as much a reflection of feasibility as importance. The aim of this work is to establish ten very different narratives of society and state experience, and their engagement with drugs, and, by contrasting them, to provide dynamic insight.

Defining 'drugs' is a thornier issue. Most of the drugs I am looking at fall into the category of illegal drugs. That is, they are considered to be illicit in the legal systems in which they may be found. That can result in decisions about inclusion that are excessively restrictive. Take, for example, qat (also spelt kat or khat in Yemen).[1] In that country, qat is not illegal. Indeed, its licit nature explains why the country is able to produce so much of the narcotic, in large and multiple harvests. Most of the drugs I am concerned with are 'dangerous drugs', but there is an increasingly vigorous debate about what constitutes 'danger'. Some argue that drugs are more dangerous when they are criminalised, and their distribution is effectively passed into the hands of organised criminality. It is frequently pointed out that this is when various forms of violence can enter the frame. It is not the job of this work to weigh into such a debate. Others have and will again exchange salvos on the subject. Suffice it to say that most of the debates in the Atlantic countries remain untroubled by such exchanges.

I began my interest in drugs in the Middle East with a preoccupation with 'hard drugs', primarily heroin[2] and to a lesser degree cocaine,[3] reflecting their importance and availability in the region. But these hardly begin to approximate the region's engagement with drugs. Cannabis-related drugs,[4] and its various by-products, notably hashish,[5] continue to be the dominant drug of use in the region. So much so that hashish has in some societies, such as parts of Egypt, become part of the very identity of its people. Field research has persuaded me to take synthetic drugs—such as the opioid Tramadol, and the amphetamine Captagon—more seriously. This applies to the realm of administrative legality, and has had an increasingly profound impact on the younger people from the region. Perhaps the last word on this subject, at least for the moment, is that this book is preoccupied with all of the drugs one finds in the Middle East—hard and soft; licit and illicit—where they profoundly and continuously exercise its people.

ACKNOWLEDGEMENTS

In a realm so thoroughly illegal, and where organised crime and violent conduct is never far away, one must inevitably be careful whom to thank and for what. Given the relatively unusual nature of research into drugs in the Middle East, perhaps the loudest thank you needs to go to those who kindled my original interest in the subject. A changing group of Masters and doctoral students have remembered my interest in the topic and have e-mailed reports and articles as they have come across them. This has enabled me to cast my net much further than otherwise it would have been.

Both field travel and project credibility require that one has strong funder support for one's work. The British Academy was generous enough to support my initial work on Turkey and drugs in the late 1990s. They were similarly helpful during the early years of the new century in funding other trips to the region, including to countries such as Lebanon and Saudi Arabia, where I had not pursued drugs-related research before. While on the issue of research funding, I should like to thank the Department of Politics and International Relations for support in the archival work undertaken for this project. I would also like to thank the School of Inter-disciplinary Area Studies for supplementary travel funds.

As ever, it is proper and correct to thank my colleagues at Oxford for providing a congenial and stimulating context in which to think, research and write. My gratitude goes to them as to so many others who must, for confidential purposes, remain anonymously thanked.

ABBREVIATIONS

AA	acetic anhydride
AJEM	Association of Justice and Mercy [Lebanon]
AKP	Justice and Development Party [Turkey]
ANGA	Anti-Narcotics General Administration [Egypt]
ASALA	Armenian Secret Army for the Liberation of Armenia [Turkey]
CPA	Coalition Provisional Authority [Iraq]
DCHQ	Drug Control Headquarters [Iran]
DEA	Drug Enforcement Administration [USA]
DFSA	Dubai Financial Services Authority
DIS	Defence Intelligence Staff [UK]
ECO	Economic Cooperation Organisation
FATF	Financial Action Task Force [G-7]
GLP	Green Leaf Party [Israel]
IADA	Israel Anti-Drug Authority
IDF	Israel Defence Forces
IHT	*International Herald Tribune*
INCB	International Narcotics Control Board
IRGC	Iranian Revolutionary Guard Corps
IRIN	Integrated Regional Information Networks
IRNA	Islamic Republic News Agency
JAD	Jeunesse Anti Drogue [Lebanon]
ISF	Internal Security Forces [Lebanon]
KCA	Keeping Children Alive [Iraq]
KOM	Department of Anti-Smuggling and Organised Crime [Turkey]
LNSADMS	Libyan National Society for Anti-Drugs and Mental Stimulants
MIKSA	Ministry of Interior, Kingdom of Saudi Arabia

ABBREVIATIONS

MWE	Ministry of Water and Environment [Yemen]
NA	Narcotics Anonymous [Iran]
NADP	National Association for Drugs Prevention / Wiqaya [Saudi Arabia
NCCIUDA	National Committee for Combating the Illegal Use of Drugs and Alcohol [UAE]
NCNC	National Committee for Narcotics Control [Saudi Arabia]
NSC	National Security Council [Turkey]
NWSSIP	National Water Sector Strategy and Investment Programme [Yemen]
PKK	Kurdistan Workers' Party
SOUL	Yemeni Organisation for Women and Child Development
UCLAD	Coordination Unit for the Struggle Against Drugs [Morocco]
UNDCP	United Nations International Drug Control Programme
UNDP	United Nations Development Programme
UNODC	United Nations Office on Drugs and Crime

INTRODUCTION

One of the more curious aspects of the rebellions against regime autocracies across the Arab world in early 2011 came in Libya, when demonstrations broke out on 20 February. Trying to explain the spontaneous unrest in his country, the Libyan leader, Mu'ammar Gaddafi, blamed the turmoil on the drink and drugs in his view given to young people by Islamists and tribal figures. Warming to his subject in a second speech delivered two days later, Gaddafi reiterated the charges.[1] He stated that al-Qaeda, the extremist Sunni Islamist organisation established by Osama bin Laden, had given 'hallucinogenic' drugs to the youth of Libya. Perhaps seeking to introduce an air of veracity into his accusations, he stated that the drugs had been given to young Libyans 'in their coffee with milk, like Nescafe'.[2] As well as dismissing the protestors as infantile, Gaddafi also let his notoriously hair-trigger temper get the better of him, describing them in speeches on 22 and 23 February 2011 as 'drugged greasy rats': 'Their ages are seventeen. They give them pills at night, they put hallucinatory pills in their drinks, their milk, their coffee, their Nescafe.'[3] The adoption of such unrelenting invective, gave a credibility to Gaddafi's subsequent threats to exact a violent vengeance against his opponents in the eastern city of Benghazi, and hence justified the consequent international military intervention against the regime in Tripoli.

The twin speeches of the Libyan leader may well have been received with some gratification on the part of the Libyan National Society for Anti-Drugs and Mental Stimulants. An NGO, to the extent that Libya had any associations that existed independent of the Gaddafi-dominated regime, the charity was established in 1994. One of its main tasks was to raise awareness about the existence of narcotic drugs in the country. In terms of the consciousness of the 'Brother-Leader of the Revolution', as Gaddafi liked to be addressed, on that

1

central issue, it seemed to have done a good job. There may of course have been other reasons why Gaddafi was sensitised to the issue of illegal substances. In November 2003 one of Gaddafi's sons, al-Saadi, who was pursuing a career in professional sport with the Italian football team Perugia, tested positive for the banned steroid nandrolone.

Whatever the precise origins of his thoughts on the subject, one may make a handful of observations regarding Gaddafi's rhetorical interventions. First, narcotic drugs had been a feature of Libyan society for a number of years, stretching back beyond 1994. Anecdotal evidence suggests that in spite of the country's nominal alcohol ban, established brands of spirits have been readily available in Libya at least since 1980.[4] Second, the consumption of narcotic drugs was deemed to have been of sufficient seriousness to impinge upon the consciousness of the Libyan leader, who presumably in notional terms at least had other things he could have been doing as far as running the country was concerned. Third, in his simplistic conflation of the major challenges being experienced in Libya at that moment, Gaddafi at least, one must presume, considered the threats emanating from extremist Islamism and hallucinogenic drugs alike as plausible ones.

Gaddafi's rhetoric about drugs was generally received with a mixture of puzzlement and derision in the West. The unexpected references to such substances seemed to fit in well with the widely held caricature of the man as both demagogic and demented. While Gaddafi may indeed have been delusional, one could argue that having the issue of narcotic drugs near uppermost in his mind actually pointed to a moment of lucidity on his part. While it was unconvincing to reduce the sustained challenge to his political authority as a reflection of drug-taking among the young, drugs have indeed been a serious and persistent problem in Libya, as in most of the rest of the region. In his fixation with drugs, Gaddafi was simply revealing an increasingly long-standing preoccupation not so dissimilar from those shared with his fellow regional leaders, from Egypt to Iran to Saudi Arabia.

* * *

There have been three reasons for researching and writing this book. The first is to fill in a large and important gap as far as the geo-politics of drugs are concerned. Drugs in Latin America, the USA, Europe, South-East Asia and even increasingly sub-Saharan Africa are arguably well covered in the published literature. Virtually the opposite is true for the Middle East. There are no region-wide studies of drugs in the Middle East in any language. There are

precious few single-country studies of drugs in the region, whether in historical or contemporary perspective and regardless of language. Those odd exceptions that do exist tend to be mainly focused upon Iran, where drugs is at least
a public policy issue that is taken seriously, and Turkey, where it is merged
with other related preoccupations, from cross-border smuggling to the PKK
insurgency. Even here, such studies are more likely to be historical, that is to
say pre-dating the Pahlavi and revolutionary eras, and the pre-1980 period
respectively. Ironically, much of the material on drugs in Turkish is doubly
problematic, being heavily reliant on translations from English-language
sources in the USA.

It is to say the least surprising that there is such a dearth of published
research on drugs in the modern Middle East, given the importance of the
European market for opiate and cannabis-related drugs, and the location of
Afghanistan as a centre of supply for hashish and heroin. One does not need
to be interested in the Middle East for its own sake in order to be interested
in drugs in the Middle East. Moving in the other general direction to most of
this heroin are precursor drugs for the refining of heroin,[5] and stimulant
drugs, bound for the nightspots of the region, with its growing 'rave' culture
among younger people.

The second reason for working on this book was to study the nature and
impact of drugs on a critical mass of individual countries of the Middle East.
The inclusion of Iran, Israel and Turkey is deliberate in order to ensure that the
study is not dominated by Arab case selections, even if they are inevitably in
the majority. The construction of ten individual country narratives has, I hope,
increased readability. It has also enabled the study to reflect the diverse experiences of the countries of the Middle East as far as drugs are concerned, without the sort of repetition that would be inevitable if an attempt at the
comprehensive coverage of twenty-three countries were to be made. The selection of ten cases for study has enabled geographical spread, coverage of producer, transit and consumer countries, and the inclusion of a range of examples
with markedly different levels of state capacity, from low (Yemen) through
middling (Saudi Arabia) to relatively high (Israel, Turkey).

The third reason prompting this research project has been the effectiveness
of using the drugs issue to generate insightful observations about the state in
action. There have been at least two major ways in which drugs may so illumi-
nate. The drugs issue is a cross-cutting one, which draws many different public
sector agencies, not to mention NGOs, into its orbit. As such, this earmarks
drugs as a public policy issue capable of exploring how and in what form
policy is created, evolves and may even be abandoned.

As well as public policy, transnational dynamics are another area where drugs allow us to explore important factors related to the region, in this case non-state activities. Whether it is tribes with lineages straddling formal borders, transnational organised criminal activities facilitating cross-border flows, or the presence of large, unregulated areas away from the concentration of state capacity, all these dynamics and more may be pivotal in the movement of drugs across borders.

One of the FAQs to be aired when it is known that one is working on drugs relates to sources. Views tend to bifurcate. On the one hand, it is often assumed that data collection will be a risky business, involving possibly reckless contact with drugs gangs and street pushers, during which one will place one's future health at stake. On the other, there is an assumption, perhaps slightly less starkly presented, that one will rely extensively if not exclusively on closed sources for one's materials, in the belief that only intelligence agencies and their ilk can put together a complete picture of the drugs trade in action.

In fact, neither assumption is correct, at least not as far as this study was concerned. The collection of data for this work involved neither three-day treks into various mountain ranges, nor one-sided conversations on park benches in the middle of London. My decision to proceed with the project was based overwhelmingly upon the conviction that it would be possible to undertake and complete the project using mainly open-source materials. Back in the mid-1990s, when I began drugs-related research in the Middle East, there was an assumption on the part of anti-drugs professionals that they enjoyed virtually a monopoly on the international domain of drugs. Since then, officials have become increasingly tentative about the nature of their knowledge. At the same time, open sources have become increasingly important, obviously enough especially with the success of the Internet. Anti-drug professionals have also become more willing to acknowledge the role that regional specialists can play, especially with regard to contextualising country experiences, even if such practices still leave a lot to be desired.

As to the sources of this work, they divide broadly into five types. First, the publications and informal briefings of the specialist UN agency, the United Nations Office on Drugs and Crime (UNODC), received and collected over a decade and more. This builds on the material generated under the League of Nations, its work on the functional theme of drugs a rare policy success. Second, published materials emanating from different branches of the state in countries with a significant state capacity and regular and respected state output in the form of publications, and oral and written evidence submitted by

US representatives, agencies, experts and critics, of which the USA is the largest and, if not handled carefully, the dominant. Most of these sources are in the public domain. Third, the aggregate corpus of reportage, generated by a range of journalists from in-country correspondents looking for new subjects on which to write, through to specialist writers, whose interest in drugs is often as recreational as it is professional. Inevitably, such material has required more weeding than most. With the exercise of shrewd and experienced judgement, this too can be an important source.

Fourth, a large number of semi-structured interviews, that seek to explore the drugs issue from a range of different backgrounds. These have included: recovered and recovering drug abusers from across most of the region; private, public and mixed-sector medical professionals; senior officials from ministries and state bodies, covering health, social development and interior ministries, the latter including specialist anti-drug police; NGOs working in such diverse areas as fund-raising, prevention and rehabilitation treatment; specialists in other areas, such as youth affairs. Fifth, there is a range of cultural artefacts, primarily from film through contemporary and historical literature, though also embracing fine and other arts. Importantly, much of this output is now generated in the Middle East, and hence is more sensitised to local conditions, where these phenomena are in practice to be found. This enables us to see what is on the minds of the creative arts as a whole.

CONTEXTUALISING DRUGS
IN THE MIDDLE EAST

Deep History

It has become something of a cliche to say that mind-altering substances have been part of the cultural and social fabric of life in the Middle East 'for a thousand years'. And indeed, narcotic drugs are hardly a recent phenomenon in the Middle East. Opium may have been brought to Iran by the Sumerians, as much as sixty centuries ago. Opium was known at the time as *hul gil*, the 'joy plant'. Narcotic drugs helped to provide a textured backdrop to life in the time of antiquity. Some of the earliest written references to the opium poppy have been found in clay tablets in the ruins of the city of Nippur, just east of Diwaniyah in present-day Iraq. The Arab engagement with narcotics stretches back at least to the sixteenth century, when nomads would feed it to their camels in addition to consuming it themselves. In sixteenth- and seventeenth-century Isfahan, Safavid courtiers liked to mix opium with wine, an early example of poly-drug use.

Similarly, hashish smoking has been a pastime in Egypt 'from time immemorial'.[1] Hardly an era has passed without some form of drugs featuring prominently in the Middle East. The warrior politicians, the (H)ass(h)assins (the Nizari Ismailis, who split off from the Ismaili sect at the end of the eleventh century), were defined by their drug of choice, hashish, as they went about the violent removal of their political foes. Opiates were consumed openly at court during rule by the Qajar dynasty in Iran. Curiously, opium was associated with the Ottoman lands, much more than it is with Turkish lands today.

The use of opium was widespread, but polite society looked down on public demonstrations of overindulgence, similar perhaps to bourgeois attitudes to wine-drinking in contemporary Europe. Napoleon Bonaparte's foray into Egypt in 1798, and the consequent enthusiasm across Western Europe for all things Egyptological, resulted in a strong interest in hashish. A rarely mentioned reason for France's capture and subjugation of Algeria from the 1830s onwards was quicker, more direct access to the drug production of North Africa. As one leading Frenchman of the day famously remarked: 'We believe we have conquered Algeria, but Algeria has conquered us.'[2]

The Euro-Middle Eastern dynamic changed with the onset of the nineteenth century. The Napoleonic engagement with the region created an unquenchable thirst for greater knowledge about the Orient, narcotics consumption included. The boom in the broader European economy created a lively market for agricultural trade in general, through commodities such as cotton. Narcotics were a component part of this commerce.[3]

In Iran, the main opium-growing areas were in the south of the country, notably around the old city of Isfahan. Iran became one of the biggest exporters of opium, especially after 1853 and the invention of the hypodermic needle. The loss of significant sections of land to national food production helped to cause hardship, most notably the 1869–1872 famine. The nineteenth century provides the backdrop against which the beginnings of a multilateral, anti-drugs regime began to emerge. Turkish opium had a reputation for being 'much superior to other varieties', and, because of the demand for the drug, capable of commanding 'very high prices'.[4] Indeed, by the early 1920s it had acquired a reputation among the diplomatic classes for being 'one of the natural products of Turkey'.[5]

Multilateral Regime Building: Illusive Members

The machinery of international drugs control began to emerge at the beginning of the twentieth century. It did so as a result of the political and economic dynamics of a weak and vulnerable China, with Britain seeking to limit opium supplies to that country. They were joined by the USA, displaying an early zealotry on the subject of drugs control that has typified American policy engagement on narcotic drugs down the years. Though both Iran and Turkey were involved in exporting opium eastwards as well as westwards, the emerging multilateralism of drugs control had little directly to do with the Middle East. Manifest in a handful of conferences and agreements, this machinery was well established, though imperfectly so, by 1920.[6]

The initial inclination of the leading Middle East states of the day was to give the emerging international regime a wide berth. The Ottoman Empire was no different. It refused to take part in the 1909 Hague Opium Conference, which would prove to be a key occasion in the emergence of a universal machinery of proscription. In refusing even to be part of the gathering, Istanbul was not acting out of perversity. It was simply taking a typical drug-producers' position, insisting that such matters were and should remain an exclusively domestic concern. More particularly, Istanbul's stance was based on the perception of its own national interest. The Ottomans were unwilling to adhere to opium conventions, where European countries, whose output of virtually any kind of drugs was negligible, actually enjoyed a substantial international policy monopoly over the production of opium derivatives. The Ottoman position was followed by those with similar interests, notably the high-volume producers of India and Iran. In 1912 Serbia and the Ottomans joined together to resist the follow-up Hague Convention, with Istanbul refusing to ratify it.

The initial reaction of the Ottoman Empire, Iran and India—all producers of raw opium—to the beginning of this process was naturally sceptical. They considered drug use a domestic issue, and hence regarded as inappropriate the intervention of external parties. They insisted on the right to export opium to those states that did not ban the import of such drugs, and to do so without restrictions.[7] The three felt that they had much to lose from an international restraint on trade, not least a significant element of their tax base, and were therefore standing in the firing line. As the framework for control began to harden, sovereign states in the region asserted their interests by refusing to be part of this new machinery. So, for example, the Ottoman state refused to attend the 1909 Shanghai Narcotics Commission, the first significant meeting of its kind; Iran only took part after the application of considerable diplomatic pressure.

Little initially came of Shanghai, other than an understanding to meet once more in The Hague. Again, the Sublime Porte, together with other significant producer countries such as Bolivia, Peru and Serbia, refused to attend. But these meetings and their declarations were beginning to build towards the adoption of a formal regime on drugs. A simple refusal to cooperate increasingly looked unlikely to head off the emerging policy head of steam. The main output at this time would be the International Opium Convention, adopted in 1912, and bolstered by a further gathering and the adoption of a protocol in 1914. Attempts to draw the Ottomans and others, such as Serbia, into the process were tried, but without success. The Ottoman position remained implacably hostile to the baby steps of the emerging international regime.

It would be an interesting exercise in counter-factual analysis to reflect on the direction that anti-drugs institution building might have taken had world conflict and its institutionalising aftermath not intervened. The outcome of the Great War changed the international dynamics of some of the leading producer countries, few more so than the Ottoman Empire. The Ottomans were a thoroughly defeated power by 1918. It was a greatly diminished and impoverished successor state that emerged after the collapse of the Ottomans in the shape of the Republic of Turkey in 1923. The Turks no longer had the international diplomatic strength to be able to face down the growing moves towards the adoption of an international anti-drugs regime. It was all the Turks could do to guarantee their independent, sovereign experience, and that they had to effect through military successes on multiple battlefields. Ankara's role in the spasmodic, global process could be little other than the speed of the slowest mover.

League of Nations

The retrospective image of the League of Nations is not an especially positive one. It is remembered largely as a failure, notably in the number and stature of states that simply walked away from it (the USA, Soviet Union, Germany, Japan), and in its further failure to prevent world conflict in the 1930s and 1940s. Such a view ignores its relative successes, especially at the more functional level, and with regard to the implementation of international norms. The creation of the League of Nations, with its permanent location, its extensive technical staff and its more formidable collective memory, represented a step away from the adhocery that had emerged in The Hague and at Shanghai. The 1925 Geneva Drug Convention was seen to be an improvement on its Hague counterpart, as it provided improved control over the trafficking of drugs.[8] Ratification of The Hague and Geneva Conventions would go on to become the badge of anti-drugs cooperation[9] against which the leading powers such as the UK would judge the actions of middle-power states such as Iran and Turkey. Indisputably, events moved in the direction of a greater degree of concerted and routinised multilateralism.

Though Turkey had not possessed any raw drug-refining capacity prior to the mid-1920s, from 1925 onwards it acquired an appreciable manufacturing capability. And, with its change in economic vantage point, a change in economic interest began to emerge. This increased its bargaining position within the unfolding multilateral structures. It had also transformed Turkey from being an essentially rejectionist power within the pre-1918 context, to being one of engagement (though admittedly unevenly so) and negotiation. Now Turkey found itself lining up alongside other drug refiners, such as France, Germany, Japan, Switzerland and Yugoslavia in arguing on the basis of an evolving definition of national self-interest. So, for example, Ankara undertook to close its domestic production as long as legitimate Western pharmaceutical companies agreed to buy their raw opium from Turkey. In spite of this emerging new posture, Turkey remained well known as one of 'the Big Four' global opium exporters, together with Iran, India and Yugoslavia.

Though Turkey succeeded in resisting the aims of the victorious powers in pursuing its physical dismemberment, it still had to make compromises in order to ensure its survival. The Treaty of Lausanne of 1923, which secured Turkey's continued existence, included such drugs conditionality.[10] An article stating that it was beholden on Ankara to ratify The Hague Convention was included in the treaty. As the post-war political context began to settle down, so Turkish political manoeuvring resulted in the drugs articles remaining unimplemented. By this stage, however, the impetus for drugs control regime building had switched to the forum of the League of Nations, an organisation from which the USA had ironically chosen to disassociate itself. With diplomatic pressure dissipating, Turkey was sufficiently robust to fend off pressure for ratification. It would take until 1933, some twenty-one years after the Hague Convention was first forged, for Turkey to take its place in formal support of an international drugs convention.

Side-stepping international pressures for the formal adoption of the drugs conditionality in the Lausanne Treaty succeeded in creating an atmosphere of perverse incentives, which would see significant exports of opium over the years ahead. As early as 1928, Turkey had been identified as being in danger of becoming 'an entrepôt for illicit traffic'. This was hardly a passing moment. In 1930, it still seemed uncertain whether Turkey would become 'the chief source of the world's supply of illicit drugs and the centre of their distribution'.[11] Istanbul was already one of the worst drug-trafficking ports in the eastern Mediterranean, along with Beirut and Piraeus in Lebanon and Greece respectively. This new reality closely reflected the growing rise in smuggling between shipping, plying the Mediterranean ports of Turkey and Egypt.[12]

Intra-Regional Focus

The Middle East's experience of the production of dangerous drugs has changed profoundly between the middle of the twentieth century and the beginning of the twenty-first. Drug trafficking was in many ways a modest affair in the region in the mid-twentieth century. During the early part of this period, drugs were produced mainly for the home market. These were primarily generated through cultivation, in the form of 'natural' products, mostly opium and hemp drugs, the latter covering mainly cannabis, hashish and bango.[13]

Small amounts of mainly hemp drugs were transported from India to the Persian Gulf. Its target market was the expatriate labour pool from the Indian subcontinent, another way of keeping the steadily growing resource of workers from making its potential political presence felt. The small number of Gulf Arabs resident in the likes of the Trucial States hardly amounted to a market at all. In the early years of the existence of the state of Israel, the assumption was that drug smuggling was an 'Oriental phenomenon', and as such would become less important over time, as Westernisation, in the form of the values of Ashkenazi Jewry, dominated the newly established state from the outset. Hashish bound for Egypt originated in the region-producing countries of Lebanon and Morocco.

The region's main opium producers were primarily Iran and Turkey, and to some extent Lebanon, with opium routinely reported as coming out of Greece actually likely to have originated in Turkey or Yugoslavia. Turkey and Iran could fend off pressure for the ratification of opium production by dint of the refusal of the USA and one another to sign,[14] with both also seeking financial compensation to desist.[15]

The hemp drugs came from Lebanon, Morocco and eastern Egypt. The refining of the former into opiates such as heroin took place almost exclusively 'downstream', that is to say outside the region. It occurred overwhelmingly at the hands of those middlemen who worked 'upstream' of the agricultural sector and the farmers who had cultivated them. Geographically, they were refined in the space to be found beyond the region, as cultivators did not possess the expertise, the capital or the sophistication to be able to do so on the ground. Small amounts of the most potent of drugs were processed closer to the source.

The Western Counter-Culture

The modest volumes of the intra-regional trade were transformed in the 1960s and 1970s, by a massive and sustained surge in demand by the rising generation of the followers of Western counter-culture, who insisted on cheap access to hemp drugs. In the 1970s and 1980s, after a short 'lead time', this demand spread to opiates. Though the demand was never as great for the latter, the profit margins to be made were definitely much bigger.

Drugs production in the Middle East responded to this surge in demand taking place across the Atlantic countries. This is important to note and remember. Western demand created eastern supply, and not vice versa. The best example of this phenomenon in practice was Morocco. Cannabis production took off there, enabling the country to traffic its hemp drug output into Europe, without jeopardising its servicing of traditional, regional markets, at home and across North Africa. It became clear that in Israel Western-style demand would typify consumption levels, rather than the piously hoped for constraint of a Western-style code of morality. Young people with a taste for the counter-culture began to flock to countries such as Morocco, Egypt, Israel and Lebanon in pursuit of a sensualised version of 'fun', with hemp drugs increasingly an integral part.

More recently, political regimes have been more directly badged with drug consumption. The last Shah, Muhammad Reza Shah Pahlavi, was widely regarded as being a user of drugs. The Egyptian leader Anwar Sadat was another leader who regularly embraced drug use. These are just two among the more contemporaneous and prominent figures.

Regional producers benefited from this surge in demand, but only up to a point. It was not the small farmers in northern Morocco, the Beqaa Valley in eastern Lebanon or the cultivators of rural Turkey who began to see their incomes multiply geometrically. The chief beneficiaries were initially the refiners and criminal gangs of the 'French Connection', who were primarily based in France and Italy,[16] though to some degree Lebanon as well. This organised, criminal activity serviced the booming markets in North America and Western Europe.

As far as opiate production was concerned during this time, Iran was largely self-sufficient in such derivatives. Turkey was the only significant producer that sent its ample harvest out of the country and in the direction of Europe, and supplier routes were mainly confined to the region. Opiates began to move more systematically westward, 'making' new markets along the way, but also leaving large areas with no appreciable hard-drugs consumption. From the 1980s the Gulf countries, notably Dubai, saw the primary drugs market alter profoundly. Drug-taking in the emirate was transformed from the use of hemp by expatriates to the consumption of opiates by nationals.

The outpouring of opiates from Afghanistan, which included increasing volumes of refined heroin, resulted in the build-up of such drugs in Iran and

Pakistan. Both countries saw significant volumes continue their journey: from Pakistan by ship; from Iran by land, primarily through Turkey and into Europe, through the infamous 'Balkans Route', but also northwards into Eastern Europe. Meanwhile, very significant amounts remained in-country, in order to feed rising levels of addiction among Afghans, Iranians and Pakistanis themselves.

Not all of the opiates entering Turkey continued into Europe. Some smaller volumes doubled back, and headed south through Syria and into Jordan. From there, they fanned out southwards into the Levant, the Gulf and Israel/Palestine.

The 'War on Drugs'

Alarmed by the impact of growing consumption habits, especially in iconic urban centres such as New York, the authorities in the recipient countries, led by the USA, soon launched a formidable anti-supply strategy in order to stem the flow of drugs from the Middle East.[17] This phase was marked by the infamous 'war on drugs' of the Nixon era, and has largely been perpetuated, though with fluctuating levels of intensity, ever since. In some producer countries, notably Iran from the 1950s onwards, the USA was helped by a strong impetus from within to reduce drugs production. In the Iranian case, it was the level of domestic addiction, for periods utterly rampant, that triggered such a move.

A decade and more into the new millennium and the issue of the abuse of dangerous drugs is still with us. Persistent and significant demand in the north Atlantic countries means that opiates and hemp drugs remain big public policy issues. The demand side saw a surge in coca-related drugs in the 1980s and 1990s. Initially, this had no marked Middle East dimension to it. This began to change, both with the use of the likes of Dubai as a transit space serving transnational criminality and the growth of the Sahel in West Africa as a more direct route for drugs from Latin America.

A Changing Narco-Geography

The east–west routes, the fixation of Western drugs policy makers, increasingly do not correspond to the narco-geography as viewed from the Middle East. The last fifteen years or so have seen the emergence of a very significant practice of smuggling chemical precursors into the Middle East from greater Europe. These are used in the refining of hard drugs, such as heroin. They are manufactured in countries such as Ukraine, and end up in markets such as

Afghanistan, where there is no manufacturing sector capable of harnessing such inputs. To the Westerners who complain about the inability of Middle Eastern countries to control the flow of drugs from their region, the riposte is offered that ending the trafficking in precursors would reduce hard-drugs flows of its own accord.

Drugs and the Middle East: Three Illustrative Cases from the Region

Egypt: Battling the Suppliers

Egypt during the inter-war years provides an excellent example of how quickly hard drugs can take hold of a society. But it also illustrates how effectively even large-scale addiction and abuse can be reversed, and its impact mitigated. In the case of colonial Egypt, there were arguably three components to this success. First, there was close collaboration between various governmental jurisdictions in the region, a process that was facilitated by the strong British profile, whether formal, as in Palestine, or informal, as in the likes of Cairo and Istanbul. This worked to the benefit of both policy and operational cooperation, especially where there was continuity of posting, such as Thomas Russell in Cairo, and strong mutual respect between colonial authorities and local political figures.[18]

The second and third advantages sprang from the first, notably in its institutional innovation. The second is the development of a specialist police force, the Central Narcotics Intelligence Bureau (CNIB),[19] charged with anti-drugs activity. Indeed, it is a matter of pride within the Egyptian anti-drugs police today that theirs is the oldest such dedicated institution in the world.

Third, the CNIB would resort to tactics comparable to those used by the smugglers, including secrecy, surprise and the use of funds to buy intelligence. The man most warmly remembered for such successes was Sir Thomas Russell—'Russell Pasha'—the long-serving Commandant of Egyptian Police, and the Director of the Anti-Narcotics Bureau of the Egyptian government. Though a committed and effective member of the Egyptian administration, Russell could not have turned the tide on his own. He readily acknowledged the need for a working partnership between competent British specialists such as himself and critical members of the Egyptian political class.

In the early twentieth century drugs were not a big issue in Egypt. Prior to the First World War the country was awash with hashish, in spite of cultivation having been banned by a law adopted in 1884.[20] Though formally proscribed, hashish remained the perennial drug of choice in the country.[21] In addition to hashish the country also produced modest amounts of opium. Efforts to reduce the impact of the latter drug were limited, partly because of the tumultuous political situation on the ground, and partly because the bulk of the population—the peasantry—seemed at least initially unaffected by it. The distractions of the day provided new opportunities for drug trafficking.

In 1916 cocaine began to enter the Cairo drugs market. It was followed by an upsurge in the availability of heroin: 'The drug that nearly killed Egypt', in the view of Russell Pasha.[22] The surge in hard-drugs supply owed much to a combination of European drugs producers identifying a potentially large and unpenetrated market and the exploitation of the Capitulations by such criminals in order to escape the rule of law. There were soon anecdotes circulating that contractors were paying their labourers in heroin.[23] The consumption of heroin further aggravated other serious medical conditions. Chief among these was malaria.[24] The number of Egyptians succumbing to the impact of drugs was partially masked by the attribution of deaths to such diseases rather than an acknowledgement of the direct impact of drugs.

By 1920 it was becoming clear that 'the white drug' habit was undermining Egyptian society, especially in the cities.[25] Russell himself referred to the appearance of 'a new slum population in Cairo', notably in the Bulaq area, 'the like of which we had not seen before'.[26] The intravenous injection of heroin exacerbated the problem. But it was also becoming clear that Egypt was bereft of a strategy with which to combat the influx of drugs. The focus of the response was initially twofold. First, to collect intelligence about the criminal organisations and the *modus operandi* of those involved in the drugs trade. Second, to concentrate on reforming Egypt's inadequate legislative framework against drugs, with its relatively modest penalties of a maximum prison sentence of one year, and a £100 fine.[27] Given the typical lead-time involved, it was not until 1925 that a new package of legal measures was introduced, aimed at tightening up law enforcement and deterring those involved in the drugs economy. For instance, the new law made the possession as well as the trafficking of drugs illegal. The main penalty for prosecution was a fivefold increase to a maximum of five years in prison, and a steep increase in fines to a ceiling of £1,000.

Though meaty enough—and some 5,600 individuals were prosecuted during a single year of the new regulations alone—it soon became clear that the margins on the trafficking and sale of contraband drugs were too great for these punishments to have real traction. By 1928 there were an estimated half a million heroin abusers out of a total population of 14 million in the country. Given that virtually all of these were males during their prime (between twenty and forty years of age), that meant that as many as 24 per cent of male Egyptians had sunk into serious dependency.[28] To meet such a demand, nearly 13 tons of illicit drugs had to be imported. In spite of this need, police seizures were only ever modest, confined to a few dozen kilograms.

Enter Russell, aghast at the impact of drugs on Egyptian society. He set about a policy of supply-side confrontation. This broke down into three parts. First, he aimed to prevent the drugs from entering Egypt. In pursuit of this goal, the Egyptian prime minister, Mohammad Mahmoud, approved the creation of the CNIB in 1929. Second, Russell sought to prevent those drugs gaining entry into Egypt from being distributed. In this, he aimed to utilise economic as well as coercive or legal means, with the manipulation of price being a key way of discouraging use. Third, he set about trying to persuade the governments of drugs-exporting countries, notably Turkey, to cooperate in the prevention of the smuggling of hard drugs to Egypt. In targeting culpable foreign governments, the focus was extended to include hashish, also produced in Lebanon, Palestine and Syria, as well as heroin.

In the end, Russell, the CNIB and the Egyptian government were successful in shrinking the consumption of cocaine and heroin, for a cluster of complementary reasons. The deployment of specialist patrols, acting on the basis of targeted intelligence, proved to be a deterrent to traffickers crossing Egypt's borders. The energetic use of the courts in the punitive imposition of fines and prison terms undermined the wholesale and retail sectors in the country, thereby further eroding distribution. Russell's dogged utilisation of the new multilateral machinery to name and shame recidivist governments led him to pay annual visits to the League of Nations meetings in Geneva, from where he was trenchant in speaking out.[29] Finally, the persistence of the anti-drugs effort eventually wore down the resolve of those involved in the drugs economy. Given that the trend in the increase could be dated back to 1920, it was not until 1935 that success against the traffickers could be claimed as a policy goal attained.

Iran: Seeking a Regimen

Iran was the first of the opium-producing countries in the modern era to limit local consumption voluntarily. It did so primarily as a result of pressure from public opinion, alarmed and debilitated by the volume and nature of hard-drug consumption. Narcotics were certainly harder to resist at certain times, such as during the Second World War, when Iran was largely devoid of foreign markets. However, such surges in demand merely added momentum for greater restrictions once the particular pressures for greater consumption had dissipated. Even in the twenty-first century, when hard-drugs consumption continues to be a serious blight for Iran, the problem remains one of external trafficking into and through Iranian territory rather than domestic cultivation and local usage.

During the period that government was responsive to popular sentiment, Tehran introduced a tax on opium production, aimed at the eradication of cultivation. Between 1908 and 1928 this tax was increased sevenfold, but without reaching its objective. In the mid-1920s the British government was making representations to its Iranian counterpart to bring about the more effective control of opium production. A League of Nations Opium Commission visited Iran during that period, headed by an American, Frederic A. Delano. It made suggestions for the substitution of a range of products, from silk to aromatic plants to oleagenous plants, as an alternative to the production of opium.[30]

In July 1928 the government created a state monopoly in opium, the so-called Monopoly Office. It assumed control of the internal trade in opium. In 1929 a new law was adopted to prevent opium smuggling outside the country or between provinces. The aim of the monopoly was to end the practice of smoking opium, with a timetable for implementation spread out over a ten-year period.[31] It was less discerning about its impact on other societies, permitting opium exports to leave for any country provided the tax had been paid. A lowering of the opium tax did reduce the level of smuggling. The government had supervised the opium production over many years, because of the importance to the exchequer of the tax revenue levied. The Iranian parliament debated the monopoly proposal vigorously. The motion was only passed because of the intervention of the new ruler, Reza Shah Pahlavi.

At its height, opium was produced in eighteen of Iran's twenty-six provinces. The value of the crop was only exceeded by that of barley and wheat. Its cultivation was estimated in the mid-1940s to have occupied some 20 per cent of the population. The revenue from the opium tax is believed to have generated around 10 per cent of government income. It was estimated that Iran produced some 30 per cent of the world's supply, though the large illicit sector made such estimates open to question.

As with the Great War, the Second World War was to have a profound impact on the Iranian opium sector. It resulted in Iran being flooded with opium, as its export markets, predominantly in the Far East, were lost. This resulted in the most widespread addiction in the country's history. Attempts during this time to curb opium production and consumption were well intentioned but largely ineffectual. Immediately after the abdication of Reza Shah Pahlavi in 1941, for example, the government in Tehran forbade the cultivation of opium in the key producing provinces of Kirman, Baluchistan and Yezd in the east. Such strictures had a patchy effect owing to the weakness of the central government. It was, however, indicative of popular feeling.[32] In 1943 the Anti-Opium and Alcohol Society, an anti-substance abuse lobby only recently established,[33] concluded that across the country Iran had 1 million addicts; 1,200 opium dens; and 5,000 opium-induced suicides per year.

More importantly from the drugs perspective, it reduced the number of addicts in Iran by two-thirds. Thirteen years later, and the strategy was once again under siege. This was because Afghan and Turkish opium was smuggled in in order to meet the shortfall in Iranian domestic supply. In response, Iran resumed the controlled production of opium domestically. Tehran certified addicts of sixty years and older, and issued them with coupons to ensure that they could purchase the drug. This only proved to be a temporary respite. Owing to corruption and negligence, these coupons became easy to attain, hence failing to regulate the distribution of opium adequately. Opium smoking became, and remains, a sign of high living.

Opium consumption, which had risen to between 25 and 50 per cent before the Second World War, was now estimated to affect as high a proportion as 75 per cent of the population. During the Second World War domestic controls on cultivation were greatly relaxed. The government did little to discourage domestic consumption. Opium could be purchased freely for smoking or eating from the Monopoly, dispensed through every pharmacy and tea house in the country. Taxes were raised, but consumers would not pay the higher, licit prices as long as the illicit sector was an established one. There was an attempt to set up a register of opium smokers in order to limit sales to registered users, but no one would voluntarily admit to being a smoker.

Post-war, the controlled production of opium resumed, with Iran producing three-fifths of the world's licit exports. In 1955, with addiction rates of up to 1.5 million, the new monarch, Muhammad Reza Shah, decided to declare war on opium and ban cultivation. Such dependency levels hardly sat well with his vision of Iran as a modern, industrialised and prosperous power. The 1955 law was the first to ban the cultivation of opium in Iran. Iranian opium production was formally ended in 1956.[34] The ban cost the agriculture sector

$60 million a year. It cost the country $30 million in foreign-exchange earnings. However, it also reduced the number of addicts in the country by two-thirds. Nevertheless, after thirteen years the Shah declared the policy to be a failure. Comparable levels of consumption would typify the last decade of his reign to 1979.

The main reason why Iran was unable to throw off its continuing dependency was that Afghan and Turkish opium continued to be smuggled into the country to meet the surfeit of Iranian domestic demand.[35] Symptomatic of the tensions generated over such trafficking was a war of words between Iran and Turkey, which dominated bilateral relations during the 1968/9 period.[36] The exchanges only waned as Tehran utilised the leverage gained from such invective in the service of its wider interests of high politics.[37] Iran though had learnt a vital lesson: that it would prove unfeasible to end mass opiate dependency if illicit opium was still being cultivated and exported in significant volumes, either from its home base or from its neighbours. This state of affairs was accentuated if the source of cultivation was either or both of two of Iran's main opium-growing neighbours, allowing the simple substitution of its own cultivation.

This period also saw the beginnings of an increased level of violence associated with the drugs sector, a reflection of the growing illicit profits at stake. This was the time of the first killings of Iranian law-enforcement officers over the control of narcotics, a harbinger of times to come. It was also the beginning of the adoption of draconian punishments for major drugs crimes. Opium users were tried and shot within three days in the northern city of Tabriz, a further harbinger of revolutionary times to come.[38]

Narcotics and High Politics: The USA and Turkey Almost Coming to Blows

Issues of 'high politics'—such as diplomacy, macro-economy and war—are supposed to trump issues of 'low politics'—such as culture, identity and resources—when it comes to states ordering and implementing foreign and security policy. In spite of this widely held assumption this is not always the case. High politics is often closely associated with elite preoccupations within a given society, and therefore of limited meaning for the wider, popular opinion. By the same token, the issues that exercise the general populace, such as immigration, often have a marginal impact for elites who rarely compete with such new arrivals in the labour market. Illegal drugs is a good example of a 'low politics' issue that has had the ability to rise rapidly up the hierarchy of priorities for state and society, often quite unexpectedly, and with potentially devastating effects. Arguably, there has been no more serious a context in which this has occurred to such potentially devastating effect than in Turco-US relations between 1969 and 1975.

Bilateral relations between the two Nato allies had already encountered some political turbulence in the early to mid-1960s, over the Cuban missile crisis—in which the USA had secretly taken steps to withdraw its Jupiter missiles from Turkish territory—and in relation to the turbulent affairs of Cyprus—where America did not share Turkey's alarm at the civil strife on the island. In response, Ankara and Moscow commenced a detente that would precede the Moscow–Washington version by five years. The relationship further declined later on in the decade, specifically over the drugs issue,[39] following a sharp growth in the number of American nationals sinking into heroin dependency in the late 1960s. This trend could be discerned both among those participating in an alternative lifestyle on the respective seaboards, but also in the rise in drug dependency among GIs fighting in Vietnam. Shocked at these developments, the newly installed Republican presidency of Richard Nixon decided to make the issue one of national interest. And there was no greater producer of opium than Turkey.

The first response of Turkey to the Nixon agenda was essentially the same as on previous occasions, when its assistance had been sought, that is, to greet American advocacy by promising big but delivering much more modestly. This rapidly frustrated the US authorities, which came to see its Turkish counterpart as venal, self-serving and lacking in compassion. The USA responded by becoming increasingly critical of Ankara in public, a style that made Turkish cooperation even less likely, in turn feeding American frustrations. It also resulted in the USA increasingly lobbying for a complete end to opium cultivation. It was with a sense of misplaced glee that Washington welcomed the indirect coup d'état of March 1971, which saw the incumbent government of Suleyman Demirel replaced by a technocratic administration with a brief to function 'above party', that is to say 'free of the restraints of "narrow interests and party politics"'.[40]

Rather than acting carefully and sensitively towards a natural ally, the USA looked to push its advantage. It browbeat the first of the technocratic premiers, Nihat Erim,[41] into announcing on 30 June 1971 that the 1972 opium crop would be the country's last. In spite of events going its way, Washington overplayed its hand, having little knowledge of or regard for the constraints of its ally's domestic politics. For example, Washington committed a massive gaffe by announcing a 40 per cent cut in military aid to Turkey during a visit by the embattled Erim to the USA.

Meanwhile, a dispute over compensation payments to farmers was becoming increasingly acrimonious, and little progress was being made on crop substitution. With the government weak and largely abandoned by the military, Erim and his successors were increasingly exposed. He was now at the mercy of Turkey's reinvigorated nationally oriented politicians, who sought to navigate a comeback. The opium issue quickly re-emerged as a barrier to improved Turco-US relations, while it became a symbol of both Turkey's stolen sovereignty and its thwarted will to return to parliamentary democracy.

With the technocratic governments failing, there was no alternative but to hold fresh elections, which took place in October 1973. The rabble-rousing, left–nationalist opposition led by Bulent Ecevit seized upon the drugs issue, and made it central to its campaign. It vigorously opposed the opium ban. Turkish popular opinion largely responded positively to such demagoguery. Ecevit consequently won the elections, a partial demonstration of the combustibility of the drugs issue. He then formed a coalition government, before announcing in July 1974 that the cultivation ban would end. At this point the drugs issue became enmeshed with the Cyprus issue, Turkish forces invading the island at Ecevit's direction in the same month. There can be no doubt that the US reaction to the drugs development was a harsh one, launching a torrent of invective from the USA, which was 'prompt, harsh and virtually universal'.[42] After all, America had come to believe that this was a policy issue that had been successfully dealt with in 1972. The prominence and intensity of the Cyprus problem, which resulted in the implementation of a checklist of sanctions, helped to provide an opening within which the drugs issue could be addressed.

In the end, the drugs issue passed surprisingly quickly, a victory for quiet, functional multilateralism. The UN specialist agency dealing with drugs helped to develop a new process for the harvesting of opium, the 'poppy straw' technique.[43] A new alkaloid factory was to be built in order to process the harvest for pharmaceutical purposes. The Turkish state was as good as its word in guaranteeing the close supervision of opium production, with farmers no longer permitted to lance the poppies they had grown themselves, for fear of the surreptitious siphoning off of the raw opium. There would be little opportunity for the divergence of the output into the illicit sector. With the appropriate US agencies confirming a speedy compliance by Turkish farmers and the state alike in September 1975, there was no longer any appreciable poppy output for even the most trenchant of journalists or congressmen to oppose.

On two occasions, in the early to mid-1970s, the drugs issue had come close to blighting the strategic, bilateral relationship fostered at the level of 'high politics'. If that risk had ended up being mitigated, it had only done so as a result of contingency and the intervention of third parties.

PRODUCTION SPACES

1

MOROCCO

'THE GREEN PETROL'

Britain's Prince Philip, Queen Elizabeth II's consort, has always enjoyed a reputation for straight talking, no matter how illustrious his audience. Among the many peoples to have felt the sharpness of his tongue have included the Moroccans, or, to be more precise, the former king of Morocco, King Hasan II, who ruled the country with an iron fist between his accession in 1961 and his death in 1999.

During the queen and Prince Philip's state visit to Morocco between 27 and 30 October 1980 numerous incidents occurred which strayed across the line of acceptable diplomatic courtesy, and the visit was engulfed in controversy. The most egregious of incidents involved what was widely seen as the king's rudeness in leaving Queen Elizabeth unaccompanied for an evening of cultural entertainment. In a 2002 documentary, which included original television clips from the trip, the queen is shown to be visibly irritated by the experience, and unsure of what to do next,[1] as she was entertained alone by a troupe of local dancers. Temperatures had reached 90 degrees Fahrenheit earlier in the day, and it was claimed that the king had spent the time in an air-conditioned building. For Britain's largest circulation newspaper, *The Sun*, it was clearly an insult. Its headline, 'Queen's Fury over Snub', left little room for ambiguity. Prince Philip on this occasion, as in so many others, was unable to contain himself. He waited for an opportune moment before asking his host a very public question: 'Why won't you give up being part of the drugs trade?' King Hasan was furious, and the rest of an acrimonious trip teetered on the brink of bilateral breakdown.

Aside from the personalities involved, the story, which is still told and retold more than thirty years later,[2] is notable for the way in which the drugs issue lies just beneath the surface of public life in Morocco. Everyone knows about it, even British royalty, yet the issue remains a raw one, and a point of potential vulnerability for Rabat. For Moroccan royalty, which has tried to eradicate output, sometimes seriously, sometimes less so, the retention of a certain level of production is expedient if it wants to maintain the loyalty of the northern part of the country at a minimum level of cost. If Morocco's historical record of the last nine decades is taken into account, the loyalty of much of the Berber-dominated northern periphery is essential to the political centre. It is the income from the drugs trade that secures that loyalty. For those who value the political role of Morocco, a country with a largely conservative elite, but where fractiousness and ideological politics are never far from the surface, it is important to mouth the need for change but not to push too hard. For those with a more parochial outlook, including traditionally some of the European countries, the cost of ending drugs production is not always viewed with the same equanimity.

A Touch of the Wild West

Most visitors to Morocco tend to avoid the north. They either head for the western coastal resorts such as Agadir and Rabat, or visit the historic cities of the interior, like Fez or Marrakesh. By contrast, they tend to give a wide berth to the louche northern centre of Tangiers. If they want to take to the high ground they head for the Atlas Mountains rather than the country's northernmost range of mountains, the Rif. They shy away from the Rif, with its stories of shoot-outs between the gendarmerie and drug bandits,[3] of break-neck car chases along the precariously twisting, mountainous dirt roads, and of locals conniving with the police to have travellers arrested for the possession of normally small amounts of cannabis,[4] in order to cover the presence of more widespread crime.

It was not always so. In the inter-war years, artists and writers from Europe and North America flocked to Tangiers in search of a bohemian lifestyle. In the 1950s and the 1960s it was the repressed gay scene that took to the city. The likes of playwright Joe Orton and novelist William Burroughs are particularly associated with Tangiers. From the 1970s to the end of the millennium, Tangiers retained the seediness while losing the atmosphere of those earlier years. Prostitution, petty theft, low-level drug dealing and incessant hassle came to define the place. Incongruously perhaps, Islamist activism also emerged alongside the buying and selling of drugs, united in a brooding resentment towards a state to which it felt it owed little. Unsurprisingly, perhaps, riots punctuated life in Tangiers, especially in the more fractious neighbourhoods such as Bani Makeda, more or less throughout the 1990s.[5]

Far fewer visitors stray further eastwards, deeper into Morocco's zone of criminality, at the heart of which lies the central Rif Mountains. This is the geographical focus of the cultivation and export of cannabis and its by-products. Cannabis, or 'the green petrol', as it is affectionately known in Morocco, is cultivated behind a camouflage of other crops, such as maize. The Rif has been described by one self-confessed 'marijuana journalist', Pete Brady, as being 'Africa's Jamaica'. By this he meant they are 'fierce, resourceful, independent residents [who] live for the most part in splendid isolation managing terraced farms, scant water supplies, and ganja fields'.[6] The Rif province of Chefchaouen was widely known for being the centre of production, a claim to fame it only ceded to al-Hoceima as late as the early 2000s. Other Rifian provinces such as Larache, Taounate and Tetouan had been major cannabis-producing areas at different times, though output has fallen in recent years. The edgy town of Ketama in the Rif claims to enjoy the dubious distinction of supposedly having the largest number of hashish dealers per capita of anywhere on earth. Together with Afghanistan, Morocco has an unenviable reputation as being one of the world's two leading sources of the cultivation of cannabis.

Tourists steering clear of Morocco's north were until recently in good company. No lesser person than Morocco's abrasive King Hasan II refused to visit the northern part of his kingdom for the entire period of his thirty-eight-year reign. His reasoning for this most extraordinary of boycotts was based on two experiences: his dynasty's existential political experience of the 1920s, when the Rif—then known as the 'Republique Rifaine'[7]—was in open rebellion for the best part of fifteen years;[8] and his own experience in the late 1950s and early 1960s, when he sought to subjugate the north on behalf of his father, King Muhammad V, and to undermine the production of cannabis.

The uneasy stand-off between royalty and Rif was underlined periodically. For example, there were two serious attempts to overthrow Hasan II in the early 1970s, from among supposedly loyal figures. Both attempts were perpetrated by Berbers, one of whom was from the north of the country. Hasan's response was to face down the north. He was disinclined to respond by doing anything that might smack of rewarding disloyalty. The feelings were entirely mutual. As long as cannabis profits were not jeopardised, a process of separate existence and development was viable from the Rifians' perspective as well as the monarch's.

With Hasan from the mid-1970s onwards investing his royal authority heavily in the future of the Western Sahara, on Morocco's southern border—another one of the throne's 'strategic obsessions', as one foreign diplomat has put it[9]—his disdain for the north was doubly reinforced. Hasan was happy to deprive the Rif of state support, funnelling available funds to the south. He was happy to let the north stew, reliant for its very survival on funds generated from the illicit earnings of drugs exports to Europe. Unwittingly or otherwise, King Hasan was extending the strategy of the state from the 1920s, which saw the Spanish colonial presence do little to develop the territory of the north, even in comparison with the French colonial presence further south.[10]

A Law unto Itself

The growth potential of Moroccan cannabis really took off in the 1960s with the explosion in the underground drugs market in Europe, and the increase in tourism from the West. This continued through the 1970s and 1980s. Songs like Crosby, Stills, Nash & Young's 'Marrakesh Express' seemed to sum up the free-wheeling spirit of the new drugs culture openly available in Morocco. During this time, cultivation was still confined to a relatively small patch of 5,000 hectares, located near Ketama, even then enjoying a reputation as something of a mafia town, a hectare yielding 5–6 kilograms of cannabis a year.

In 1995 it was estimated that cannabis production in Morocco had grown tenfold.[11] Up to that stage, cannabis production had been intermittently banned by the French Protectorate, which only ended its colonial engagement in the centre and south of the country in 1956. Ironically, it was Spain, France's imperial twin, that permitted the continuation of output from the Rif, which it controlled.

The cultivation of cannabis in Morocco very quickly expanded, in order to meet this overwhelmingly external surge in demand. It remains the case that, as in so many countries of cultivation, precise figures are difficult to come by. Estimates oscillate quite starkly: out of ignorance; vested interest; strengthening demand from abroad; and natural fluctuation, born of the climate in the predominantly rain-fed uplands.

In 1993 cannabis cultivation was estimated at between 64,000 and 74,000 hectares.[12] In 1998 an estimated 57,000 hectares were supposedly under cannabis cultivation. The EU's estimate during this time was 70,000–75,000 hectares. An Interpol study estimated the cultivated area at 85,000 hectares. Still others placed cannabis cultivation for the late 1990s at 120,000 hectares,[13] as demand took off once more on the back of a European market that was now more permissive in its stance towards drugs. By 2003 some 134,000 hectares were reckoned to be under cultivation, rising to 250,000 hectares, an area the size of the British county of Oxfordshire. In the latter situation, as much as 300,000 tonnes of fertiliser a year was being used to support this level of output.

As the cultivation of cannabis increased, so the agrarian sector of the north became increasingly dependent on its production for the limited wealth enjoyed by that part of the country. It was very much a monoculture in its production profile. Attempts to produce tomatoes or wheat as part of an alternative cropping strategy were shown to be an abject failure. A UNODC survey, reporting in 2005, found that approximately 75,000 villages and 96,000 farms in the Rif region were involved in cultivating cannabis. This comprised around 6.5 per cent of all the farms in the country, Morocco continuing to be a predominantly agrarian society. The UN study also revealed that about 800,000 Moroccans, an estimated 2.5 per cent of the country's population, were actively involved in the production of the drug, out of a total population in the north of around 5 million people.

As with cultivation, there are big discrepancies as to the volume of cannabis that is produced and trafficked. Estimates seem to range from around 98 metric tonnes each year to more than 1,000 tonnes.[14] The potential hashish production is believed to be up to 2,000 tonnes; in 1993 some 200 tonnes of hash was seized, of which 112 tonnes were apprehended in Europe.[15]

Alongside the growth in hashish production, the government of Morocco stepped up its institutional involvement with the adoption of anti-drug rhetoric. In 1988 the UN adopted its latest convention on the restriction of illicit drugs. Rabat quickly endorsed the convention to make itself formally compliant. In doing so, Morocco had certainly shown policy consistency, having endorsed the two preceding drugs conventions, in 1961 and 1971. Beyond that, however, it was doubtful that Morocco wished to take the lead. For Rabat, recognising the convention was a means by which to manage and delay pressure, rather than to place it at the centre of its policy response.

At a bilateral level, Morocco and the USA concluded a drugs accord in 1989. Much depended on whether real political will would be galvanised behind implementation. Facing mounting pressure for action from the Americans and the Europeans, King Hasan took the initiative in the form of a 1992 anti-drugs campaign. Some 10,000 extra police were posted to the north of the country. Two hundred checkpoints were established on the main roads. Rabat claimed that up to twelve drugs networks had been broken up, and several of its members arrested. By 1996, however, the Moroccan parliament had still not published the necessary legislation to fulfil the terms of the 1988 convention. In January 1996 a Coordination Unit for the Struggle Against Drugs (UCLAD) was established by the Moroccans. External cooperation was beefed up, with, for example, an increase in coordination with foreign specialist enforcement officers.

Morocco's partners were not, however, impressed. UCLAD was viewed in Europe as seriously underresourced. These new, sector-specific measures were judged to be ineffectual as long as corruption in the country was to remain 'widespread', and government officials in the north 'involved in the drugs trade'. Mule trains circumvented much of the road system. The proceeds from illicit drug sales were easy to dispose of. As late as 1997, the USA observed that it was still the case that 'the Government of Morocco makes no serious effort to trace drug or contraband money'. Indeed, there were no laws against money laundering that would enable the Moroccan government to prosecute offenders 'effectively' in the first place.[16]

Attempts by European states to persuade or cajole Morocco into preventing the production and exportation of cannabis to Europe resulted in perfunctory gestures in this direction and little else. Pressure on Rabat proved difficult to galvanise, especially in the 1990s, when Morocco's neighbour Algeria was racked by a long and bloody civil war, and the likes of France feared the spread of radical Islamism right across North Africa and into continental Europe. With these geo-political factors more intense even than normal, King Hasan II could always rely on his close allies in Europe, of which Jacques Chirac's France was the most egregious example,[17] to defuse such external pressures. The outcome was low-level crackdowns implemented on a periodic basis, to little long-term effect. In short, a situation that all parties could just about live with always seemed to prevail.

BOX 1

KIF IN THE RIF

Much of the cannabis smoked in Morocco is known colloquially as 'Kif', meaning 'perfect bliss',[18] a rough-and-ready mixture of resin glands and plant debris freshly harvested, and therefore at its most potent.

Sometimes Kif is mixed with tobacco and smoked; sometimes it is consumed in a purer form using a pipe called a *sebsi*. Kif was only outlawed as recently as the early 1960s. There are still Moroccans who are old enough to remember its open consumption. Some still resent its arbitrary criminalisation, though this narco-nationalism is passing. Somewhere between an estimated 15 per cent and 40 per cent of the harvested cannabis crop is used for domestic consumption.[19] Moroccans are estimated to smoke 1.1 billion 'joints' a year, that is, about sixty for every adult in the country.[20] In Morocco it is socially acceptable for male friends to meet and consume Kif, especially in the functional cafes of the Rif. By contrast, the consumption of soft drugs by women in public is greatly frowned upon. Whichever way it is imbibed, Kif is usually consumed together with endless rounds of mint tea. For more discerning consumers, Morocco is better known for the hashish it produces, harvesting the resin, or *chira*, of the cannabis plant. The adulteration of the hashish is routinely somewhere in the vicinity of 30–50 per cent, the rest of the drug on sale being made up of a range of additives, including anything from powdered milk to, infamously, goat dung.[21] The hashish sold in the Rif makes as little as $2/gram for its vendors. By contrast, the sale of such hashish in Holland, under 'brand' names such as 'Golden Maroc', 'Honey Maroc' or, in an earlier age, 'King Hasan Supreme', would involve a price mark-up of some fifteenfold. Given that Morocco's per capita income is only around $4/day, a basic starter income for locals of $50/day for working in the hash trade represents more than good money.[22]

A New Regimen

The death of King Hasan II was perceived from the outside to have created a significant vacuum in Morocco as far as policy and governance more generally were concerned. There was never any real doubt that Hasan's eldest son, acceding as Muhammad VI (aka M6), would be the man to take over. But his personal diffidence, his distaste for foreign travel and the conduct of foreign affairs, and the much lighter touch he brought to matters of state, in contrast to his father, all created a sense of uncertainty about the future. Indeed, some speculated about whether Crown Prince Muhammad had even been interested in becoming king.

One of King Muhammad VI's earliest acts was to sack the hardline, long-serving and Hasan II loyalist at the Interior Ministry, Driss Basri—the tough's tough—after twenty years in office. These were the notorious 'years of lead',[23] when Moroccans died for political crimes. Perhaps it explains the initial caution towards the early signs of reform following the succession. Nevertheless, this did indeed provide the prelude to wider reform. If change occurred somewhat incrementally at first, then the same pace and direction of travel applied to the issue of illegal drugs. As late as October 2003, some four years after the accession, press reports still routinely referred to the 'l'habituelle passivité des autorités marocaines', as far as the drugs issue was concerned.[24] A UN-led survey in 2003 stated clearly that 'large-scale illegal cultivation of cannabis in the country remains a prime concern'.[25] Indeed, this had been growing steadily over the past few years.[26]

First appearances, however, proved to be misleading. In spite of the slow start, Muhammad VI was in fact happy to move the country forward, at least in certain respects. Less over-bearing and more forgiving than his father, the new king moved quickly to make his peace with the north. He adopted a range of cultural concessions, designed to placate his Berber subjects in particular. These included the establishment of a body responsible for the preservation of the Berber language, and the integration of this language into the country's education system. There are approximately 12–15 million Berbers living in Morocco, mostly in the north and north-west, comprising some 40–50 per cent of the population.[27]

M6 quickly reversed his father's self-imposed internal travel ban. Indeed, his first tour of the country after his accession, made in a white Cadillac and hence thoroughly visible to all, was to the Rif, the new king being given a rapturous welcome in Tetouan. He responded shrewdly by announcing that he would build a new palace in this, one of the most hardened drug towns in the Rif. In heading northwards, M6 soon discovered Tangiers, both personally and commercially. It soon emerged as the focal point for his recreational activities. The king is now often to be found holidaying in Tangiers, where he is reportedly an enthusiastic swimmer and jet-skier. The potential for turning Tangiers into a modern, coastal resort, comparable to Malaga or Marbella, just across the Straits, the latter the summer playground of the Saudi set, has not been lost on him.

A slew of industrial projects and tourist services have also ensued, in prototype at least. These include a strategy for the transformation of the commercial port, marketed under the collective vision of 'Tangier Med', the construction of a new city centre and plans for an upmarket hotel sector. When finally completed the former will form the largest container port in the entire African continent. It will enjoy a container capacity some 2 million units larger than that in Dubai. Revealingly, some €200 million were set aside by the EU's European Investment Bank (EIB) in order to help in its financing.

Table 1: Area Cultivated for Cannabis (hectares)

2003	134,000
2004	120,500
2005	72,500
2008	60,000
2009	56,000
2010	47,000

Source: Government of Morocco.

A second port is currently being built, in the north-eastern city of Nadour. This city also has a reputation as being a staging point for the movement of drugs. From its eastern Rifian location, less than two hours' drive from al-Hoceima, it is an important conduit for the flow of drugs into Europe. An important reason for developing Nadour as a busier, more versatile port is to try to incentivise its growth and hence broaden its economic hinterland. With its planned hotels, tourist complexes and real-estate development—all classic money-laundering sectors—new Nadour may simply end up helping the old centre to expand as a focus for a different type of criminal activity.

Of course, change is seldom uncomplicatedly straightforward. A boost in container traffic will also give a huge fillip to smuggling, illicit drugs included, comparable to that which has taken place in the free port of Jebel Ali in Dubai. In the run-up to the inauguration of the Tangier Med initiative, the Moroccan and American authorities have been working closely together to try to minimise such anticipated side-effects. Both training and the acquisition of appropriate technologies feature prominently in this joint operation. Perhaps it is more than just irony that Muhammad VI wishes to turn greater Tangiers into 'Morocco's answer to Dubai'.[28]

If Tangiers was the immediate eye-catcher as far as the vision of M6, the new king, was concerned, a willingness to address the issue of illegal drugs soon followed. In 2001 the Moroccan government announced that it planned to eliminate all hashish production in the kingdom within seven years. The broad commitment to take action on illicit drugs followed in concrete terms in 2003, when Rabat called in the UNODC to help definitively to judge the volume of cannabis produced in the kingdom.[29] This was a bold gesture by anyone's standards. The fact that the country is reputed to earn between $2 billion and $3 billion from hashish production of 2,000 tonnes points to the existence of significant vested interests in preventing such change. In the overall context of Morocco's black economy, in which drugs are the dominant commodity, cannabis-related output accounts for between one-third and one-half of the country's total earnings.[30]

The problem was not easy to grapple with from the outset. For instance, getting to grips with the subject was profoundly difficult when so little was known about the scale of the problem. Take the issues of cultivation, the cannabis harvest, the exportation of cannabis and its derivatives by way of illustration. By 2010, however, it was beyond doubt that the output of cannabis farming was falling. According to the Interior Ministry, the area of cultivation had fallen to around 50,000 hectares, as the figures in Table 1 illustrate. The avowed goal of the state was to see cultivation drop to as low as 12,000 hectares by 2012.

BOX 2

DRUG CORRUPTION

Signs that the anti-drugs crackdown in Morocco was to have real teeth came in August 2006, when the authorities arrested the head of security at the royal palaces, Abdelaziz Izzou. He was prosecuted for the close relationship that had developed with a major drugs baron when he was head of the Tangier judicial police from 1996 to 2003. After a protracted trial, Izzou was found guilty and imprisoned for eighteen months. Around $100,000 of his personal assets were seized. In Morocco, legal punishments are much more proportionate for connections with illicit drugs than they are across much of the Middle East, especially in the Gulf. Izzou's was not the only high-ranking arrest. The son of a former president of Mauritania, Khouna Ould Haidalla, was caught trying to smuggle 18 kilograms of cocaine into Morocco, an early sign that north-west Africa was becoming a conduit for growing levels of trafficking from South America. He was convicted in October 2008 and sentenced to seven years in jail. December the previous year had seen the dramatic escape from Kenitra prison in the north of

---

Mohamed Taleb Ahmed, aka 'El Nene', the little kid, illustrating that in Morocco apprehending drugs-based criminals has not been the only challenge for the state. His flight was expedited by local prison guards, whose families were almost certainly in receipt of the patronage of the traffickers. The guards were given sentences of up to four years for their complicity, while El Nene was recaptured after five months on the run,[31] indicating that the anti-drugs crackdown on this occasion was serious.

Regardless of the base area of cultivation, what seems incontrovertible is that the area given over to cannabis cultivation had begun a marked downward trend that was to characterise the following eight years. Within a year, the 2003 base rate cited above had dropped by 10 per cent to stand at 120,500 hectares. The year 2004 marked the beginning of a sustained reduction in the production of cannabis. With a consistent trend being established over a five-year period, by 2009 Morocco's friends were able to go on the offensive in its favour. So, for example, in its relevant drug evaluation report, the US State Department was able to refer to 'a significant reduction in cannabis and cannabis resin production' in 2010. A year later the *Washington Post* wrote about the 'considerable effort' expended in order to achieve cannabis eradication. Elsewhere in the same report it could go on the offensive, referring to Morocco as continuing to pursue 'an aggressive counternarcotics strategy'. Indeed, the word 'aggressive' was used twice in that year's response. A year later, the Department of State could refer to the 'impressive inroads' made in seeking to reduce production.

Table 2: Seizures of Illegal Drugs in Morocco from 2007

	2007	2008	2009	2010	2011
Hashish (tonnes)	117,710	113,703	187,590	118,168	129,131
Kif (tonnes)	209,445	221,923	223,000	186,630	138,490
Cocaine (kg)	248,775	33,791	22,800	58,400	57,090
Heroin (grams)	1,906	6,325	28,085	4,855	2,006
Psychotropics (units)	55,243	48,293	61,245	105,940	60,917

Source: Government of Morocco.

There are other ways of judging success in a sector where tools of measurement are notoriously imprecise. One of these would include the perception of the drug-importing countries. This benchmark too has favoured the narrative of the Moroccan state. In 2003 the proportion of European countries naming Morocco as the origin of hashish in their home markets stood at 31 per cent; three years later this figure had declined to 18 per cent.[32] Another measurement would involve studying seizure rates, for which see Table 2. Between 2007 and 2011 the level of Kif seizures declined by approximately one-third, presumably because there was markedly less of the drug available circulating on the black market.

By the end of the decade, however, it looked as if Morocco had reached the extent of its potential as far as limiting cannabis cultivation at home was concerned. It had reached its limit, that is, if it did not want to risk triggering the type of unrest in the Rif that had been evident periodically throughout the twentieth century. By 2010 the Moroccan authorities had clearly relaxed the pressure that had been sustained throughout most of the decade. In part, this reflected the continuing problems of a region dependent on the monocultural agriculture of cannabis production for the basis of its meagre levels of wealth. Such a development also needs to be set in the context of the underdeveloped nature of the Moroccan economy more broadly. In part, it represented the manifest failure of the Moroccan state and its partners abroad to develop a strategy for alternative cropping. In that, Morocco was hardly alone. From Afghanistan to Lebanon, the anti-drugs community of nations has failed to develop profitable and sustainable alternatives to the potential of illicit narcotics presented by organised criminality around the world.

Hard Drugs

Prior to the middle of the 2000s, hard drugs barely featured in commentary about Morocco. This was partly because such drugs tended to be prohibitively expensive as far as ordinary Moroccans were concerned, for the middle class as well as the working class, and hence there was no effective market in existence. The hard drugs that did exist tended to be the preserve of the 'party scene'. The exorbitant prices in turn reflected the modest levels of demand on the ground. Social mores were also important. While smoking Kif was regarded as a widespread, well-established and culturally acceptable pastime, the consumption of hard drugs, such as cocaine, was viewed with considerably greater suspicion and distaste.

The balance between hard and soft drugs in Morocco began to change in the mid- to late 2000s, when the kingdom suddenly emerged as a 'zone de transit'.[33] While there were discernible increases in heroin and synthetic drugs such as methamphetamine entering Morocco, it was seizures of cocaine that proved to be the most startling. In 2007 Moroccan law enforcement seized nearly 250 kilograms of the drug (see Table 2), in stark contrast to the 45 kilograms in 2006 and just 1.8 kilograms the year before, though since then seizure levels have greatly fallen. In spite of this increase in seizures, the price of a gram of cocaine counter-intuitively fell from $130 per gram in 2004 to $70 per gram in 2007, according to local press reports. The trend in price suggested that attempts were being made to 'make' a new market in the kingdom. Both trends were symptomatic of the fact that suddenly Morocco was awash with cocaine.

Ominously, these seizure and price shifts took place against the backdrop of Morocco's greater involvement in a wider cocaine connection. The number of South American drug-smuggling 'mules', bringing cocaine through Morocco's main Casablanca Airport, was on the rise, as established by the evidence of the number of arrests. By 2007 some 85 per cent of these individual smugglers were now drawn from West Africa, with each carrier trying to move 1–2 kilograms into the country. More tangibly, a number of airline pilots from Latin America had been arrested since 2005 for flying aircraft loaded with contraband between the Rif and airstrips in Spain. There was no doubt that Rabat was 'extremely worried' at this emerging threat from illegal cocaine transit, something it regarded as 'a destabilising factor', thereby posing a threat, euphemistically expressed, to 'various nations'.[34] There can be little doubt that such sentiments were expressed with the danger of such threats at home in mind.

Since 2009 cocaine trafficked from Latin America, through West Africa and then on into Europe has arguably become the big geo-narcotic story of the world. This threat has become even more pronounced as a result of regime change in Libya, political turmoil in Guinea-Bissau, and a coup d'état and possible secession in Sahel states such as Mali. In the midst of this pronounced trend, the role of Morocco has perhaps surprisingly become somewhat uncertain. Morocco has certainly continued to be important as far as cocaine supply is concerned. But it has not emerged as the missing piece of the jigsaw connecting the Sahel countries with southern Europe, in the way that a geographer might have predicted when it first emerged as a transit supplier. Relatively few Moroccans have been seduced by the supposed glamour of the drug, at least so far. The government still describes the situation as 'particulièrement inquietante' (particularly worrying).

Consider the wide range of damage that drugs theory says the impact of the high end of drugs might have had on Morocco. It is really remarkable that there has not been: a surge in domestic demand for the consumption of cocaine; an entrenching of organised criminal gangs, profiting from the illegal business; an erosion of the relative sturdiness of the state (compared to those states further down the cocaine supply chain); the descent of the cocaine-related drugs trade into ever-increasing spirals of violence, this area presenting a special vulnerability if one bears in mind that the origins of such drugs flows are from Colombia, still one of the most violent countries in Latin America.

How to explain this? The favourite theory as seen from Rabat is that the absence of such extreme social ills reflects the fact that Morocco has indeed not become the 'primary artery' as far as cocaine transit northwards is concerned. It remains the case that other routes are of greater importance to the drugs criminals. Perhaps the relatively successful securitisation of the smuggling route from northern Morocco across into the EU best explains Morocco's peripheralisation with regard to these flows. Potential smugglers have simply been deterred by the presence of surveillance technologies and active law enforcement, and have not wanted to place at risk a more high-return commodity like cocaine.

Such a profile also points to the possible bifurcation of gang operations, and for that matter, smuggling routes. It may indeed be the case that the trafficking of cannabis and that of cocaine are being carried out by different criminal organisations, operating different routes and with different external partners. Under such circumstances switching between the two might not be as easy as students of transnational organised crime have tended to assume.

The European Market

A preoccupation with the supply side of illicit drugs would lead one to the conclusion that Morocco was the villain of the piece as far as drugs production and consumption was concerned. Of course, in reality there would be a much reduced level of drugs production if the demand for such narcotics ceased to exist. The relationship between market and producer in the case of Europe and Morocco is particularly compelling. Morocco does not have a market that is as affluent and as sophisticated with regard to drugs as that in southern and western Europe. Nor does Europe have a replacement market for cannabis and its derivatives produced in Morocco, certainly not an immediate one. Afghanistan is too far away; Lebanon is a smaller producer, the output of which is determined as much by the undulating nature of national and regional politics as interregional markets. As one senior official put it to me in Rabat: Morocco is 'the victim of its geographical situation'.[35]

In 1991 Morocco supplied an estimated 27 per cent or perhaps a little more of the European market for hashish, the equivalent of 52 tonnes.[36] It remains the case that Morocco supplies around 70 per cent of the European market for the drug.[37]

The big challenge for drug producers in Morocco is to get their illegal goods across the 17-kilometre land and sea divide and into the European Union. Once they have made this leap unapprehended the contraband is difficult to interdict, other than in predominantly intelligence-led operations. In 2000 the Portuguese honorary consul in Tangiers was arrested for having hashish hidden in his car, thereby illustrating that virtually anyone, regardless of background or prominence, can function as a smuggler, such are the potential financial rewards.

From southern Spain, organised gangs can transport the narcotics northwards through the country, with the pick of the EU markets lying beyond. The drug gangs moving their contraband northwards tend, in the first instance, to be French and/or Spanish. National officials in such countries have been accused of involvement in these criminal activities, such are the large margins to be made. There are estimated to be some 1.5 million Moroccan expatriates in Europe, some of whom are involved in illicit drugs. Beyond that, criminal gangs from other countries, such as Romania, have been charged with drug-trafficking offences, suggesting that the drugs distribution trade is larger than merely the preserve of one or two nationalities.

There are two ways to try to move illegal drugs from Morocco into the EU: outrunning the authorities; and outwitting them. The former involves the harnessing of modern transport in order to deliver the merchandise across the Straits of Gibraltar and unload it before the authorities on the Moroccan and Spanish sides are alerted and able to intercept or apprehend them. Such vehicles as fast 'Zodiac' speedboats, rubber ribs, helicopters[38] and even light aircraft have been regularly used at different times to effect such rapid transfers. The speedboats, which can handle volumes of up to 2 tons or 5,000 kilograms, have been the preferred method of transportation in recent years. The round-trip journey time to Spain and back sometimes can take as little as forty minutes. American sources indicate that such vehicles are increasingly likely to carry armed guards on board for protection of supply.[39] This method is particularly useful if the cargo is cannabis related, as the volumes are greater than those carried by individuals, and the rewards commensurate.

The latter method involves trying to exploit the volume of total traffic travelling between the south and the north across the Straits in order to move narcotics, literally under the radar screen. Existing transport options, such as ferry services, are favoured, as are the use of yachts and fishing boats, which tend to be utilised for the movement of large consignments.[40] An additional option is to make use of the two Spanish enclaves of Ceuta and Melilla,[41] which form a contiguous territorial link in Morocco. These apparent political anomalies have in fact existed since the fifteenth century. The enclaves have been described as 'frontier economies'.[42] They are subject to a significantly less rigorous inspection regime than the ports of the EU or even Tangiers. Ease of crossing into the enclaves is also subject to the payment of bribes. Drugs tend to move by car and truck into the enclaves before then crossing the Straits by ferry to Algeciras. It is alleged that African migrants bound for the EU are trafficked through Melilla. Such smuggling may involve the transportation of cannabis-related drugs, but the volumes would be smaller for practical purposes. The risk per volume would therefore present much less of an incentive.

The perceived threat from Moroccan cannabis in continental Europe has spawned responses on both a multilateral and a bilateral basis. The chief vehicle for the former was the Trevi Group,[43] which was established in 1976. This was an ad hoc arrangement among the existing twelve members of the then European Community (now the European Union), directed at resisting transnational threats, such as terrorism and money laundering, as well as illicit drugs. Within the Trevi process, it was actually a subsequent bureaucratic iteration, 'Trevi 3', that was given responsibility for addressing the challenge of organised crime, especially drug trafficking. It too was a slow-burning institution, with no formal meetings held before June 1985, when it actively took over the portfolio of organised crime. Though it only existed for some seven years, Trevi supporters claim that a handful of important developments took place during this time. Among them was a decision to establish a network of drugs liaison officers in post outside the member states of the EC. This network is still in place and active. A second example would be the decision to create a national drugs intelligence unit in every one of the core group's member states.

Trevi subsequently morphed into the prototype for the ad hoc group on Europol, which came into being in June 1992. Europol was formally created on 6 April 2009 and remains a central institution in the law-enforcement efforts made against drugs and organised crime.

The Spanish have not been idle while such trafficking practices have emerged and evolved. Since 1999 Spain has been developing an Integrated System of External Vigilance. This is a strategy for identifying and interdicting those involved in smuggling across the Straits. It includes a network of fixed and module radar, infra-red and video censors. It has been successful in that it has forced smugglers working in Morocco to seek longer and more vulnerable routes, thereby at very least increasing the de facto costs of failure. This relative success has been called into question as a result of the collapse in living standards in Spain. This is partly because desperate people are trying to smuggle drugs as a way to rescue themselves from their economic predicament in the context of the 2007/8 world economic crisis, and partly because law enforcement have seen their budgets cut, even in such controversial areas as drugs smuggling and people trafficking. Spanish officials in the port town of Barbate in Andalusia complain of not being able to afford even to replace two broken surveillance cameras,[44] such have been the severity of the government cutbacks.

BOX 3

JOE ORTON

The English playwright Joe Orton, infamous for his black comedies, spent an eighty-day holiday in Tangiers in May and June 1965, together with his lover, Kenneth Halliwell. The trip coincided with his newly produced play, *Loot*, which was suffering from bad reviews, and would soon close after a limited run. It was the first time they had been on holiday together abroad. The drug-fuelled holiday features prominently in the diary that Orton was keeping at the time. It lists a series of sexual encounters, many allegedly with underage boys. However, one must take the entries with a pinch of salt. The diary was always meant for publication, and has been described as being too polished merely to be a record of events. At the end of the holiday Halliwell launched a violent physical attack on Orton. It was a dress rehearsal. In less than two years, on 9 August 1967, Orton was dead, aged thirty-four, bludgeoned to death at the hands of his partner, increasingly consumed by jealousy. Orton was one of a long line of leading lights from the British arts scene, from Oscar Wilde to Kenneth Williams, who found Tangiers an enjoyable escape. From further afield such figures as Truman Capote, Gore Vidal and Tennesee Williams were also enthusiastic visitors.[45]

Conclusion

During its extended engagement with French and Spanish colonialism the drugs issue hardly featured in Morocco. There was some consumption, notably in the north of the country, from where cannabis was locally grown. This was tolerated as a local tradition. This situation changed radically with the emergence of the youth counter-culture of the 1960s, in which the consumption of cannabis and its derivatives quickly came to be an integral part. This externally generated demand resulted in a surge of supply, and subsequently of drug trafficking. Cannabis came to dominate crop production in the Rif Mountains, where its profile turned into an agricultural monoculture. The response of the Moroccan state, then commanded by King Hasan II, was to isolate the politically fractious north of the country. In exchange for the *quid pro quo* of political introspection, the king would de facto allow the cannabis economy to prosper. From the 1980s Morocco became known for having 'la culture du cannabis'.[46]

Things changed in 2000, with the death of Hasan and the succession of his son, Muhammad VI. The young king wanted to reintegrate the Rif and the north more generally into the political economy of the kingdom. He did this firstly through a series of political gestures of inclusion, followed by new investments, particularly in Tangiers. In 2003 M6 embarked upon a bold strategy to curtail cannabis production in Morocco. In spite of initial international scepticism, the palace proved to be as good as its word, with land used for cannabis production falling steadily over an eight-year period. By 2011 it appeared as if such a trend was beginning to bottom out. This reflected the tough economic conditions being experienced in the north generally, and the Rif specifically. The Moroccan state choked back on its output-curtailment strategy for fear of political unrest in what is still a peripheral and generally impoverished part of the kingdom.

As Rabat addressed its cannabis profile, the country faced a second drugs challenge in the shape of cocaine trafficking from Latin America. Over the last handful of years the West African route has proved to be dynamic and growing, leading to speculation that smuggling through failing states such as Mali might eventually integrate Morocco into the mass movement of drugs that eventually ends up in Europe. Though such fears are real enough, they do not appear to have been justified, despite an aggressive attempt to 'make a market' for cocaine in Morocco in 2007. With the future of such criminal intent uncertain, it is, however, too soon for complacency.

2

LEBANON

LOCAL FASHION, REGIONAL POLITICS

In Beirut, the fashion industry had wanted to play its part in the campaign against illicit drugs for some time. To this end, on 28 September 2010, taking advantage of a very hot autumn, a well-known local designer, Nathalie Fadlallah of Nathalie's Agency, held a bold and spectacular fashion event. It was aimed at raising funds for and promoting awareness of the work of one of the country's leading NGOs active on the drugs issue, Jeunesse Anti Drogues (JAD).[1] The specific aim was to help the JAD increase its capacity to assist those suffering from the effects of narcotic drugs; the NGO had room for only sixteen beds in its long-term, in-patient rehabilitation centre, while there were several dozen names on its waiting list.

It was with this worthy cause in mind that Nathalie Fadlallah organised the 'Sky Fashion' show. In order to maximise the impact of the fashion event, the agency looked hard for a high-profile venue capable of drawing a mass audience, and ingeniously hit upon the idea of occupying a road bridge over a busy highway in the middle of the city. Having obtained permission from the local highways department to close the bridge, models dressed up in evening gowns and wedding dresses and showed off their lingerie as the event got under way in time for the morning's rush hour. As hoped for, the event generated considerable media interest, and was well covered in the national press. From a publicity angle, the occasion seemed to have been a roaring success.

But that was only the half of it. Taking over the bridge caused Beirut's traffic—a noisy and slow-moving crawl at the best of times—to come to a standstill. Rat-runs filled up fast. Those who had no business that morning took to their cars to view the extraordinary event. It is doubtful whether Beirut has ever seen so much 'rubber necking' from drivers using the road under the bridge, at least since the end of the Lebanese civil war in 1990. But as the effects of the traffic fumes spread from the roads, and pedestrians gasped at the additional fumes in the atmosphere on that day, the inhabitants of the Lebanese capital became more and more irascible and impatient than usual at the hold-ups. As the populace began to realise that the congestion had been caused by the fashion trade, and was entirely man-made, they became belligerent. The original motivation for this public event became obscured from view, and people cursed the designer and her 'eccentric' event.

Noisy cars, flaunting lingerie, drugs and their consequences, the ire of the people, high fashion over breakfast: to say that this had been a very Lebanese story on a very Lebanese morning was an understatement. To put things in these terms entails both a criticism and a compliment. The criticism is that here was yet another example of Beirut society at its most shallow: a self-conscious, self-important city tagged on to the extremity of the Middle East, whose collective attention span on the original concerns of illicit drugs did not last a morning, but was rapidly displaced by the city's usual parochial fixations.

The compliment is that, in contrast to much of the rest of the Arab world, Nathalie Fadlallah's fashion show to highlight the struggle against drugs showed that Beirut society was mature and open enough to have a debate on the issue. In short, it was not a society in denial about its drugs problem. Yet the conclusion has to be drawn that, while Beirut society is capable of focusing on such matters, it does not have enough internal momentum to affect the outcome of such issues. As with so many things concerned with Lebanon, it was as much external actors who would determine the fate of such problems as the issue of drugs in the community itself.

Drugs, War and the State

The Beqaa Valley has historically been a centre for agriculture in Lebanon, famous originally for supplying wheat to the Roman Empire. More recently, it has been the source of 40 per cent of the country's agricultural production and around 8 per cent of its gross domestic product.[2] High-grade hashish, known colloquially as 'Red Leb', has long been grown in the Beqaa Valley. Before the outbreak of the civil war in Lebanon in 1975, the country was part of the international trafficking chain, especially in opiates. Much of the opium harvested in countries such as Turkey, and trafficked under the control of 'French Connection' 'mafias' in France and Italy, would have geographically looped down into Lebanon, where 'laboratories' converted some of the morphine base into heroin.

Civil War and Criminality

The outbreak of the Lebanese civil war, with its associated factors of a breakdown in central authority and the arrival of occupying forces from Syria and Israel, provided fresh opportunities for smuggling and racketeering. These were no less present in the Lebanese agricultural sector than in any other part of the economy, which had become less transparent, making it difficult for outsiders to discern the volume and nature of the output. This provided opportunities for both the changing of the cropping profile and the expansion of the area under cultivation, with the possibility of increasing profits for those who controlled production and trade.

The shift in output from cereals to more profitable, though illicit, crops, such as hashish and opium, was palpable. For example, annual land devoted to wheat production, which had been at a record high of 76,000 hectares in 1974, fell to 45,000 hectares per year in the late 1970s, and as low as 9,000 in 1987. This took place even as the area of land under drugs cultivation expanded as far south as the Beirut–Damascus highway.[3] The shift in hashish production during this time stood almost in inverse proportion to the decline in wheat output. Annual production rose from around 30,000 tons at the outbreak of the civil war to 100,000 tons in the early 1980s. During this time hashish accounted for 80 per cent of the output of agricultural land in the area of Baalbek, which had by this time been taken over by Iranian Revolutionary Guards, and the more inaccessible northern stretch of the Beqaa known as al-Hirmal, the original centre of hashish cultivation.[4] For Lebanon's hashish producers, 1975–90 were 'the golden years'.[5] Opium was also increasingly grown in the Beqaa Valley during this time.

As institutional politics broke down in the early to mid-1970s, to be replaced by the militarisation of Lebanon, so the competing paramilitaries of the day fought for supremacy. This included control of the sources of income, of which the movement and export of drugs was one of the most important. The victory of Bashir Gemayel's Lebanese Front in its intra-Maronite trial of strength with the Chamounist 'Tiger' militia followed a protracted militia struggle for power. Of comparable importance was Gemayel's takeover of the

Mediterranean ports, through which drugs exports flowed. By 1978 Gemayel's faction was estimated to be earning around $100 million a year in illicit income,[6] of which much of this was a result of his control of the drugs trade.

Though the intra-Maronite struggle for power and wealth was real enough, it was a very local conflict when compared to the interests and impacts of the regional powers, one of which—Syria—came to occupy much of Lebanon during the civil war and its aftermath. In the words of veteran American journalist Jonathan Randal, the Syrian army 'fell prey to very Lebanese vices', and soon had a big stake in a range of rackets from hashish production, through heroin labs to car theft.[7] Owing to their superior fire power the presence of the Syrians obliged compliance on the part of Lebanese elements already involved in the drugs field. Hashish was Lebanon's biggest export earner. By 1990, and the end of the civil strife, Lebanon's annual heroin trade was worth around $1.4 billion a year.[8]

The Syrian military were active in smuggling scams during much of their occupation of Lebanon. They were especially engaged in the movement of hashish and opium, involvement in which a Syrian officer could pocket an income some tenfold greater than his military salary.[9] Western intelligence sources estimated at the time that such an expanded income would have been in the bracket of $20,000–$30,000 a year, even after paying off both the middlemen who delivered the crop from the farm gate and the more senior military and political bosses in Damascus.[10] Syrian officers would then be rotated out of the lucrative positions to ensure that the benefits of patronage were widely circulated within the regime core, and that no single faction or clan gained disproportionate influence. By 1987 up to half of the cultivable land in the Beqaa had been turned over to opium, as a result of 'the breakdown of law and order' in Lebanon. Numerous informal laboratories had been set up in Lebanon, and to a lesser degree Syria, in order to refine the raw opium into heroin. The smaller loads and the greater portability of the drug in this state turned it into a more practical and lucrative export commodity.[11]

By the mid-1980s Lebanon had become one of the world's most important drugs-trafficking centres. Prior to the civil war most of the drugs were transported by light aircraft from the valley itself. Once the Syrians had got a grip on the trade, and volumes had increased exponentially, sea and land routes were preferred, for ease of 'taxation', and for fear of the vulnerability of the air option. The three main routes of choice in the 1980s were: via Christian-controlled Mediterranean ports to the island of Cyprus; overland to Syria; through Israel and on to Egypt, said by some to be the largest hashish market in the world. The sizeable volume of the illicit earnings, together with the inclusive nature of the trafficking, meant that most of the major political organisations in Lebanon's multiple confessional communities, together with their militias, benefited from the drugs trade.

Making up with the USA

The Syrian-controlled Lebanese drugs production and trafficking industry came dramatically to an end some three years after the end of the civil war, in 1990. One moment, the Beqaa's half-million people working in agriculture were making annual foreign currency earnings of $500 million a year;[12] a couple of years later the floor had dropped out of the market. In a graphic illustration of how quickly the political economy of the region can change, the Asad-led, Ba'thist regime in Damascus had not only choked off existing production, but had used the drug issue as a device with which to repair its tattered relationship with the USA. In other words, drugs production in Lebanon was subordinated to the overall strategic priorities of the geo-politics of post-civil war realignment.

The Lebanese civil war ended entirely on Syria's terms. The last Lebanese warlord to try to face down the Syrian occupation, the former head of the army and prime minister, Michel Aoun, had been chased out of the country and into a long and chastening exile in France.[13] All of the major confessional communities had been cowed, undermined by a series of microcosmic civil wars in their respective sectarian communities, and the oppressive hand of Syrian occupation. Only the radical Shia militia Hizbollah, closely allied with post-revolutionary Iran, Syria's strategic partner in the Middle East, was permitted to retain its heavy weaponry. With Israel only hanging onto its enclave in southern Lebanon by its fingertips, pending its complete pullback in May 2000, Damascus was to enjoy hegemonic control of Lebanon for the next decade and a half. This left Syria free to calculate its own interests in Lebanon and to pursue its goals accordingly.

Top of the list was to end Syria's regional isolation. This aim had become increasingly acute as the leadership succession loomed in Damascus. Long-time incumbent, Hafez al-Asad had no choice but to look beyond his signalled successor and eldest son, Basil, who had been killed in a car accident in 1994. With the ailing president obliged to look to a younger and less charismatic son, 'Dr Bashar', the British-trained eye doctor, it became all the more imperative that the father should neutralise potential external threats. It was on this basis that President Asad Senior used the drugs issue to forge more coopera-tive relations with the USA.

Under the oversight of Damascus, a joint Lebanese/Syrian narcotics eradi-cation programme, introduced in 1992, had within two years posted notable successes. In 1994 less than 90 hectares of opium poppy was available for harvest, a fall of 80 per cent on the previous year. Hashish cultivation was also in marked decline, with a fall of 50 per cent to just 8,100 hectares in 1994. Seizure levels were also up in 1994, with 1,100 arrests in that year, well over four times the level of a year earlier. In addition, there was tangible evidence of greater cooperation between the various Lebanese and Syrian law-enforce-ment bodies and their European counterparts. Furthermore, the government in Beirut took steps towards endorsing the 1988 UN Convention on Narcotics,[14] having ratified the earlier anti-drugs conventions of 1961 and 1971, placing it in step with the prevailing outlook of the Western-led world towards illicit drugs.

There was initially some scepticism on the part of the US government towards these positive gestures from Damascus. Suggestions were made that while domestic production had been cut right back, this had been in part compensated for by the arrival of drugs from outside. Moreover, the US authorities pointed to the importation of chemical precursors for the purposes of refining drugs. The USA also complained about the absence of credible banking laws to combat money laundering.[15] During this pre-9/11 era many countries had inadequate legal infrastructure as far as the latter was concerned. Lebanese banking secrecy, routinely opaque at the best of times, surpassed even that of Switzerland.[16]

That these issues did not in the end prevent a reconciliation based in great part on drugs was best demonstrated by the fact that in 1995 the specialist UN agency formally removed Lebanon from the list of world drug-producing countries.[17] The more sceptical USA took a little longer to fall into line. By the end of 1997, however, when President Bill Clinton had noted that both Lebanon and Syria had successfully eradicated opium cultivation, both were removed from the list of countries suspected of producing or shipping illegal drugs.[18] Even the Clinton White House still maintained that both remained transit countries for South American cocaine, and for the refining of opium from south-west Asia into heroin for the European market. While Syria dropped off the USA's thirty-odd member list of countries deemed narcotic offenders (the 'majors list'), it remained on the list of a roughly equal number alleged to be supporters of terrorism.[19]

Beqaa Valley: Impoverished, but Fighting Back

If the Beqaa Valley farmers had prospered during the dark days of the Lebanese civil war, by the end of the 1990s they had fallen on hard times. Though the national per capita GDP average for Lebanon in 2001 was $3,500, the rate for the northern Beqaa area was just $500.[20] International donors, who had pledged around $300 million in aid to fund a broadly based crop-eradication programme, were only able to distribute around 1 per cent of these funds during its first phase, thereby only enabling the UN Development Programme (UNDP) to help some 1,500 farmers. Neither were the substitution schemes well thought through. The possibility that the keeping of dairy cattle,[21] or the production of apples, might compensate for the high margins to be earned in growing hashish or producing opium appeared fanciful to say the least.[22]

BOX 1

CROP-SUBSTITUTION ATTEMPTS IN LEBANON

Lebanon's first attempt at crop substitution in the Beqaa Valley came early in the 1960s. On that occasion farmers were told to desist from planting cannabis and to grow sunflowers instead. However, the plan lacked the sort of infrastructural investment that might have made it a success. The absence of irrigated water meant that the sunflower yields were low and the price of production high. The Beirut government was caught in a trap of having to buy the output at double the price in order to ensure that farmers did not slip back into their old production patterns. This gross distortion of the market continued until the onset of the civil war, when the subsidies were stopped, the scheme collapsed, and farmers returned to their former ways. A second and even less plausible exercise in production substitution came in the late 1990s, when Holstein dairy cattle were introduced into the Lebanese agricultural sector with the help of a loan scheme provided for under a US programme. Though the farmers displayed little enthusiasm for the idea, Lebanon went ahead, paying some $6 million for 3,000 cows, which were distributed among 1,000 farmers, a third of them located in the Beqaa Valley. In 2000 the project was expanded, with a further 5,000 cows arriving at a cost of $11 million, including the cost of training farmers. This expansion did not mask the general disappointment at a

---

scheme where imported feed costs proved higher than expected, while milk yields languished due to a combination of disease and inexperienced management. The regional rivalry between the USA and Iran even extended to cropping innovation in Lebanon's farm sector at this time. One Iranian team arrived offering Lebanese farmers $50 million in aid, covering such a range of investment activities as bee keeping, fish farming and food processing.

Such concerted attempts were not limited to reducing the production of illicit drugs. They came in partnership with a broader attempt to impose central authority on the peripheral areas of Lebanon, itself a reflection of Syrian control of Lebanon. So, for example, in 1998 Lebanese security had sought to demonstrate that their control of the valley from Baalbek, now minus its Iranian Revolutionary Guards, to al-Hirmal area, in the northernmost area of the Beqaa Valley, was permanent. In 1998 the Lebanese state also raided the offices of Hizbollah, then led by the controversial, radical figure Shaikh Subhi Tufaili, whose supporters had attempted a year earlier to stop the illicit production of opium and hashish in the mountains of the Beqaa.[23]

But if such developments were expected to preface a most un-Lebanese situation in which the central government asserted and enforced its control over the eastern periphery of the country, such expectations were to be short-lived. The two sides were to stare resentfully at one another up and down the valley: on one side the farmers of the Beqaa, trying to get away with as much illicit production as possible; on the other, the specialist Lebanese police bridling at the boldness of a community that should not have been powerful enough to lord it over government authority. A typical exchange went thus. The authorities would drop leaflets threatening life imprisonment with hard labour and a fine of $75 million against anyone cultivating illicit drugs. The farmers would then proceed to hand the leaflets to their fellow confessionals in Hizbollah, by now a more formidable adversary. By doing so, the Shia farmers and militia would dare the Beirut administration to risk a standoff with the country's best-organised and best-armed militia.[24] The farmers would then attempt to intimidate the anti-drugs police, threatening to 'kill one policeman' for every cannabis plant that they might chop down,[25] a very Lebanese notion of proportionality, which would result in the police reluctantly drawing back.

The outcome of successive stand-offs was to track the undulating fortunes of Lebanese politics more generally. Every time the security situation deteriorated at the political centre, such as in 2005 (the assassination of Rafiq Hariri),

2006 (Israel–Hizbollah conflict) and 2007 (insurgency of Fatah Islam),[26] the farmers of the Beqaa were more likely to get away with planting and harvesting larger volumes of illicit crops.[27] At times when Beirut was not under pressure, and was able better to assert its authority, such as in 2001 (after the Israeli withdrawal from southern Lebanon) and 2002, 'the year of combating drugs', as the interior minister described it[28] (following 9/11), it was the farmers' turn to feel the pressure. The year 2008 was a very good one for hashish production, though with the harvest having to be sold locally.[29] The year 2009 saw a particularly successful eradication campaign in response, with large stockpiles of hashish seized,[30] as a result of operations coordinated between the Internal Security Forces (ISF) and the Lebanese army.[31] The farmers would deal with the deterioration in the political environment by seeking balancing benefits, such as new areas to plant, especially in the more inaccessible terrain.

The ultimate sanction for the farmers was a recourse to arms,[32] though that had to be managed carefully, for fear that it would bring the state authorities down on their heads. Under these circumstances, the role of local militia-style or 'kingpin' figures emerged to bridge the gap between the farmers and Hizbollah. For a long time the role of local 'kingpin' was occupied by Jamil Hamieh from the village of Taraya. With Hamieh's 'retirement', this role has increasingly been identified with Beqaa Valley strongman Noah Zaiter, known as the 'Robin Hood of the Beqaa'. Still only in his late thirties, and with over 480 criminal charges against his name, he has put himself forward as the hero of the farmers. He has cleverly bought the allegiance of farmers on the ground by distributing monetary benefits, in turn making his private militia available for their protection.[33] His importance, together with the resentment of the police over the challenge he represents, is evident in the fact that a five-kilometre security zone exists around Zaiter and his home in the valley, and he is regularly attended by fourteen or more bodyguards, for fear that he might be the victim of an assassination.[34]

Domestic Consumption

Lebanon has always been a status-conscious society, characterised by extremes of wealth. Both social and political hierarchies are very steep, with personal loyalty rendered by the individual to the *za'im*, the local boss. Though the civil war disrupted some of these relationships, the basic pattern still applies. There are different ways of gauging where individuals lie on this social hierarchy, with yardsticks such as social background, fashion, education and wealth all important indicators of standing within society. Drugs have to some extent been added to that list.

There are five types of illegal drugs that are routinely available on the social scene in Lebanon. These are: cocaine; hashish; heroin; amphetamines; and other synthetic drugs, of which Ecstasy and Valium,[35] especially imported from Western or Eastern Europe,[36] are the best known. The abuse of substances, whether alcohol or drugs, lends itself to perceptions of hierarchy, most obviously because of the differential pricing of different drugs, a casual, night-time signifier of wealth. This is likely to become a more acute gauge as the consumption of drugs increases in the country.

'Party Drug Nation?'

Research on substance use and misuse in Lebanon is rare.[37] Best guesstimates by the NGO community put the number of 'addicts' in Lebanon at between 10,000 and 15,000,[38]—most of them aged under twenty-five—out of a total population of some 4 million. This figure may well be understated, owing to the tendency of families to hide problem users because of the shameful nature of their addiction. At least these issues are a matter of public discussion in Lebanon, in contrast to the 1980s, when such matters would have been studiously avoided because of the social stigma attached. The signs are that these figures are growing. The average age of illicit drug use has fallen from around nineteen, in the mid-2000s, to as young as fifteen at the end of the decade, although the age of the first use of substances can be as early as nine.[39] Increasingly, drugs are being regarded as fashionable.

In the Lebanese party scene cocaine is considered to be a 'status drug'; 'pour le snob', as the local patois would have it, as one gram can cost between $60 and $100, depending on its purity. By contrast, the price of heroin is as low as $20 per gram, making the poor more susceptible to its attractions. In addition to being taken on its own, cocaine is often consumed in conjunction with alcohol, increasing an individual's tolerance to alcohol and enabling substance consumption to continue through the night. Poly drug use is one area where the impact of substances is unclear, with the attendant level of risk. Some men also claim that an additional attraction of cocaine is that it increases their sexual prowess.

For those with fewer resources at their disposal MDMA (Ecstasy) is a familiar drug available to clubbers and partygoers, an established form of recreation in night-life Lebanon. High range logos are appropriated for status value: Yellow and Red Ferrari branded pills have been widely available, as have

Blue Mitsubishi pills, which sell for around $25 each. In 2008, before it was a priority for law enforcement, just 400 Ecstasy pills were confiscated in Lebanon; a year later this figure had risen to 17,312, giving a better insight into the amount of the drug available.[40] Anecdotal evidence suggests that supplying Ecstasy at raves can net dealers an income some tenfold that of the minimum monthly wage.[41] The drug Ketamine, 'marketed' as 'Special K', is another popular drug, widely available.[42]

Hashish holds less reputational value for those taking drugs, partly because it is home grown and partly because it is much cheaper to buy than its imported counterparts, but this does make it a more favoured substance among students, many of whom have limited disposable income.[43] Indeed, hemp-based drugs routinely represent the most commonly used illicit drug among high school and university students.[44] Though price often reflects the outcome of the stand-off between producers and the ISF rather than market preferences, there would appear to be less cachet in falling prices. In 2009 the 'street price' of an ounce (25 grams equivalent) of hashish fell from $500 to $200.[45]

Drug consumption is also reported as growing in the Palestinian refugee camps of Lebanon, together with stress-related illnesses and mental break-downs. However, much of the reporting of such changes is anecdotal. In the absence of a systematic investigation of the phenomenon, the situation remains sketchy.[46]

Drug Tourism

It should not be supposed that all of the drug consumption in Lebanon is perpetrated by the Lebanese. Beirut continues to be a fashionable destination for Arab tourists in particular, and much real estate in Lebanon is owned by Arabs from the Gulf. A previous government minister identified 'drug and alcohol tourism',[47] as part of the attraction of Beirut as a destination. He may have added sex tourism too, which Lebanon also has to offer.

Lebanon has been described as playing the same role as Bahrain in another geo-social context: providing a social safety valve for dissolute Gulf Arabs, keen for some edgy recreation during their vacation time.

Hasan Nasrallah and Drugs Concerns

In 2010 the issue of illegal drugs began to catch the attention of prominent politicians in Lebanon, and they do not come more prominent than the serving secretary-general of Hizbollah, Hasan Nasrallah. Whereas in the past political parties and their militia had shamelessly exploited the drugs market with the aim of maximising income, Hizbollah, with its claim to represent the Lebanese resistance, had set the moral bar somewhat higher for itself.

Moreover, Hizbollah found itself in a potentially uncomfortable position. It claimed to represent the Lebanese Shias, the bulk of whom were concentrated in the poorer suburbs of the south of the capital, Dahiyah, where social problems and increasing drug consumption were at their greatest. However, Hizbollah also had to maintain its relevance for the Shia communities in the south of Lebanon, adjacent to the Israeli border, because it was from there that the Lebanese 'resistance', Hizbollah's greatest source of legitimacy, was organised. Finally, in order to make its comprehensive claim to represent the country's Shias a credible one, Hizbollah had to represent the interests of the Shia farmers of the northern Beqaa Valley.

In many ways Hizbollah had begun life as a Beqaa Valley party. Its first two secretaries-general, Subhi al-Tufaili—long estranged from the organisation—and Abbas al-Musawi, both came from that part of Lebanon. In the 1998 municipal elections in Lebanon, Hizbollah easily won all six municipal elections in al-Hirmal, with the exception of Tufaili's home town of Brital.[48] Squaring the circle of income for the Beqaa, a drugs-free society in the southern suburbs and the centrality of the south was never going to be easy.

It was against the background of this complex sociology that Hasan Nasrallah decided that he had no choice but to enter the debate on drugs and their effects in Lebanon. He did so by devoting one of his prominent annual Ramadan speeches in 2010 to the drugs issue. In doing so, he chose to emphasise the challenge posed by illegal drugs, which he described as 'a cross-sectarian' issue, and the need for Lebanese society to respond to the threat as a whole. It was almost as if Nasrallah was offering Hizbollah as the social resistance against drugs in Lebanese society, an analogy for its wider resistance against Israel. In recognition of the insidious social impact of drugs, Nasrallah drew attention to the availability of drugs in schools and universities. He also pointed out that even some of Lebanon's prominent families had been left lamenting the impact of illicit drugs on their own number.[49]

Though the frankness of the Hizbollah leader was laudable, he and his organisation have been less forthcoming over the years since the speech, as far as solutions were concerned, even at a practical level. So, for example, Hizbollah allowed anti-drug experts from the Shia community to attend national NGO-organised training sessions, but then refused to allow such specialists to be an active part of national networks of cooperation, which, due to the fact that the Shia community is the largest in Lebanon, could not but have favoured their own. Information gathering from the Shia areas has also proved to be painfully slow, owing to the sensitivity of some of the issues concerned. Hizbollah had to be coaxed repeatedly before it agreed to data on sex workers in Shia areas being collated centrally, which meant the statistics moving out of their exclusive control. Most notably, Nasrallah has failed to address the contradiction that it was Beqaa Valley Shias who were in part producing the drugs that were degrading the families of poorer Shia in the southern suburbs.

Hizbollah and Wider Concerns

It was not only at the domestic level that Hizbollah faced difficulties in assuaging competing interests. There has been growing evidence over the last decade that Hizbollah is an organisation with global aspirations, notably through the mobilisation of the large Lebanese Shiite diaspora, notably in Latin America. While the party's activities are predominantly political and security oriented, illegal drugs are nevertheless an integral part of these operations, both in terms of revenue raising and the creation of synergies with other illicit organisations.

Revelations about the presence of Hizbollah in Latin America has been the most notorious. Hizbollah is one of a cluster of armed groups that is to be found in the so-called Tri-border area, which is to say at the confluence of the borders of Argentina, Brazil and Paraguay. Of even greater concern has been the relationship that Hizbollah has established with Mexican organisations involved in trafficking,[50] and with certain groups in the likes of Colombia and Venezuela,[51] which are reliant on illicit activity. To date, such activities seem oriented towards raising cash for the main organisation in Lebanon. Wisely, Hizbollah appears to have avoided moving known operatives across the border, and indeed has avoided any major violent attacks inside the USA, in contrast to the Mexican drugs cartels. While there is little concrete evidence to suggest that Hizbollah is itself involved in smuggling drugs into America, the company it keeps has led to a lot of expert speculation that it could be drawn into inter-gang power plays in Mexico. It has also spawned some flaky conspiracy theories.[52]

More recently, it has appeared as if Hizbollah was intent on penetrating the European continent. In early 2010 the German press carried reports linking it with national drugs crime, notably the trafficking of cocaine, and money laundering. Lebanese nationals resident and travelling in Germany in order to raise money for the organisation were identified as a threat by the authorities. A party spokesman dismissed the claims out of hand. The Israeli government has long maintained that Hizbollah has been involved in growing and selling drugs for profit, though these were the first reports linking the organisation with the European drugs trade.[53]

Such speculation did give an opportunity to Israel's publicity campaign against Hizbollah. In 2008 Israel's Anti-Drug Authority ran a domestic campaign showing Hasan Nasrallah as a genie emerging from a drugs pipe with the slogan: 'At the end of every joint sits Nasrallah ... whoever uses narcotics are lending a hand to the next terror attack.'[54]

NGOs and their Limitations

In Lebanon the state is weak, while society is strong. The upside of this is that the state cannot easily bully the country's confessional communities, as has been the pattern in many of the authoritarian regimes in the Arab world. This means that NGOs tend to thrive in the permissive atmosphere of Lebanon's civil society. The downside is that society is itself deeply divided, with organisations being replicated according to sect, rather than being functionally organised on a secular basis. For instance, there are around forty-five universities in the country, in order to reflect the multiplicity of communities, and the associated principle that each community should have its interests represented.

It is also a fact that the very weakness of the state makes it hard to elaborate and implement ideas, even when there is a widespread NGO consensus on the direction and substance of reform. Under this situation, the Ministry of Social Affairs acts as a conduit for the distribution of state funds as patronage to bankroll the 4,500 NGOs in Lebanon, rather than to implement a central policy agenda.[55] This reality on the ground in Lebanon has prompted the quip: 'There is only one dictator in each of the Arab countries, except in Lebanon, where there are many.'

There is no better illustration of the coexistence of strength and weakness on the part of NGOs in Lebanon than Law 673, passed in 1998. In a narrow sense, the drafting and adoption of the bill was a triumph for the NGO anti-drug community in Lebanon. The groups had lobbied relentlessly and effectively for its adoption. They won over the cabinet and the majority of the parliamentarians of the day. At its centre, the law stipulates that drug addiction in itself is not a crime. Those suffering from any form of drug addiction should be treated as though they were suffering from an illness. What this means in practice is that drug abusers should not be criminalised. Rather than going to prison, they should be placed under the jurisdiction of an 'addiction committee', a de facto body of experts, responsible for elaborating protocols under which patients would be referred for treatment. Those subject to referral would then be placed in a rehabilitation centre for long-term treatment.

More than fifteen years later, however, the 1998 law has gone largely unimplemented. The addiction committee was never activated. There are woefully few in-patient facilities to provide rehabilitation services for all of those seeking them. Perhaps most tellingly, a dedicated budget line for drugs at the Ministry of Interior was never established.[56] The fact that drug users are not a priority for just about anyone in Lebanon explains why this fleeting political will for reform so easily drained away, and follow-up was so difficult to achieve on the issue.[57] The philosophy behind the 1998 law was to eradicate drugs not drug users, though the outcome might suggest otherwise.

Oum el-Nour

The oldest, best known and most widely admired anti-drugs NGO in Lebanon is Oum el-Nour.[58] In spite of its rather venerable status, it has only been in existence since 1989, established by a group of friends following the death of one of their number from a drug-related problem. In addition to its longevity, it is almost certainly best known because it is the NGO in Lebanon with the most beds for drug addicts wishing to go through rehabilitation: sixty for its men's centre and thirty for its women's facility, though the numbers are actually modest compared with demand. With JAD, one of the best known but most controversial NGOs having space for only sixteen beds, the modesty of provision is there to see.

One of the strengths of the Oum el-Nour approach is the seriousness with which admission is taken. The charity's reception centre, staffed by professionals, is the sufferer's first entry point. With beds in short supply and much at stake in this initial consultation, the process is despatched with thoroughness. Strenuous efforts are made to understand an individual's background, including their family life, given that addiction is often symptomatic of a wider set of problems. Particular effort is made to decide whether an addict is serious about confronting their addiction, especially given that potential patients are often in denial or deeply ambivalent.

If the judgement of the reception centre is that a drug abuser is sincere about ending dependency, then he or she will be sent to a hospital for detoxification. If this process is completed successfully, the patient is sent to one of Oum el-Nour's rehabilitation centres, where they remain as part of a therapeutic community,[59] usually for between twelve and fifteen months. Since 1995 the provisions offered by Oum el-Nour have expanded to include the establishment of a follow-up centre to monitor patient progress over the twelve months or more when they are readjusting back into society. It is often the shock of reintegration back into daily life, especially with drugs available all around and the same peer group for company, that tips former sufferers back into addiction. During the first two decades of its existence Oum el-Nour has helped 3,305 people, of whom 2,974 were men and just over 10 per cent women.[60]

NGOs such as Oum el-Nour are fiercely adamant that they operate on a cross-sectarian basis. And it is certainly true that they employ members of staff from across confessional communities. But it is also the case that the charity is inextricably identified with the church, the president of its board being a Maronite Catholic priest, and the church having provided the land upon which the rehabilitation centre was built. Moreover, an overwhelming majority of both the board and the charity's important public relations committee are Christians. As a reflection of this, Oum el-Nour remains a conservative organisation and was hostile to the proposal to establish a collective anti-drugs NGO committee in 1999. Still, Oum el-Nour remains more inclusive in its approach to drug rehabilitation than some, with three faith-based rehabilitation centres in Lebanon using the concept of Christotherapy as the basis of their rehabilitation work.

BOX 2

ROUMIEH PRISON

The prison in Roumieh, looking down onto the coastal plain from the hills above Beirut, is the largest such establishment in Lebanon. It has an inmate population of around 4,000. In composition it is 'Lebanese society writ small'. An estimated 30 per cent of the inmates are drug abusers, falling to 22 per cent if the whole prison population of the country is taken into account. Of the 500–600 new arrivals in the prison each month, more than 100 are regular drug users. The police tend to arrest drug users rather than dealers, and place the onus on the user to try to avoid jail by finding in-patient care. Such concentrations of drug users make it difficult to put effective palliative care into practice. Roumieh has suffered in the past from a reputation for having a harsh regime. Similarly, some of the long-stay inmates, especially those connected with radical, violent groups such as Fatah al-Islam, have gone out of their way to disrupt its organisation. Running prisons in Lebanon is currently the responsibility of the Interior Ministry. The NGO sector is campaigning for the Ministry of Justice to take over this function. In a potentially innovative experiment, the Catholic charity the Association of Justice and Mercy (AJEM)[61] has been given responsibility for drugs rehabilitation in the prison. AJEM is innovative in a prisons context because of the efforts it makes to try to understand why drug users acquire such dependency. The charity also appreciates that it is not only the individual that suffers from the abuse, but the family of the addict as a whole. Rehabilitation is therefore organised with the wider social context of addiction in mind.

Conclusion

Lebanon is one of the most sophisticated countries in the Arab world as far as the issue of dangerous drugs is concerned. It has a dedicated anti-narcotics security agency. It has some extremely well-qualified health-service personnel. It arguably has the most savvy associations dealing with drugs issues anywhere in the Middle East. The country's NGOs ooze professionalism, whether in the provision of recovery services or in the realm of public affairs. If they go about their work with the pazzaz associated with modern Lebanon that is because they are part of it.

The frustrations are also evident, in Lebanese multiples. The potential of both society and state are dissipated by the requirements of consociational governance, the reducto duplication of civil society, and the vertical, sectarian rigidities militating against promotion on merit. Both law making and implementation remain intractable, again because of the confessional fragmentation of a small entity. But it is in its regional context that the fortunes of Lebanon are, as ever, contingent on the actions and wars of others. Left to their own devices, the Lebanese can curb much of the local production of cannabis and opium, and warn against the dangers of what remains. Buffeted by the likes of Israeli invasions, Syrian civil conflict and Iranian transnational influence, drugs and drugs policy in Lebanon will reset itself every decade or so.

3

QAT IN YEMEN

JEOPARDISING DEVELOPMENT

Introduction

On the first day of the football World Cup in South Africa in 2010 the website of the Ministry of Defence in Yemen announced that the price of qat, the euphoria-inducing drug, had shot up in price. The price of the ordinary-quality leaves had doubled or tripled in price to stand at between $5 and $7.50; higher-quality leaves, usually around $10 a bunch, were selling with a 70 per cent mark-up. Like their fellow football supporters in England and elsewhere it seemed as though Yemeni fans too were settling down to watch the matches in the company of an intoxicant, but with the green qat leaves substituting for beer. That, however, seemed to be the extent of the parallel. After the end of the tournament, beer and football would return to their position as important but essentially peripheral parts of modern life. In Yemen, qat would continue to dominate the lives of the people, albeit it at lower retail prices. No wonder that the issue of the price of qat was deemed of sufficient importance for the Defence Ministry to be the arm of the state most closely monitoring developments.

In Yemen's poverty-stricken, war-ravaged society,[1] qat has emerged as one of the few methods for dealing with the realities of daily life. As the habit has entrenched itself, Yemeni farmers have abandoned traditional crops such as coffee and cereals, the former (as mocha) for which they were long best known, and have given over increasing areas of prime agricultural land to qat production. The fact that the narcotic is not illegal means that the daily rush to market, before the leaf dries and loses its intoxicating sap, is unimpeded by law enforcement. With remittance money in the 1970s and 1980s, and the recycling of the modest proceeds of Yemen's small hydrocarbons sector after that, new levels of disposable income have resulted in qat consumption rising to dominate the Yemeni way of life. The cost, however, has been considerable. The routine consumption of qat, from early afternoon well into the evening, has hit productivity.[2] The deployment of large volumes of water to nurture the plant has jeopardised Yemen's delicate developmental equilibrium, and even its long-term survival as a viable economy and society.

Belatedly, foreign institutions, local NGOs and government agencies are wrestling with the problem. They do so at an unpropitious moment. Yemen remains one of the three or four Arab countries in the eye of the storm of public pressures for governance reform. The Yemeni state has been trying to stifle a rebellion in the north. A secessionist movement appears to be emerging fitfully in the south. The hard end of the al-Qaeda movement in Arabia is regrouping in parts of the unpoliced tribal heartlands of the country, notably Marib. This, in turn, triggers impatient complaints from the USA about assumed Yemeni complicity in terrorism. For the leadership in Sanaa, which functions more as a broker of national politics than as a commander, the intensity of such challenges is not easy to grapple with, especially when many of those who work for the state are themselves enthusiastic consumers of qat.

The Qat Way of Life

The tradition of chewing qat goes back at least 500 years. It is unclear whether the plant originated in Ethiopia or Yemen. Historically, qat chewing was limited to one day a week. Moreover, it was largely the preserve of the wealthy and the social elites. Traditional farming practice was seriously eroded in the 1960s, when Yemen was flooded with cheap grain, and farmers looked to switch crops in order to maintain their margins. At the time, Yemen was practically self-sufficient in cereals and other crops.

A further boost to the qat monoculture came in the 1970s, when qat for the first time became 'a majority practice'.[3] Ironically, this came with the expansion of the Yemeni economy. This was driven by the large number of Yemenis working in the oil-wealthy Gulf states, and the remittances that they sent home.[4] The growing economy stimulated an expansion both of the consumers of qat—to embrace the middle classes and then in turn the poorer parts of society—and the extent of its cultivation. As the anthropologist Martha Mundy has observed, the chewing of qat became 'an indispensable form of conspicuous consumption'.[5] The unification of the states of North and South Yemen (previously known formally as the Yemen Arab Republic and the People's Democratic Republic of Yemen respectively) in May 1990 gave demand a further boost in the south, as the socialist government there had in the past strongly discouraged excessive consumption.[6] The absence of an attractive alternative leisure pursuit has left qat largely unrivalled in recreational terms in Yemen.

Since those days, the Yemeni economy has fallen on harder times, with 800,000 expatriates being sent home from Saudi Arabia in the early 1990s in response to the Iraq–Kuwait crisis;[7] a civil war briefly blighting the country in 1994; a rise in the kidnapping of foreigners, involving increasingly uncertain outcomes; and oil exports dwindling more recently. Qat has been immune from such hardships, with demand spreading, and other crops, notably wheat, being sacrificed in order to expand its production. Qat has become a coping mechanism for dysfunction at home.

Qat comes from the *Catha Edulis* shrub, which contains the amphetamine cathinone. While the qat leaves are initially chewed, the defining act of consumption is that they are 'stored' in an ever-expanding ball (usually somewhere around the size of a golf ball) in one of the cheeks of the partaker, thereby ensuring that as much of the drug as is possible enters the user's system. This practice is known as *takhzin*. The sap of the plant is ingested, triggering—albeit slowly—the narcotic experience. This is no swingers' drug!

The leaves have to be consumed quickly, as the cathinone begins to break down after twenty-four hours, and the leaf is virtually without intoxicating effect after thirty-six. Swallowing the leaves is discouraged, and is believed to trigger a range of ailments, including constipation. There are different types of qat plants, with differing narcotic effects, thereby making it difficult to generalise about the precise impact of the drug. This variety has given rise to what Tim Mackintosh-Smith has called 'qat snobs' in Yemen, to rival any wine snob in the West.[8] The plants are given different names to differentiate their effect, with the brands associated with the district of the country from which they originate.[9] The best is reputed to be al-shami, though it is now hard to obtain because of the conflict between the government and Zaidi rebels led by the Houthi clan in the north of the country, the origin of the strain. For a strong effect on the mind, al-hamadani and al-arhabi 'brands' are preferred.

Mostly males take part in chewing sessions, which occur in a special room in the home, the *mafraj* or salon for receiving visitors, evocative of the *diwaniyah* system in Kuwait.[10] The home is the focus of social life in Yemen. Up to fifty guests may take part at any one time. A small number of Yemenis seem interested in enhancing the natural aspects of the 'highs', and are beginning to do things such as drive into the mountains to consume qat, where they can marvel at the spectacular scenery. An increasing minority of women also partake,[11] though in smaller quantities and almost always on the basis of gender segregation in the home. Women are reported as being more animated than men during their qat sessions, with dancing not unusual. Children too, some as young as seven, are said to have joined in these sessions, with speculation that up to 20 per cent of minors may take part. Meanwhile, others run wild in the streets, neglected by family members more intent on the direct experience of the qat.

Supporters of qat say that chewing sessions result in periods of clarity, during which business may be transacted,[12] mediation furthered[13] and political issues negotiated. The ultimate goal of qat sessions is to achieve a state of *kif* or well-being, though this is not by any means automatic.[14] These are enjoyable sessions, which promote individual and corporate self-esteem for the host and his clan alike, with music, story-telling and poetry recitals sometimes part of the experience. Qat is also used on more formal occasions, such as at funerals, where mourners use the drug as a stimulant to reflect on the life of the deceased. It is also used to facilitate enjoyment at circumcision parties and marriage ceremonies.[15]

Qat, 'this baneful little tree',[16] or 'the philosophical leaf',[17] depending on one's point of view, has come to dominate Yemen and its way of life. At least 70 per cent of households report that they have at least one user in the family. It is estimated that the average Yemeni household, desperately poor at the best of times,[18] spends between 10 and 30 per cent of its income on qat, and a further proportion on tobacco. A recent report from the Ministry of Agriculture estimates that Yemenis collectively spend around $1.2 billion a year on qat.[19] Little wonder then that production now covers about one-third of the country's cultivable land. This has caused alarm because an estimated one in three Yemenis (7.5 million people) suffer chronic hunger.[20] Somewhere between 14 and 20 per cent of national employment is related to the production, distribution and sale of qat. Such is the economic and social attraction of the drug that increasingly every spare space is given over to its cultivation, including grass verges, gardens and the grounds of historical attractions administered by the state.[21] There are believed to be between 300 and 500 million qat shrubs in Yemen, covering around 130,000 hectares (compared to 8,000 hectares in the 1970s). Qat is currently to be found cultivated in fourteen out of Yemen's twenty-one governorates.[22] Qat cultivation has been expanding at a rate of 12 per cent per year, at least up to 2010. Each shrub may fruit up to four times a year, depending on the availability of water, making its production a particularly cost-effective exercise, especially compared to possible alternative crops.

Barriers to Development

As qat production steadily increased during the 1970s and 1980s, a debate emerged about whether this cultivation profile was good for the economy in developmental terms. Those who argued that it was a virtuous change pointed to the excessive dependence on oil rents, which generates 75 per cent of Yemeni national revenue. Though modest in overall output terms, the impact of oil exports on the economy was still a disproportionate one. Furthermore, it was argued that coffee, one of the country's best-known crops, and frequently advanced as a potential substitute crop, was actually little different to qat, being a mild stimulant with little nutritional content.

The supporters of qat pointed to many of the business efficiencies that characterise the production and distribution of the shrub,[23] driven by the short life of its leaf. They also pointed out that the profitability of qat was likely to keep the people on the land, thereby avoiding a precipitate rural-to-urban migration, the like of which has been seen across most of the rest of the region. Finally, the qat debate has raged every bit as ferociously among foreigners working in and on Yemen, with the defenders of qat—who include at least one former Western ambassador—taking a romantic view of the country and its practices,[24] while its critics have looked disdainfully on the qat chewing, and often Yemeni society more generally.[25]

By the early 2000s the qat debate appeared to have reached a decisive outcome. The key arguments were twofold. First, the production of qat had continued to grow rapidly, thereby increasingly squeezing out every rival in the agricultural sector; in short, qat was becoming almost as economically dominant as oil and gas in the neighbouring economies of the Arabian Peninsula. Second, the clincher, was that qat production was having an alarmingly detrimental impact on the country's meagre water supplies. The Ministry of Agriculture estimates that 30 per cent of Yemen's available water is being spent on qat production.[26]

Though qat has a widely held reputation for being a water guzzler, some contend that it is not a particularly greedy plant. The problem is that farmers tend to over-water their qat. They also water their crop later in the agricultural year (qat being an evergreen), in order to squeeze out more yields. Irrigation systems in Yemen more generally are notoriously wasteful. This water debate was taking place against a backdrop of broader concerns at Yemen's ability to supply its rapidly increasing population with potable water. The alarmist *cri de coeur* has it that the underground aquifer that supplies the capital could run dry as early as 2017.

That the water argument had won the day can best be understood if one appreciates the history of developmentalism in the sector over the last forty years. The advent of new drilling technologies in the 1970s, and their ability to access Yemen's aquifers, was hailed as a great breakthrough for the country by much of the developmentalist community. It was even regarded by some as a democratising innovation. Yemenis were encouraged to take the initiative. They were often egged on by a public policy environment that favoured such a strategy. For example, the Cooperative and Agricultural Bank of North Yemen for 'many years' extended credit for the purchase of water pumps at interest rates of 9–11 per cent, while market rates hovered around the 20 per cent mark.[27] Meanwhile, the government spends an annual $700 million subsidising diesel prices, much of which goes towards powering technologies that deplete the country's water supplies more rapidly.[28] The World Bank, which has had a long-standing presence in North Yemen, has shown comparable inconsistency in the past. More generally, the government lost control of the process. Of the estimated 55,000 wells in operation across the country, only a small percentage are state owned.[29] The cost to Yemen of four decades of incoherence has been a water system that has left only one underground aquifer relatively undamaged.

A belatedly broad consensus on the part of the specialist and developmental communities in Yemen has not, however, proved to be a basis for positive action. Over the years a powerful qat lobby, comprising direct and indirect beneficiaries of the harvest, has built up within the political system. With the qat trade being controlled by 'syndicates' that buy qat at the farm gate, and distribute it through a network of middlemen across the country, some commentators have claimed to have identified the existence of a 'qat mafia'.[30] The direct beneficiaries divide into three complementary groups.

- the farmers, who cultivate qat, some of whom are large landowners, but most of whom are smallholders;
- those involved in the country's transport sector, who ensure that the shrub gets to market speedily before drying, in spite of Yemen's inhospitable geography;

- the retailers who sell the leaf at the various qat markets that have sprung up around the country.[31]

The first two groups are often further bound together by tribal ties, which are arguably stronger in Yemen than anywhere else in the Arab world. With tribal sinews providing additional solidarity, and arms freely available in the countryside, changing policy is not simply a matter of winning intellectual or even institutional arguments.

The indirect beneficiaries of the crop are less visible, but no less important in qat's political resilience. Notable among this group are the police, who have the ability to disrupt the swift delivery to market if not brought into the coalition of vested interests. Then there are those government employees who levy taxes on the movement of qat at a governorate level; much of this revenue fails to find its way into the central government budget, being lost to corruption at a more local level.[32] Finally, there is the state itself, enfeebled in nature, which benefits from the collection of even reduced levels of taxes, such is the poor position of the government's coffers. With groups involved both directly and indirectly in the qat economy having a collective vested interest for the continuation of production, changing priorities, either at the political centre or the rural periphery, will not be easy.

Strategies for Reform

The first signs of a concerted fightback against the spread of qat came in the early 2000s, notably with the adoption, after years of debate, of a Water Law in 2002. Its impact, however, was limited. It resulted in institutional evolution, with the creation of the Ministry of Water and Environment (MWE) in 2003. Though presentationally bringing water management and the environment together represented a public policy breakthrough, the process was left ham-strung. Most crucially, the MWE was not given jurisdiction over anywhere near all of the bodies involved in the sector. So, for example, it had no control over the National Water Resources Authority, which was responsible for basin-level management; the National Water and Sewerage Authority, which led on urban water matters; the General Authority for Rural Water Supply Projects, which controlled water in the countryside; and the Ministry of Agriculture, which is responsible for the country's inefficient irrigation management, and hence is the main client of the non-renewable aquifers. Consequently, management and coordination has remained weak.

The main water-sector donors have been the World Bank and the governments of Germany and the Netherlands. Unfortunately, this triangular relationship has often been characterised by rivalry and disagreements over strategy. The Dutch have emphasised the need for tighter water management for much longer, with obvious implications for qat, while the World Bank has until relatively recently pursued contradictory policies. The main outcome of a newly galvanised triangular cooperation has been the establishment of the National Water Sector Strategy and Investment Programme (NWSSIP). Following its initial three-year focus (2005–7) the NWSSIP has been updated, and now contains a costed list of planned activities. However, fully funding such a programme remains a challenge, while the organisation's attempts to reconcile diametrically opposed views through the crystallisation of a user consensus appears naive.[33] The Yemeni government and the World Bank have also formulated a partner strategy for qat called the Integrated Qat Demand Reduction Agenda, which began functioning at the end of 2009.

Attempts to break the alliance of vested interests for qat production have focused on crop substitution. This is a familiar story from past and current experience of narcotic production as diverse as Turkey in the 1960s and 1970s, and Afghanistan and the Andean countries today. In Yemen the situation is not as acute as for some, at least as far as agricultural fertility is concerned. Yemen has relatively good soil, on which a range of crops may successfully be grown. Traditional crops such as wheat, barley, sorghum, vegetables, grapes and coffee have been frequently mentioned as appropriate for substitution agriculture, as have other items, for example bananas, guavas and papayas. There have been experiments with the state distributing seeds to farmers in an effort to encourage crop rotation.

The fecundity of the land does not obviate the problem. Bottom-line economics dictates a reality under which qat growers can increase their income up to fivefold by switching away from grain production. Richard Tutwiler, an anthropologist with over twenty years' experience of working on Yemen, states that an irrigated qat farm one hectare in area can net twelve times the poverty level.[34] The role of the syndicates in supplying agricultural inputs for qat producers, notably through the provision of credit, together with the efficient process for the marketing of qat, have left the leaf with a strong comparative advantage, resonant of the experience of opium production in Afghanistan. Sanaa has proved reluctant to introduce an effective tax regime to disincentivise the production of qat. It is unrealistic to expect such a poor and low-capacity state as Yemen, or the modest enabling funds provided to it in the form of overseas aid, to meet the sort of cost that would be required to break the market grip enjoyed by qat. Anti-qat advertising across the country has made little material impact.

There have been dark mutterings about other strategies for limiting qat production at home, beyond that of crop substitution. This could involve the importation of qat, currently proscribed, as a means through which to divert demand from home production. Acutely aware of the possible deployment of such tactics, the 'qat mafia' is alleged to have threatened to shoot down cargo planes in the event that flights begin to bring in such foreign output.[35]

Furthermore, pressures have been building from below for action to limit qat production and consumption. A 'large segment' of society, it is claimed, have come to the conclusion that qat is a major problem for contemporary Yemen.[36] For some members of the middle class, 'Qat in today's Yemen is what smoking was in Britain a generation ago',[37] the focus of a steadily rising social opprobrium. There are now several organisations, largely functioning disparately, that are concentrating on different aspects of the undesirability of qat and its consequences. One organisation, for example, has been promoting qat-free weddings.

The al-Afif Cultural Foundation was one of the first civil society organisations to expand into the area. 'Good citizenship' groups are involved in distributing posters and booklets, and organising seminars about the 'qat habit'. Much of the NGO activity has focused on the health implications of qat. While many of these are contested, some seem more clear-cut. For example, there has long been concern about the effect of qat chewing on breast-feeding mothers, and on the birth weight of the newly born.[38] The Yemeni Organisation for Women and Child Development (SOUL) has been particularly active in warning of the dangers of the former to secondary school and university students.[39] Health concerns can be secondary as well as primary. The use of pesticides in order to maximise qat production has certainly been a worrying development.

BOX 1

POETRY AND QAT

Since at least the days of Samuel Taylor Coleridge and Kubla Khan, narcotics and poetry have frequently gone together. Such is also the case in Yemen, where poetry and story-telling are taken extremely seriously, and feed off one another. One of the more pleasurable aspects of qat-chewing parties is the poetry that is recited or even composed at such events. Though most of the poetry in Yemen tends to be about such subjects as personal and clan heroism, national unity, mediation and the like, the debate over qat has spawned its own sub-genre. Songs lauding the virtues of qat were prevalent at one time. More recently new stories have emerged, some prompted by official intervention no doubt, about children, women and families who have been impoverished and divided as a result of their brush with the narcotic. Yemeni poetry, whether about qat or other subjects, is characteristically rough and tough. One poet mobilised in one of the early campaigns against qat, dating from the early 1970s and now making a comeback, Ahmed al-Mu'alimi, does not mince his words:

> And as an opinion to fight the qat
> Since the qat is an evil and its cure is uneasy
> Qat is an insult and a shame on us
> Which is soaking us with mud
> Qat is a plague and its least harm is
> Spending hours without a work
> Qat is a time's killer and it is an evil
> For our youths, old men, and middle-aged men
> We live in the space era and we no longer
> Are still living the unenlightened life of camels and mules
> Our era invades other planets whereas
> Some of us still walk barefooted[40]

A more recent viewpoint is just as critical and lyrical. In an interesting juxtaposition of images, a well-known Yemeni writer, Abdul Karim al-Razihi, says: 'Qat ... is the opium of our people. It is the green Imam who rules over our republic. It is the key for everything and it is central to all our social occasions. It is the unexplainable that explains everything.'

Regime Politics

A joke circulated in Sanaa in June 1978 just after the assassination of the president of North Yemen, Ahmad Hussein al-Ghashmi, who had lasted just eight months in power, following the killing of his predecessor, Colonel Ibrahim Muhammad al-Hamdi. The joke has it that after his arrival in heaven Hamdi had launched a tirade of invective against Ghashmi, because he had forgotten to bring any qat with him. Ghashmi had placated Hamdi, saying that his successor, Major Ali Abdullah Saleh, had promised to take care of the qat—'and he would be joining us any time now'.[41]

The story is interesting for a number of reasons: the centrality of qat to the cultural practices of North Yemen; the fact that qat consumption extends right to the very top; the association of qat with the vicissitudes of regime politics; the chronic instability of regime politics in Yemen; and the constant, almost casual presence of political violence in the country. The joke may have given an insight into the Yemeni body politic, but in another way the joke got things spectacularly wrong. Thirty-two years later both Hamdi and Ghashmi are still waiting for Saleh, who, while no longer in power in Yemen, is still very much alive, to bring the qat. It may be the case that since his ouster in 2012 Saleh is no longer president of the country, having been succeeded by Abed Rabbo Mansour Hadi, who is also a qat-chewer, but not as regularly and with as much compulsion as his prime minister, Mohammed Salem Basindwa. But Saleh is still a player in Yemeni politics, where he hopes to secure the succession for his son, Ahmad. His personal conduct is also indicative of how the leadership of the country has tried to address the qat issue.

There is a chance, though perhaps not a very big one, that Yemen's two dead leaders will have to remain qat-free for eternity. Saleh periodically associated himself with civil associational campaigns to reduce the consumption of qat. In doing so, he resembled a Yemeni version of Mikhail Gorbachev, intent, futilely so in the end, on stopping or at least containing the deleterious impact of vodka abuse on Russian society. Saleh was trumpeted by his supporters as having given up the qat habit.[42] Moreover, he associated himself with a national campaign under the slogan 'Yemen Without Qat'. It showed him making appearances on Yemeni television, mostly in sporting attire: Saleh was shown jogging, swimming and even diving, thereby emphasising what feats of physical prowess may be achieved if the debilitating effects of qat are eradicated. Another favourite pose of the ex-president is that of working at a computer terminal or browsing the internet. Again, the image is supposed to convey vigour, focus and modernity:[43] what the Yemeni economy would be capable of if only it could end its collective dependency on qat.

Saleh's involvement in such public demonstrations are, however, sometimes of a more equivocal nature. He also proclaimed on television that he only chews qat at weekends. At other times, such as in 1999, he committed himself to giving it up altogether—without, it is assumed, more than a few months' success.[44] Saleh knows that qat remains extremely popular at home. It would not do for the national leader to spend too much time chiding his own people for their consumption. And besides, diving and swimming are hardly viable recreations open to the vast majority of the country's impoverished population, searching for an alternative pursuit.

Some efforts have been made to control or limit the use of qat within the public sector. In 2002 all government employees were formally banned from chewing it altogether,[45] an empty gesture that has been all but forgotten. There is also a ban on consumption for those wearing uniform in Yemen. In practice, soldiers chew the leaf, even while under arms. More concerted attempts have concentrated mostly on the regime's elite forces,[46] frequently in different forms the bedrock of military rule. Key among these is the 20,000-strong special forces division, since 1999 commanded by the ex-president's son, Ahmad. A special guard unit is headed by a nephew of the former president.[47] Saleh's professional background demonstrates that it was his position as a senior army officer that brought him to power in the first place. It illustrates his reliance on the elite military for continuing regime support.

The lot of the majority of Yemen's troops is not so privileged. Take those rebels fighting in the north and centre of the country, best known as Houthi rebels, after their commanders, but more properly as Zaidis, after their religious affiliation. The insurgency began in the north of the country, in the governorate of Saadah,[48] on the Houthis' home turf. More recently the insurgency has spread to the centre of the country. The conflict, having erupted in 2004, has only been punctuated by the odd short ceasefire since. The basic wages of the combatants have only been around $100 a month. The troops, who range in age between fifteen and twenty-five, are permitted to supplement their income by taking whatever booty the rebels might leave behind after battle, from food to equipment. The military has a reputation for being corrupt.

When not actually engaged in combat, many soldiers while away their time chewing qat leaves—that is, if they are able to find any. The supply of qat in the north has been greatly curtailed, owing to the devastation of many of the fields in which it grows. There were around 150,000 internally displaced people in the northern fighting zone, exacerbating the chaotic nature of the region. Troops haggle with vendors in the conflict areas. Qat is reported to be the only aspect of the economy that still thrives in the war zone. Commanders and enlisted men join together to consume qat in the afternoons and evenings.[49] Lacking basic military gear such as helmets and body armour,[50] there is little appetite for prosecuting the campaign on the government side. Sanaa lacks the killer instinct to force a victory, perhaps in part due to qat. This has only been overcome as a result of the intervention of a Saudi-backed conventional military force, intent on decisively affecting the result in the government's favour. Even qat has its limitations.

It is far from being an unusual story. This book reveals that different types of narcotics have been used by soldiers across the region, from Israel to Iran to Yemen. This is not just the case in the Middle East. Many African paramilitaries have given their fighters narcotics before going into battle. In the war for the Yugoslav succession in the early to mid-1990s, Serbian irregulars were periodically described as fighting under the influence of alcohol.

Within the civilian sector, one in three Yemenis are unemployed. Chewing qat is a simple way of passing the time, and keeps such people away from the altogether more pernicious substances, such as alcohol or hard drugs. Critics of the government point out that qat is a great diversion from politics. One opposition figure is quoted confidentially as saying that 'when people are chewing qat, they don't ask awkward questions about where Yemen's oil revenues are going'.[51] If accurate, for a country that has recently experienced riots by unemployed young people, and where poverty and corruption are a structural part of daily life, qat is a stabilising force. Not all agree with this proposition. J. E. Peterson, for example, informs us that reformers in early 1930s North Yemen used the mosque and qat chews as platforms from which to demand liberal political change.[52]

Qat is frowned upon by radical Islamists. This in spite of the fact that qat is not mentioned, let alone proscribed, in the Qur'an. By contrast, some Yemeni religious leaders are regular chewers. Devout Yemenis used qat in the past in order to remain awake during all-night prayer sessions.[53] Reports suggest that ordinary Yemenis experience no particular unease in attending Friday prayers and immediately afterwards jostling one another to purchase the best-quality qat.[54] The one area of a religiously inspired restraint relates to the Islamic holy month of Ramadan, though even here qat is often used to stave off sleep. As with the public consumption of food, it is generally frowned upon to chew qat openly during the period of fasting. This may cause some anguish, but a tolerable level of public discomfort is seen by many as a sign of taking one's religious practices seriously. Many Yemenis then chew qat during the period for the breaking of the fast, rather than waiting until the end of the month before resuming consumption. Indeed, some Yemenis speak of religious holy days, such as Ramadan and the pilgrimage season, as being the times when the greatest volume of qat is consumed.[55]

Qat and its Wider Context

Unlike better-known narcotics, such as marijuana and opium, qat has not been brought within the net of global proscription. Formally, this has been because it was not included in any of the anti-drugs conventions that have punctuated the last hundred years of multilateral negotiation, and which formed the basis for a steadily encroaching illegality, as adopted in the legal codes of the members of an emerging world order. Qat has therefore benefited from relatively low levels of awareness, even on the part of those responsible for this widening net of illegality. Historically, the crucial factor at the root of this situation has been the poor communications hub of which the underdeveloped nature of Yemen has been part. With the narcotic component of qat quickly dissipating, it has until recently proved to be practically impossible to distribute it much beyond Yemen's neighbours. Of crucial importance, the exportation of qat to the USA was a practical impossibility, at least until recently.

The marginalisation of the 'qat question' has not prevented international organisations from venturing to give a view on the subject, when inclined or pressed. Notably, in 1980 the World Health Organisation classified qat as a drug of abuse that can produce mild to moderate psychological dependence, though less than alcohol and tobacco. It did not consider it to be an addictive drug, but it did describe it as 'dependency inducing'. In short, this determination viewed qat as a narcotic, but not as an especially harmful one. This meant that, as in Ethiopia[56] and Somalia, the world's other two main country consumers, there was no appreciable pressure on the Yemeni state to outlaw the practice.

The development of modern communications, notably mass air transportation, has obliged the adoption of a wider view towards qat. This has perhaps inevitably propelled the regime in a more restrictive direction. Take, for example, Britain, one of the few Western countries not to have banned the plant,[57] where it was mainly consumed by the Somali and Yemeni communities in such widely spread areas as the cities of Birmingham in the Midlands, Cardiff in south Wales, Sheffield in Yorkshire and, of course, London. It is brought twice weekly by Yemen Airways in 400 kilogram consignments, and is distributed through cafes and markets. Sheffield is home to a Yemeni community believed to be in excess of 9,000, with at least 20 qat sessions going on virtually every afternoon in the city. Ultimately, this was all too good to be true. In mid-2013 the British government decided to make qat a controlled substance. However, it was only elevated to a Class C substance, the most benign of classifications, and is presumably still enjoyed, but more clandestinely than was the case before 2013.

The ability to transport qat to the USA has raised the issue of whether the shrub should be brought firmly under the global anti-drugs regime. A series of prosecutions were brought in order to develop the legal infrastructure on the matter. The fact that two alkaloids found in qat—cathine and cathinone—were banned by federal law in 1988 and 1993 looked ominous in terms of the future free availability of qat. In reality, these test cases failed, leaving qat importation and consumption as a grey area of legality. A central issue of this is that in the USA cathinone is classified as a Schedule I drug, compared with cathine, which is Schedule III or IV. The bulk of the prosecutions were brought under the former, because of its greater seriousness. However, the presence of cathinone in qat is small, 36 parts in every 100,000 when freshly picked. Owing to the short shelf-life of the narcotic content of qat, this would mean that even this element would dissipate rapidly. It was beyond the ability of US law enforcement to test the drug and register its mood-altering component before it ceased to exist. It remains the case that qat does not appear on the US list of banned substances. Without giving 'fair notice' that a substance is illegal, a successful prosecution is unlikely.[58]

The fraught issue of qat and US–Yemeni relations has also had an airing on the ground in Sanaa. The case surrounded whether US diplomats should be allowed to attend qat-chewing sessions as part of their work of engaging with and getting to understand local society. A further debate involved whether they should be permitted to ingest the leaf. At first, caution and a sense of social superiority decreed that the embassy's diplomats not engage in such practices. However, the range and importance of business transacted at qat-chewing occasions, together with the associated accessibility of senior government and regime figures, meant that the logic of doing business in Yemen saw the regulation quietly rescinded. The search for intelligence to prevent terrorist outrages originating on Yemeni soil—such as the December 2009 'underpants bomber', a Nigerian student, who had been trained in Yemen—has overridden the niceties of diplomatic convention and political correctness.

That does not mean that qat is not causing problems for Yemen in its foreign relations. The source of the tension is much closer to home than the USA: Saudi Arabia is becoming concerned at the increasing levels of qat being smuggled illegally across its border with Yemen. One source has even put the value of the annual contraband going to the Saudi market at $1 billion. The image of qat as a 'natural' substance has enhanced its appeal in Saudi Arabia, in turn fuelling demand,[59] in spite of official attempts to deter usage.

The qat issue is just one more problem in a lengthy list that preoccupies bilateral relations. Riyadh has been concerned at the spread of the Houthi rebellion, not just across the common border. The Saudi government believes that Iran has been aiding the Zaidi rebels, giving an additional edge to its military response. Relations between Riyadh and Sanaa have also been strained over Islamist extremism, with some of Osama bin Laden's most implacable supporters, drawn from Saudi Arabia and Yemen, seeking solace in the latter. Finally, the problem of 'what to do about Yemen' has been exercising Saudi Arabia, as the richest economy in the area, for many decades. Foremost among these concerns is how to manage the perceived threat from Yemen, based on a high birth rate, high poverty levels, poor development prospects and a chronic shortage of water. In addressing this, qat is very much an important, though not the key, determinant of future relations between the two countries.

Conclusion

There has long been a debate in Yemen about the nature of qat, its effect on the individual and the impact that it has on the development process. That debate has apparently been resolved over the last decade in favour of those who believe that a qat monoculture has emerged in Yemen, to the detriment of the economy and of society alike. In particular, the debate has focused on water. The depletion of the underground aquifers has had a detrimental effect on the country's long-term ability to supply itself with water.

The logic of agricultural cropping and of water management does not, however, mean that a strategic reduction in qat production is around the corner. Cultural values, especially in the politically dominant part of the old North Yemen, discourage such prudence, as do daily mastication habits. More crucially, an embedded set of clustered vested interests have emerged that will make it very difficult for Yemenis to desist from the production and consumption of qat. These extend across small farmers, police, state officials and urban market sellers. Most of these primarily material interests have been complemented by strong tribal affiliation.

In all of this, the state in Yemen remains frustratingly weak, and disinclined to take on the special interests. The military is poorly motivated and often ineffectual. It is distracted by a host of patchy insurgencies. The domestic leadership of the country is divided. Qat is therefore likely to remain a staple of farming in Yemen for the foreseeable future, in spite of the growing risks involved.

CONSUMPTION SPACES

4

EGYPT

THE LAND OF THE HASHISHEEN

Egyptians are famous in the Arab world for their sense of humour, and a healthy ability to laugh at themselves. This extends to narcotic drugs, notably hashish, as well as other features of everyday life. An old favourite story that has stood the test of time goes as follows:

> The Egyptian army had been mobilised prior to the outbreak of hostilities against Israel in June 1967, the third Arab–Israeli war. Two soldiers from the Egyptian countryside were assigned responsibility for a tank. In order to while away the time before going into battle they decided to smoke some hashish. One thing led to another and the two soldiers were soon completely stoned. It was a hot summer's day, and they became drowsy, and soon fell into a deep sleep. While they were comatose, the 'Six-Day War' began. Israel launched a lightning pre-emptive strike, destroying the Egyptian air force, after which their ground victory in the war was assured. So sweeping was the success that Israel took over the Sinai Peninsula, and captured the tank in which the two soldiers lay fast asleep. The Israeli army towed the tank to Tel Aviv, to show it off as a war trophy. Its entry into Israel coincided with the awakening of the two Egyptian soldiers. They roused one another and, upon seeing Tel Aviv before them, both cheered loudly in praise of the great victory that they assumed had been won by the Egyptian side.

This story is a good place to start the process of evaluating drugs in Egypt. It illustrates the ubiquity of hashish, even extending to such important institutions as the military. It indicates how extensively narcotics circulate for personal use, and how their use complements a sense of fatalism for which lower-class, rural Egyptians are most renowned. Implicit in the joke is a social snobbery on the part of the city towards the countryside.

Direction of Travel

After the 1940s,[1] but before 1980, narcotic drugs were not considered to be a particular problem in Egypt.[2] Hashish was freely available, especially in Cairo, where, in the poorer area of el-Batniyyeh, to the rear of the famous thousand-year-old al-Azhar University,[3] hashish was sold from trestle tables, which were erected out in the open. Though they had a manned guard box in the area, the police turned a blind eye to the trade. The authorities were warned off or bought off by those making money from the business, sometimes by roughnecks threatening the use of violence. So infamous were the practices that in 1980 Hossameddin Mustafa made a film about the area, which was named after it.[4] So-called sophisticated drugs, such as cocaine, were theoretically present in the country, but their price placed them well beyond the reach even of the middle classes, let alone of the working man. The same could be said of heroin.

The situation began to change in the late 1970s/early 1980s. First, the US president Jimmy Carter actively started to pressurise Cairo to crack down on the public supply of narcotics. The fact that Egypt was now increasingly dependent on US aid, in the wake of the Camp David peace settlement with Israel, meant that the USA could wield greater leverage on the subject than it had been able to before. But the increasingly activist response was not a success. It backfired badly. The effect of this greater involvement was to help drive the drugs trade underground. The el-Batniyyeh operation was closed down completely: a renovation project in an adjacent area, paid for by the Aga Khan, helped to hide its traces. The criminalising of drugs had an impact that was perverse and has since proved all too familiar. It simply offered more lucrative opportunities for those involved in the trafficking and distribution of drugs than had existed in the past.

A parallel boost to the drugs market came from the domestic front. Increasingly, drugs came to be viewed as glamorous. This growing attraction of drugs increased under the presidency of Anwar Sadat between 1970 and 1981. Sadat himself was known to enjoy hashish. He even had a reputation for chewing opium, and was reputed to do so when making speeches. The success of his 'open door' (*infitah*) strategy, which stimulated the private actor and economic activism in general, could not fail to give a boost to drugs-related criminality, as well as legitimate business. For hashish consumers the Sadat era has come to be known as something of a golden age.[5]

The effect of this internal change was that by 1989 there were estimated to be some 2 million regular drugs users in Egypt,[6] out of a total population of perhaps 45 million. In spite of attempts to stem this trend, for instance through the imposition of punitive prison terms,[7] the number of regular users continued to increase steadily, and had reached 6 million by 2007, when the general population topped 80 million. By this stage, however, there was a much greater range of illicit drugs on offer in the country, including Ecstasy, methamphetamine and pharmaceutical drugs. Meanwhile, cocaine, which had not been evident between the inter-war years and the early 1980s, was beginning to become more widespread, especially among the monied. By the end of the first decade of the new millennium approximately $3 billion was being spent in Egypt each year on the procurement of illicit drugs, the equivalent of about one-third of the figure in the UK economy, with its entrenched hard-drugs problem and considerable levels of casual usage. At this time, around 8.5 per cent of the Egyptian population was estimated to be drug dependent, approximately 6 million in total[8] (rising to over 7 million, as a proportion of the World Bank estimate of the Egyptian population in 2009, 83 million). Of this number, 439,000 were believed to be children.

Somewhat surprisingly, as late as 2009 Egypt's International Narcotics Control Strategy Report concluded that Egypt is not a significant consumer of narcotics.

Hashish, the drug of choice

It is often remarked that if for Christians in the Middle East the drug of choice is alcohol ('the drug of the infidels'), the equivalent for Muslims is hashish. Nowhere are the proportions of that split better illustrated than in Egypt, where 90 per cent of the population is Muslim and 10 per cent Coptic Christian, and some 85 per cent of Egyptians who are substance users consume cannabis.[9] With a mixture of affection and mild contempt Egyptians as a whole are widely referred to as the '*hashisheen*' across the rest of the Arab world, in recognition of their fondness for the drug. Specific Qur'anic invocations against the use of alcohol, as well as gambling, alongside the absence of any such a dictat against hemp drugs, are often cited as justification for this socio-cultural cleavage.

In reality, things are rarely so clear-cut. Alcohol was used by wealthy Muslims at various times, and hence became a symbol of wealth and title.[10] By contrast, the poor tended not to access alcohol—finding its cost prohibitive rather than necessarily being deterred by its status as forbidden (*haram*). Moreover, there have been no shortage of attempts to limit the circulation and consumption of hashish in Egypt and beyond, with concerns over the effectiveness of Egypt as a fighting machine, along the lines of those described in the introduction, often uppermost in mind. Nevertheless, hashish, and its botanic cousin bango, or 'Egyptian marijuana', still dominate as far as national consumption levels are concerned.

Consumption levels[11]

Generating hard figures about the drugs issue is as difficult in Egypt as it is anywhere else in the Middle East region. Indeed, this challenge is greater than for most, partly because of the physical proportions of the country, its long borders, its large population and the dynamism of its social context, with a pronounced rural-to-urban drift and extensive outward economic migration. It would not therefore be easy to quantify Egypt's narcotic experiences even if considerable resources were available, which, considering Egypt's modest per capita income, they are not. These structural disadvantages are, however, at least partly mitigated by the existence of a small but well-trained and dedicated set of anti-drugs professionals, active in the universities, the specialist state sector and among NGOs, and the willingness of the state modestly to fund data collection on the ground. These are further complemented by experts working in associated areas, such as HIV/AIDS, and supported by the presence of the regional office of the UN's drug and crime agency, the UNODC.

On the basis of research carried out especially since 2007, which has a traction rarely witnessed across the region, it has been possible to build up the following profile of drug abuse in Egypt. A typical drug user will therefore more than likely be:

- A young adult. People have a mean age of 20.8 years at the point of the onset of substance misuse (alcohol included). To some extent, such a figure masks the range of ages at which first use begins. For example, 29.3% of users first consumed substances when aged 16–19 years of age, while 19.4% first experimented while in the 8–15 age group. A more recent report identified children as commencing the consumption of hard drugs as young as 11.[12] The high point of substance use among users is in the age range 26–30, when 37.9% of abusers are likely to be consuming.
- Predominantly male. The prevalence of substance abuse in males is 13.2%, compared to 1.1% for the female population. In most societies males tend

to be the greater and heavier users of narcotics and alcohol. In Egypt this is likely to be exacerbated by the strict social norms, which restrict a woman's access to social interaction, and therefore to the sort of people and places where drugs would be available, whether for purchase, sale or use. It may also be the case that females are less likely to admit usage, distrusting the confidentiality of the surveying process, because of the far-reaching implications that such an admission might entail if it became public. There is, however, no room for complacency. Substance abuse among females is unquestionably creeping up as a proportion of the whole.[13]

- Resident in urban or desert areas. Residential prevalence figures indicate that urban rates are 10.6% compared to rural experiences of 7.9%. These, however, pale alongside prevalence rates for bedouin, many of whom are still to be found resident in the desert fringes, and for whom rates are as high as 30.5%. More specific research on the bedouin in the Negev, the desert area of southern Israel, which abuts the desert of the Sinai Peninsula, indicates a wider vulnerability, with 14% of adults reported as having consumed alcohol, and 11.1% users of illicit drugs.

- Located close to the drugs routes, especially on Egypt's coasts. Historically, Alexandria has been a key entry point for contraband, owing to the size and sophistication of its port, and the level of corruption of its administration. Suez and the ports of the province of Sharkia are also important as they lie across the Red Sea from the Sinai, from where much of the drug smuggling originates. The Suez Canal is also important for the transit trafficking of cannabis and heroin for other destinations. The prevalence of substance abuse is the greatest in Suez, Alexandria and Sharkia, with 13.7%, 13.2% and 12.9% respectively.

- Someone with some education and a reasonably good job. Of those polled using substances in the job categories offered, 22.8% were found to be skilled workers, 21.8% were literate and 20.8% were tradesmen. This was well above higher-status, professional positions, but also higher than lower-status categories, and even the jobless, 11.7% of the unemployed admitting use. The inference behind such figures is that those using substances will need a better-paid job in order to be able to afford the luxury of substance consumption over and above the basics of life. At the same time, the lower incomes of the poor will make procuring illicit drugs less feasible.

- The socially distressed. Though the samples are small, there is powerful evidence to indicate a correlation between acute stress in family life and the consumption of substances. For instance, over 63% of males separated from their wives were likely to be regular substance abusers. This figure was at 47% for divorced men. Interestingly, of those men with more than one wife, prevalence stood at almost 59%, polygamy being a potentially stressful life-style choice, and hence linked closely to the consumption of drugs.

BOX 1

MUHAMED MOUNIR

Muhamed Mounir is one of Egypt's best-known popular singers and actors. Now more than fifty-eight years of age, Mounir has made over twenty albums, and has been well regarded in the music business for three decades. This durability has earned him the sobriquet 'al-Malek Huwa al-Malek' (The king is the king). Mounir originally comes from Aswan in Upper Egypt. His musical style places him firmly in the Arabic music genre, but blended with Nubian music and more catholic influences such as blues and reggae. As much as anything Mounir is famous for the use of hashish at his public concerts. By the end of his gigs a thick film of smoke invariably hangs in the air. Mounir is an enthusiastic and public consumer of hashish himself, leading to worries that younger, more impressionable fans will embrace the habit by fol-lowing his example. Mounir underlined his continuing relevance in the field of Egyptian popular music when he recorded a song, 'For Egypt, Revolution', to mark the 2011 protests against President Husni Mubarak. This was not unexpected, as Mounir has specialised in patri-otic as well as popular and romantic songs in the past. He let it be known that he would like to perform on stage in Tahrir Square as the protests against the old regime grew.

Bango

A lower-status alternative to hashish from among the hemp family, a drug known locally as 'bango' has become a popular substance for consumption over the last twenty or so years. Local drug experts say that, in spite of the bedouin referring to it as 'green tobacco', in fact bango should be considered as part of the cannabis family. The main difference with other forms of canna-bis-based drugs seems to be that more of the plant, such as the stem, flowers and seeds, are utilised in this preparation than would normally be the case, either with cannabis resin or marijuana. This more rough-and-ready concoction perhaps helps to explain why bango is popularly regarded as being more potent than regular forms of cannabis.[14] The consumption of bango has on occasion, whether fairly or unfairly, been associated with violent acts, including rape and murder, the implication being that taking it makes such crime more likely.[15]

Bango is a drug closely associated with three somewhat incongruously diverse consumer groups: the young; manual labourers; and intellectuals. Tens of cases of artists and performers, such as the well-known comic actor Said Saleh, have been caught consuming bango. Part of the attraction of the drug for intellectuals has been that it has helped them to associate with the lives and experiences of the working man. This sense of empathy has increased their tendency to speak out about their social and political predicament.

It is among ordinary labourers that the social effects of the drug appear to have been most harmful. Manual workers justify the regular consumption of bango on the grounds that it makes them more active, and hence capable of working longer hours. Professional opinion is much more critical, with one professor of sociology, Aza Kuraim, calling the consumption of bango 'a social infection'. Professor Kuraim notes that it is usually the families of consumers who suffer the most within a context of dependency, with the head of the household frittering away much of his income on the drug, and even seeking to borrow against future wages, in order to be able to afford larger current purchases.[16]

In spite of these social problems, the prevailing attitude towards bango is much more ambivalent. This applies especially in Egypt's rural areas. Here, the drug is associated with an authentic lower-class Egyptian experience, typified by its melancholy wistfulness. The feelings it elicits helps to make the drug popular, in spite of its more harmful side-effects upon the individual's long-term health. Such mixed feelings are nowhere better illustrated than in a well-known song entitled 'El Bango', by the popular singer Sha'ban Abdul Rahim.[17]

The song, which is addressed to Egyptians at large, tells of the dangers of bango, as Abdul Rahim sings:

The guy Gareeei and the guy Lango, lost their life in the bango.
They are lost in the hospital, and they are dancing baladi [country-style] and tango, tango, tango, tango.
The guy Gareeei's name is Peachi.
And the bango is not dependable and makes you dizzy, dizzy, dizzy.

In every street and quarter, they made the bango in boxes.
In every street and quarter, they made the tango in boxes.
And every day a person is lost and say more five or six, six, six, six.
Bango is very hard on your health and ruins you.
Why do we let it ruin our lives?
This is something should be fought, should be fought, should be fought, should be fought.

Nevertheless, in the mid-2000s it even fleetingly seemed as though bango might displace hashish as the most widely consumed drug in Egypt. In 2007, of the 12.1 per cent of Egypt's students estimated to be regular drug users, 9 per cent favoured bango, while 3 per cent were reported as preferring hashish.[18] Seizures of bango were also rising during the first decade of the 2000s, from some 60,000 kilograms to 80,000 and above,[19] indicating, in the absence of a more general breakthrough in law enforcement, a rising volume of bango coming onto the market. By the end of the decade bango consumption had died back, and hashish had re-established its pre-eminent position among consumers.[20]

The bango consumed in Egypt is cultivated in the Sinai by the bedouin, or imported from Sudan, although there is evidence of cultivation elsewhere, such as in the governorate of Assiut, 320 kilometres south of the capital.[21] Periodically, the bango fields are subject to crackdowns by the authorities. For example, in 1999 an estimated 120 bango farms were discovered and shut down in Egypt, following official action.[22]

The re-emergence of hard drugs

The domination of hemp drugs in Egypt should not be allowed to obscure the fact that hard drugs have been re-emerging as a real medical and social problem over the last three decades. The reason for this increase is most likely explained by a combination of lower prices, higher disposable incomes, greater availability, greater poly-drug use and, if the biographical fiction book *A Quarter Gram* is to be believed, the boredom, idleness and self-indulgence of some of the offspring of the country's well-to-do.[23] Included in the list of opiates that are increasingly abused in contemporary Egypt should be added opioid painkillers, notably Tramadol,[24] which are obtained in tablet form. The use of Tramadol, according to Cairo University head of psychiatry, Professor Imad Hamdi, is 'spreading like wildfire'.[25]

In the 1980s and before, heroin used to cost in the vicinity of $275 a gram. In the socio-economic setting of the age, price proved a very effective deterrent to purchase and consumption. By the end of the first decade of the 2000s, an equivalent amount of the drug could be purchased for as little as $20 a gram, even with the American dollar not having the buying power that it would have had three decades before. While still price prohibitive for Egypt's $2-a-day lower-income earners, students from well-to-do backgrounds and members of the middle class more generally now have the means to indulge temptation,[26] should they wish to do so.

As with cannabis, Egypt is one of Africa's highest cultivators of the opium poppy.[27] This is grown primarily in the Sinai. In addition, Egypt imports significant volumes of heroin and to some extent opium. The opium for the former comes from Afghanistan, and is increasingly processed at source. According to the Anti-Narcotics General Administration (ANGA), the Egyptian drug squad, and the longest established anti-narcotics police force anywhere in the world, heroin imports tend to take place through the Sinai ports of Nuweibeh and El-Arish, in the south and north of the Sinai Peninsula respectively. Seizure levels for heroin in 2010 were, at 222 kilograms, much higher than usual.[28]

By 1988 Egypt had an estimated 250,000 heroin abusers. About 300 kilograms of heroin were sold in that year. It was at the end of the 1980s that a significant amount of drug-related crime began to emerge in Egypt.[29] The reality of a deteriorating narcotic drugs situation is amplified by the proportion of drug takers using injection as a method of consumption. In 1996 0.3 per cent reported that they had used such a method; in the 2005/6 survey the proportion had risen to 2 per cent.[30] In 2011 the number of IV drug users in Egypt was estimated at some 800,000, still well above the 1 per cent mark.

A big problem in Egypt has been identifying and reaching those parts of society most at risk, and reaching them especially with early, preventative treatment in mind. Because of the family-focused nature of Egyptian society, it is the case that a very significant proportion of the country's hard-drug abusers continue to live in the family home.[31] According to one senior drugs policy official, this could account for as many as 52 per cent of regular users. With families trying to conceal a source of shame, they tend to hide the problem from specialist help until the drug taking has reached unmanageable levels. This predicament is accentuated in those areas where anti-drugs advice is not available. This tends to be the case in the poorer suburbs in the big cities, notably Cairo and Alexandria. With outreach work depending heavily on peer education, provision for the middle classes is relatively easily developed. It is much harder to tackle the problem when it is caused or exacerbated by poverty and other social ills.

Other areas of special vulnerability are to be found in prisons and detention centres. Here, as in so many countries in the Middle East and beyond, needles and syringes and other drugs paraphernalia are easily smuggled into such institutions. In prisons,[32] which tend to be grossly under-resourced, especially in terms of experienced warders, it is assumed that 'everything gets in'.[33] Bad practices, notably multiple needle-sharing, are rife.[34] Where needle access has been effectively denied, it has even been asserted that drug abusers have resorted to the use of pen shafts as a means by which to ensure that the drug enters the bloodstream. Moreover, needle-sharing has raised concerns about the spread of HIV among intravenous drug users, although at present this is generally held to be a relatively low risk.[35] The HIV epidemic expected in the mid-2000s did not take place. So, for instance, research from that period finds that 4.1 per cent of AIDS cases in Egypt are injecting users, mainly from the cities of Cairo and Alexandria.[36]

BOX 2

A QUARTER GRAM

This novel was a runaway success in Arabic and English for its debut author, Essam Youssef.[37] First published in 2008, the title of the book refers to the weight of a wrap of heroin, and, in the words of the book's subtitle, 'what it did to a group of friends'. The plot traces the decline of a group of well-to-do university students, with the world at their feet, into a downward cycle of addiction, dishonesty and despair. Arguably the biggest impact of the book was the way in which it described the innocence and powerlessness of family members, as they battled to protect their sons from the ravages of the drug. The city setting of Cairo and its suburbs, not for their historical monuments or aesthetic qualities, but to describe the narco-geography of the capital, was also an eye-opener for readers. With Youssef claiming over one million readers, a majority of whom are said to be female,[38] the book has become a hit comparable to Egypt's other contemporary word-of-mouth classic, Alaa el-Eswany's *The Yacoubian Building*.[39] A film of the book is now planned, with the award-winning director Ibrahim el-Batout said to be signed up. Though Youssef says that he has written his 'drugs book', he has no intention of leaving the subject behind. He is a regular speaker at universities and high schools in Egypt on the subject. Together with a group of friends, Youssef is trying to establish an anti-drugs NGO, which is planned to operate an ambitious twenty-eight-day recovery programme in a hundred-bed facility. According to Youssef the only people not to like *A Quarter Gram* were the critics, who viewed it as insufficiently literary, perhaps in part because it is written in the patois of the street. Egypt's reading public has begged to disagree.

The Sinai and the Bedouin Gangs

Social tensions within Egypt are deep and enduring. Those among city, countryside and desert are particularly acute, beset, as they are, by deep cultural differences, social snobbery and material resentments. Nowhere is this social tension so real and immediate as between the bedouin of Egypt and the settled populations of the country and town. The friction between the bedouin and the rest has a long historical resonance, bedouin tribes having raided the livestock of the settled farmers as a regular part of their economy. Such activities were regarded as both honourable and a necessity. They matched the bedouin's self-image, of displaying courage and disdaining manual work, while camels were used as the main form of transport, especially in moving rapidly beyond the grasp of the law. For the bedouin, with their aboriginal life chances, there was in any case little alternative. For their main victims, the farmers, this *modus operandi* amounted to little more than extortion and theft.

In the twenty-first century four-wheel-drive pick-up trucks have largely replaced the camel as the bedouin's favoured option for flexible, efficient and speedy transportation. Furthermore, the machine gun has replaced the dagger and the Lee Enfield rifle. The bedouin continue to try to leverage their intuitive knowledge of the desert to make a return on the movement of goods, with illegal trade by definition the most lucrative source of income. Egypt's long desert borders in the west with Libya, and to the east in Sinai, home to between ten and twenty bedouin tribes (depending on one's definition) afford the best opportunities. On the Peninsula the bedouin divide into the northern and southern tribes, each with their geographical hinterland, and their activities and problems.

The urban focus of the northern tribes is el-Arish. It is a desperately impoverished place, with up to 90 per cent unemployment among the male workforce between twenty and thirty years of age. Periodically since the onset of the twenty-first century el-Arish has been the scene of clashes between the Egyptian security forces and tribesmen. The symbols of state and regime have been the target of retaliation against heavy-handed crackdowns, especially when they have been aimed at bedouin livelihoods, such as drugs and weapons smuggling.[40] Such penury makes illegal economic activity even more appealing, as there is little by way of licit commercial opportunity to rival such sources of income.

The lot of the northern tribes has been one of structural disadvantage since 1982 and the completion of the restitution of Egyptian sovereignty in the Sinai from Israel. Such was the bitterness of some tribesmen that a few were recruited to take part in sporadic terrorist bombings of tourist centres on the southern coast. In the main, this was prompted by grievance rather than ideology. Fears of radicalisation by Iran, Hizbollah and/or al-Qaeda persist, however. Since the late 1990s opportunities for trafficking have grown, with the increasing reliance of the Gaza Strip on a system of tunnels for the delivery of smuggled goods. The lucrative nature of this illicit trade multiplied in 2007, when the Egyptian–Gaza border was closed, following Hamas's seizure of power there, and the Strip was left economically isolated.

The southern tribes fare better than their northern counterparts, at least having a tourist industry to integrate with. This, though, is no panacea. While the southern tribes have benefited materially from the successful surge in the economic success of the sector, they too are resentful at the role of the Egyptian state. The main origin of the bad blood between the southern bedouin and the state is the land sequestered from the bedouin. This occurred when the high-end tourist developments were being established in the likes of the rapidly expanding Sinai coastal resorts, such as Sharm el-Sheikh, Dahab and Nuweibeh over the last three decades. Anecdotes abound, whether apocryphal or otherwise, of President Mubarak himself overseeing the land seizures and sales. Without ownership of this land, the bedouin's commercial interests in the southern Sinai were marginalised and restricted to the likes of heritage services, such as providing camel rides and making sweet tea in traditional tents for tourists. Meanwhile, *nouveau riche* elements from the cities made bumper profits on the likes of hotel construction as a result of their cronyism and cosy relationship with the Mubarak regime.

Illegal operations offered the best prospects for the tribes to rectify this financial imbalance. For instance, the bedouin became well known for supplying drugs to tourists. Russian nationals, for example, are reputed to be enthusiastic and wealthy consumers. It became well known that designated points on the main road skirting Sharm el-Sheikh were places where drugs were traded. Such regular business does little to assuage the simmering resentment of the tribesmen. It still boils to the surface intermittently. For example, when the protests in Tahrir Square were steadily weakening the position of President Mubarak, it was reported that groups of bedouin raided Sharm el-Sheikh, extracting protection money from hoteliers and robbing those visitors who had ignored government advice to remain in their hotels.

The Sinai desert has been described as having 'long been something of a lawless no man's land'.[41] This is in great part because of the Egyptian state's limited projection of authority into the Sinai, as required by its bilateral peace treaty with Israel. During its anti-drug operations the Egyptian side was reticent about returning in force to the Sinai for fear of contravening the basic force limitation provisions contained in the treaty. *In extremis*, the Egyptian side feared a re-eruption of tension with Israel, springing from such miscalculation. The reticence of the Egyptian state was also a reflection of the values and outlook of its core population. The centre of political and social gravity in Egypt is the Nile Valley. The thought of being deployed to Sinai, with its harsh and arid terrain and unfriendly inhabitants, to interdict armed smuggling operations would hardly appeal to Egypt's mainstream police force, or indeed the country's basically conscript army.

Located between the hard-power states of Egypt and Israel, different bedouin clans have at various times sought to try to play off their neighbours against each other. This has been done rhetorically, by, for example, praising Israel as a better jurisdiction to live under, as a way of embarrassing the Egyptian authorities in the wider Arab world, where the general view of Israel is deeply pejorative. Israel has been accused of encouraging such behaviour at various times.[42] For example, it has been alleged that Israel supplies cheap drugs to the bedouin for export to Egypt in exchange for intelligence cooperation, especially with regard to the Gaza Strip, about which Israel is so perennially exercised. On occasions, some of the tribes based in Sinai have even tried to relocate to Israel.[43]

The trafficking activities of the bedouin of the Sinai have not been limited to an east–west axis between Israel and Egypt. The bedouin also smuggle drugs from the Peninsula south into Saudi Arabia. The distance between the two is in any case proximate, amounting to about 15 kilometres at its shortest point. In developing this route the bedouin have demonstrated their versatility: replacing their camels and pick-ups, and operations in the desert, with jet-skis used on the Red Sea. Distributing drugs by sea is in any case easier and less costly than trying to cross two land borders, through Israel and Jordan, in order to access Saudi soil. On the Saudi side there appears to be only low-level capability to intercept such 'runs'. The fact that the Saudi authorities have, however, been able to apprehend expatriates wind surfing to Saudi Arabia from Egypt suggests that an element of corruption may be involved in such smuggling.

BOX 3

CINEMA AND DRUGS

Historically, Egypt has been the cultural centre of the Arab world. This has been nowhere better witnessed than in the realm of cinema. This is also the case with soap operas, which enjoy a special popularity in the region during the Islamic celebratory month of Ramadan. Though Egypt's cultural pre-eminence has come under challenge in recent years, notably from Turkish-made Ramadan 'soaps', dubbed in Syria, Egypt's reputation persists as a major centre of cultural production.[44] Egyptian Ramadan soaps proved to be particularly controversial in 2015 because of the leading production's treatment of heroin addiction.[45] Egyptian cinema in part reflects the social preoccupations of the day. This includes the area of narcotic drugs. The longevity of the drugs issue in Egyptian cinema is best illustrated by the film *al-Kukayin* (Cocaine), released in 1934. A significant genre film from the 1950s, *Rasif Nimra Khamsa* (Quay number five, 1956), is based in the port of Alexandria, where a naval captain battles drugs smugglers, reflecting the importance of Egypt's second city as a conduit for trafficking. *Tharthara foq al-Nil* (Chatter on the Nile, 1971), in which intellectuals fritter away their days through hashish abuse, is based on a Naguib Mahfouz novel about the decadence of the Nasser era. The Sadat period spawned a lot of films about the *nouveau riche*, some of whose wealth was based on crime, especially drug smuggling, *al-Sa'alik* (Vagabonds, 1985), being a good example. A companion film about the dangers and opportunities of drugs are explored in *al-Kayf* (Addiction, 1985), about an unemployed graduate who is drawn into a world of dealing and abuse by his brother, a chemist. Most recently, drugs in Egyptian films are as likely simply to provide the basis for a good suspense movie, where morality may be absent or difficult to apportion. In *Ard al-Khauf* (Land of Fear, 1999), a cop goes undercover for so long that he forgets who he is, and is unsure whether his loyalties lie with the police or the drugs gang;[46] a parable for the time.

Drugs, Crime and Politics

The Mystery of Hiking Prices

Anyone requiring firm evidence of complicity between the Mubarak regime and large-scale drugs trafficking and distribution in Egypt need look no further than the early months of 2010, and the unexpected volatility in hashish prices.

Hashish prices may adjust up and down from time to time in Egypt; rarely do they sky rocket. Yet this is mysteriously what they did between February and May 2010, as the country geared up for parliamentary elections in November and December 2010. This also provided the immediate backdrop for what soon would become known as the 'Arab Spring' in Cairo, on 25 January 2011. Without a sign or a serious, market-distorting problem, such as a bad harvest or an insect blight, no one expected the doubling in price of a 150-gram 'hashish brick', which normally sold for E£180. In other contexts, drug prices were said to have trebled or even risen more steeply than that. At the sharp end of the retail market, dealers expressed themselves mystified by the acute nature of the price shift.

The one narrative that no one seemed to accept was the one emanating from the Ministry of Interior. A headline in *al-Ahram* newspaper on 3 April 2010 announced that 'The Interior Ministry imposes its control over the drug market', thereby suggesting that the dearth of supply had taken place because of good police work.[47] The head of the anti-narcotics bureau in the ministry, General Mustafa Amer, announced that 7.5 tonnes of hashish and 250 kilograms of heroin had been seized during the previous quarter, the vast majority of which was coming in through the Mediterranean port of Alexandria. Furthermore, the ministry estimated that more than 300 distributors of drugs had been arrested, between them triggering the steep rises and reflecting the sudden hole on the supply side. Even with the publication of such figures, few were taken in. The rounding up of 300 sellers is hardly a big number in terms of impacting price in a market the size of Egypt's, the more so given that arrests in most contexts tend to be those of retailers rather than wholesalers or those further up the chain of criminality. Meanwhile, the UNODC undermined the credibility of such claims, pointing out that drugs seizures in Egypt are invariably rare and small.

The pervasive scepticism of such claims reflected both the history and the present as far as the relationship between illicit drugs and the ministry are concerned. Casting back, Egyptians remembered the experience of Ahmad

Roshdi, who held the interior portfolio between July 1984 and February 1986. He was the only interior minister in recent memory who tried to clean up the hashish market, and it even looked at one stage as if he might succeed. So successful did Roshdi appear to be that he was removed from office, as the vested interests connected with the market, both inside and outside the state, made their displeasure with him known. Roshdi apart, the rest of the time the symbiotic relationship between the police and the drugs suppliers has prevailed. On occasion, this relationship was bolstered by some of Egypt's local religious leaders, who would intervene to protect the local drugs trade.[48] This dominated the market, to the benefit of both parties, with the assumption that bigger actors in the Mubarak regime gave protection within the system to both sides. Also indirectly complicit in the hashish market was the ordinary consumer, without whose effective demand such market shifts would have been untenable.

The interior minister in the cabinet of Ahmed Nazif when the initial 'Arab Spring' challenge to President Mubarak was made was Habib el-Adly. He held the post for a prolonged stint, between 1997 and 2011. He spoke approvingly in public of Roshdi, and talked tough as far as choking off the supply of hashish in Egypt was concerned. With drugs no-go areas in both Upper Egypt and Sinai, the gap between posture and performance was a significant one.

There were no shortages of potential explanations lying behind the sharp rise in prices in 2010, all of which contained at least some conspiratorial dimension.

- Perhaps the least persuasive was that hiking the price of hashish was aimed at driving the consumer away from the purchase of hashish and towards other substances, with anything from alcohol through heroin to pharmaceutical drugs being mentioned as potential market fillers. As well as being uncontrollable and therefore of little manipulative benefit, it is unlikely that those involved in the hashish market would easily have accepted the loss of market share to other drugs, rendering such an interpretation fanciful.

- A second and more plausible explanation was reliant on big hashish suppliers and their 'partners' in the police and other parts of the state facing down competition from potential rivals, perhaps in the form of new market entrants. With relatively few actors in the market, this would conform with a narrative of a more successful market manipulation.

- The final explanation was a jockeying for money, power and influence among rising groups of politicians in Egypt at a time of growing uncertainty. After all, Egypt was in a state of political flux at the time, accentuated both by parliamentary elections and the more momentous presidential elections, which would be held later on in the year. However, this description of a more fragmented market lies uneasily with the quick success chalked up in raising prices.[49]

Finally, the hash price hike demonstrated just how confused, opaque and uncertain Egypt was at that point in time. The whole country waited nervously for the outcome of the elections, with the lack of transparency exacerbating worries, and in turn precipitating radical responses.

'Shahid' (Martyr) Khalid Said

There were arguably three pivotal moments in the emergence of the chronology of protest that prefaced the start of the Egyptian 'revolution' in January 2011. One was the New Year's Day bombing of a Coptic church in Alexandria, in which twenty-one people were killed. This was the worst case of anti-Christian violence in Egypt since 1999. A second was the flight, on 27 January 2011, of the Tunisian tyrant, Zein el-Abideen Ben Ali, who proved to have no stomach for a fight. This encouraged young and idealistic young protesters to try their luck against other octogenarian despots. A chronologically earlier event, and one whose full impact was not appreciated by those outside the region at the time, was the death at the hands of two policemen of a young man in Alexandria, Khalid Said.[50]

Khalid Said was a twenty-eight-year-old, who has routinely been described as a businessman. In fact he was a baby-faced young man, whose iconic martyr's picture features him wearing a 'hoody'. He lived at his parental home and seems to have spent a lot of his time blogging and chatting on the internet. On 6 June 2010 he was sitting in an internet cafe, having posted a clip allegedly showing corrupt policemen sharing confiscated drugs and their proceeds. By doing so, he was purporting to expose the structural involvement of the police in petty street crime in the cities of Egypt. Soft narcotic drugs were at the top of the substances traded under police control.

Two plain-clothes policemen subsequently went to the cafe and confronted Khalid Said about his actions. An argument ensued, which quickly turned to violence. During this confrontation, Khalid Said sustained terrible injuries, especially to the head. His face was beaten to a pulp and he lost teeth. His head was rammed against a table and then a metal door. He sustained a fractured skull, and serious injuries to his rib cage. His body was later dumped outside his parents' house.

The official version of events could not have been more different. It said that Khalid Said had swallowed a bag full of hashish on being approached by the policemen, and had consequently died from an overdose. This view was 'confirmed' by two autopsies carried out by the state, the second following the exhumation of his body. The police response was to try to defame Khalid Said by calling him a drug addict. The official narrative referred to previous arrests for theft and, of a more sinister nature, on morality charges. This, however, failed to persuade. The cafe owner was filmed confirming the brutality of the assault. Khalid Said's brother let it be known that the family considered the killing to be an act of revenge by the police in the face of his attempts to enforce a citizen's accountability.

The case was quickly taken up by young people and bloggers across Egypt's major cities,[51] in spite of the scepticism of some. It spontaneously became a rallying point against police brutality. A number of demonstrations took place over the ensuing month. One of these was attended by the presidential hopeful and anti-Mubarak campaigner, Mohamed El-Baradei. Human rights activist Aida Seif al-Dawla, who works closely with torture victims in Egypt, spoke for many of the young people by stating: 'We live in a country where there is absolutely no law;' she demanded the sacking and trial of the head of police.[52]

In the face of this concerted campaign, the authorities changed tack. Two policemen, Warrant Officer Mahmoud Salah and Sergeant Awad Ismail Suleiman, were subsequently arrested, the Alexandria prosecutor charging them with 'illegal arrest, using physical torture and brutality'.[53] As late as April 2011, and well after even the downfall of President Mubarak, the case against the two, which had been moved to Cairo to try to dissipate public pressure, was still being routinely opened and adjourned. It was not until March 2014 that the case was finally dispatched, with each of the policemen receiving ten years' imprisonment. Khalid Said's face remains prominently affixed on the various martyr display boards and websites set up to acknowledge the sacrifice of those who lost their lives in trying to make the revolution a success. Khalid Said remains a reminder of police corruption and the force's routine use of thuggery against its own people. He exposed the moral ambiguity of the police in Egypt and the place of illicit drugs in topping up their earnings through the use of dishonest practices.

Borders and Policing

Soon after the successful removal of President Mubarak, the Arab protest contagion spread to one of Egypt's neighbours, Libya. Within a matter of days the Libyan situation had developed very differently. The country had divided into two camps, one in support of the Libyan leader, Colonel Mu'ammar Gaddafi, mainly in the west and centre of the country, and the other predominantly based in the east at Benghazi, backed by a series of smaller towns in the east and the far west. The Libyan case was also very different from the Egyptian one in that it quickly came more to resemble a conventional conflict between two military formations than a struggle of the people against a ruler and his clique. Nato's decision to join the fray supported the perception of it as a conventional conflict.

The main concentration of the conflict was on the ribbon pattern of desert towns located between Tripoli and Benghazi. The existential nature of the conflict meant that military forces otherwise deployed were switched to the main struggle. Police on the streets of these towns either defected or were redeployed for work more crucial than conventional policing. Military formations with responsibility for regulating the affairs of Libya's wide expanse of desert were posted back to the main arena of conflict. In the three months from the start of the fighting precious little capacity, whether state or oppositionist, had been deployed with fighting crime in general and drugs in particular in mind.

Theory developed inductively on the experience of organised crime and illegal drugs suggests that a country with a diminishing level of state capacity will become increasingly susceptible to the ravages of criminal activity. This may apply to the movement of contraband across North and central Africa, with its ultimate destination in Egypt. According to the Egyptian anti-narcotics police, the main conduit of the hashish from Morocco was the wide expanse of desert between Algeria and Libya, which lay between the point of cultivation and the destination of a major market.[54] A consequence of the unrest of the 'Arab spring' was simply to make these routes even more porous.

What is also clear is that the vulnerability of Libya to trafficking in illegal goods is being complemented by developments on the Egyptian side of the border. Since the ousting of Mubarak the military has taken on an overt role as the transitional political authority in Egypt, principally through the creation of a higher military body, the Supreme Council of the Armed Forces. This body has pronounced on a variety of policy issues. The common thread of these has been a concentration on domestic political issues at the expense of external factors. Just as Libyan territory has become more porous, and in effect an invitation to transnational organised crime, so have the barriers on the Egyptian side become less effective. Unsurprisingly, a further consequence of these parallel developments has been a situation where neither party can conceive of effective coordination. Regular meetings provided for under the auspices of the Egyptian–Libyan bilateral convention to combat narcotics have simply ceased to take place because of the war on the ground.[55]

Crime in Egypt

If the military has come to play an increasing role in keeping the peace at home, the police themselves have been a lot less visible and assertive than has been the case in the past. Initially, internal security organisations including the police began by trying to confront the demonstrators, increasingly focused on Tahrir Square. Many of the early casualties among the demonstrators resulted from the robust methods used on the ground by the police and government paramilitary formations. Once it was clear that a violent onslaught would not be allowed to clear the demonstrators, the police and other units were withdrawn from the streets, or simply melted away, as the country's leadership sought increasingly desperate measures, such as opening the prisons holding common criminals. This seemed to have been a deliberate move by the transitional authorities to distract the protestors on the street and to prompt a return to both property and work.

Once withdrawn from the streets, the police proved to be unenthusiastic about a return to the beat. By this stage dozens of police stations had been torched, with the loss of criminal records; many police firearms had been looted. The burning of the Ministry of Justice building, with the loss of court records, will also be a blow to law enforcement long term. Marginalised by the military, little trusted by the public,[56] with their authority undermined, and robbed of the scams that would previously have been used to supplement their modest incomes, the police seemed to have no appetite for a return to the fray.[57] Though numbers are vague and anecdotal, a substantial proportion seemed not to have returned to work even some two years after the fall of Mubarak.

Those that had returned seemed to adopt a more reticent attitude when on the streets. For example, many working police disappeared after nightfall, either for fear of retributive attacks or because of an unwillingness to work a sixteen-hour shift in return for such low pay. Unsurprisingly, given this deterioration, there was also a very marked fall-off in the number of drug-related arrests since the onset of Egypt's political protests. In Upper Egypt policemen were regarded as avoiding drug dealers in order to side-step public confrontations in which they might find themselves outgunned.[58] The alleged cosy relationship of the past between some policemen and pushers, whereby the police were able to reach their arrest quotas thanks to tip-offs from the latter, seem to have at least partly broken down.[59]

The absence of the police and the presence of newly released criminals triggered a surge in crime, preliminarily estimated to have grown by 200 per cent since the fall of Mubarak. Initially, affluent areas, such as Maadi on the outskirts of Cairo, were targeted. Though fear of this surge in crime has receded somewhat since the end of Mubarak, it has certainly not disappeared. Indeed, fear of crime has become a major impediment to the return to a settled society.[60] The basic formula of less external supervision, increased criminality and a much-reduced police profile is almost bound to result in a rise in the availability and consumption of drugs in Egypt over the short to medium term.

Conclusion

Hashish consumption in Egypt is a good example of the ingrained nature of drugs in the leisure pursuits of the well-to-do. Even the proud but less well-off would aspire to such practices, as illustrated by bridegrooms laying the tables for their wedding breakfasts with pieces of hash, alongside the more traditional fare of sweetmeats and tea glasses. This is reported to include the weddings of policemen![61] It was into this practice of 'cultural authenticity' that Egyptians were suddenly expected to desist from such practices, as the global anti-drugs regime spread itself steadily into the international illicit drugs periphery, of which Egypt was a significant part.

The criminalisation of drugs made the trade across North Africa more lucrative. It offered enhanced opportunities for the country's poorly paid police to supplement their wages through the seizing of substances and their resale back into the economic cycle. Established centres of the drugs trade, which at least had spatially confined and contained it, infamously el-Batniyyeh, were soon put out of business, with the drug trade defusing in fragmented form across Cairo. As the abuse of drugs grew, so new sources of informal revenue began to accrue.

With the new realities of the supply side established, from both west and east, drug efforts have grown into more of a concern with the profile of those consuming drugs. Thanks to the Egyptian medical profession, we now have a broad profile of the country's typical drug user: young, male, educated, damaged, urban or desert based, located near a drug route. No sooner was this earnest attempt to quantify levels of prevalence under way than the 'Arab

Spring' arrived on the scene, expanding the previously held parameters. Gone were the external controls on drug smuggling; surging was the use of synthetic drugs such as the manufactured opioid Tramadol; on the rise once again the affordability of hard drugs in Egypt: a regional leader anew.

5

ISRAEL

CRIME AND ETHNICITY

One of modern Judaism's leading poets, Haim Nachman Bialik, once famously said that he would not be content until a Jewish society had been created that was just like any other.[1] The measure of whether the country had attained such an endpoint would be whether it contained the less attractive but generally ubiquitous social groups that characterise all societies, such as thieves and prostitutes. He might reasonably have added drug addicts, pushers and traffickers to his list. More than seven decades after his death in 1934, Bialik's objective has certainly been realised. There is little likelihood that Israeli society will ever succeed in eradicating any of these socially undesirable categories. In that sense Bialik's vision was well drawn. Israel is a real society and there is no going back.

Of course, there is nothing new in the link between Israel and drugs. For middle-aged, middle-class, male Ashkenazi (European-origin) Jews, a couple of joints are much more likely to be the source of a weekend's relaxation than, say, alcohol. But this felicitous scene is not the extent of Israel's engagement with mind-altering substances. This is notably the case among Israel's younger population, whose consumption levels tend to be significantly higher. The youth debate has focused on the causes of this recreational practice. It is widely assumed that this reflects the stress of military service, compulsory for three years for Israeli males after leaving high school. Such pressures have been exacerbated over the last five years in particular because of the proximity of active war zones on Israel's Gazan, Syrian and Lebanese borders.

Many Israelis have a second experience with drugs that goes much less noticed. Heroin has come to rival cannabis as the most prevalent narcotic in Israel. Moreover, in the course of the last twenty years Israel has seen the emergence of serious organised criminal activity, much of it built upon the drugs trade. Many attribute this trend to the arrival of immigrants from the former Soviet Union, though such crime also has a local base. For these activities, drugs, together with other scams—such as people trafficking, the sex industry and fraud—has emerged as part of what one might call a national portfolio of criminality. It even moved such a stalwart conservative, nationalist figure as Moshe Arens, a long serving minister of defence, to describe Israel in 2010 as 'a state of organised crime'.

The reason why heroin goes much less noticed than hashish is that it is not associated with the elite of the country, but rather with ethnic groups that are less economically and socially successful. The trade in and consumption of heroin is much more likely to embrace Sephardi and Mizrahi Jews, who comprise the other half of Israel's Jewish population, and Israel's 20 per cent population of Palestinian Arabs, whose presence designates Israel as a deeply divided society.[2] The ethnic group at the bottom of the social hierarchy, at least as far as the Jewish populations are concerned, are the so-called 'black Jews', the Falashas, who arrived from Ethiopia as recently as a generation ago.

An estimated one in three of Israel's prison population is drawn from the latter minority ethnic community, a figure comparable with the incarceration of black Americans for drugs and associated offences in the USA. Given the *tour d'horizon* above, it is now routine to say that there are few communities in Israel left unaffected by narcotics. Indeed, it can be argued that the profile of the drugs market in Israel has more impact on and is more potentially harmful to these communities than is the case with Ashkenazi 'tokers', whether young or more seasoned in age. As ever in Israeli society, though, it is the Ashkenazim who attract the greatest attention.[3]

Delineating Narcotics

One of the state of Israel's first drugs reports, released in 1955, noted that 'the territory which is now Israel' had served as a transit route and point of contact between the ancient civilisations of Mesopotamia and Egypt 'since the beginning of recorded history'.[4] Relating this to narcotics, the report noted that the largest volume of seizures were of hashish, mainly grown in Lebanon and Syria, bound for Egypt, and using Israel as a land bridge. The routes for trafficking such narcotics were varied during this period. These included a variety of smuggling routes by land—either across the Israeli border or through Aqaba on Jordan's Red Sea coast, notably by bedouin, taking advantage of the difficulties of passage through arid desert areas. They also included smuggling by sea in small fishing boats. In such operations the fishermen would attach their contraband to the back of their vessel and tow it through the water, making it easier to jettison the illicit cargo in the event of interdiction.[5]

The tone of the 1955 report illustrates how drugs issues were reflective of wider social tensions within Israel even then, just eight years after the declaration of the state. In this case it was the country's newly arriving 'Oriental Jews', who had immigrated from a clutch of Arab countries in the aftermath of the 1947/8 Israeli war of independence, with which the report was preoccupied. Its tone reflected the view of a disdainful political establishment, the authors almost certainly being Ashkenazi in ethnic origin. This was a time when Israel was seeking to promote mass immigration from among Jewish communities around the region. It then housed them semi-permanently in tent cities through much of the 1950s, or obliged them to move into slum-standard housing, recently vacated by Arabs fleeing the war zones.

The report pointedly noted that 96 per cent of the new immigrants to Israel involved with narcotics were Sephardi Jews, newly arrived from the likes of Iran, Morocco and Turkey. It held these new arrivals as being the reason why 'the use of hashish is now known among a growing number of Jews in Israel itself'. It further complacently noted that 'comparatively few people of Israeli descent [for which read Ashkenazis] have become addicts'. The report was quaintly naive in viewing education as the panacea for the eradication of the drug abuse that did exist. The report concluded blithely that 'the [drugs] problem is not a serious one from the viewpoint of the national [sic] health and welfare'.[6]

Contrast the 1955 report with the realities of the narcotics problem in Israel more than fifty years later. According to the Internal Security Minister, Yitzhak Aharonovitch, a senior member of the hard-right Yisrael Beitanu party, led by Avigdor Liebermann, speaking in mid-2009, Israel had a total of 320,000 illegal drug users out of a total population of around 7 million (5.6 million Jewish; 1.4 million Palestinian Arab), a prevalence of between 4.5 and 5 per cent. This number included about 60,000 young people in the twelve to eighteen age range, some 10 per cent of this total category. Of this number, UN sources suggest that 1.9 per cent of Israelis, or around 11,400 people, had used heroin at least once over the course of the previous twelve months.[7] The oft-repeated statistic in Israel for the number of addicts in the country is

25,000. By 'addicts' is meant people 'whose entire life is devoted to obtaining the next drug dose'.[8]

The growing social blight represented by narcotics has been exacerbated by alcohol abuse, in this case largely spirits, a phenomenon unknown in Israel until the mass arrival of immigrants from the old Soviet Union. Alcohol has become a coping mechanism for many of the recent immigrants from Russia, especially in the 1980s, as they sought to adapt to a new and in many ways unfamiliar society. But the presence of alcohol and its frequent abuse now makes young people more susceptible to the lures of hard drugs because of its role in triggering domestic violence and fracturing family life. In turn, the strongly corporate nature of Israeli society has been steadily eroded over the last three decades. In part, this reflects the rise of economic and social individualism in an age of Reaganism and Thatcherism, Israel having been one of the countries most quickly, enthusiastically and effectively to embrace the market economics of the 1980s. In part, it represents the diminishing importance of a secular Zionist ethos, which had bound the Jewish component of the country together since well before its foundation, and the consequential diminution of its institutions in society.[9] It represents the loss of a safety net that leaves the individual that bit more vulnerable to acute social ills, such as substance abuse.

Aharonovitch further indicated that Israel was a country awash with illegal drugs. He stated that every year around 5 tons of heroin, 4 tons of cocaine and 3.5 tons of hashish are consumed. Lebanon is the biggest single source of drugs reaching Israel, especially of hemp drugs. Significant 'busts' have been made against smuggling rings in Jordan. Favoured routes for the latter include crossing the Dead Sea by boat, and traversing the Rift Valley, known in Jordan as the Wadi Araba, by land. Indeed, Israel's largest single seizure of heroin, 82 kilograms in weight, was made in the valley in 2008.[10]

The volume of cocaine apprehended in Israel, compared to heroin, underlines the fact that the drug is no longer one that only the affluent can afford. Israel is now mentioned in the same breath as Brazil as far as the cocaine trade is concerned. The last official surveys indicated that the amount of cocaine used in Israel in the four years between 2005 and 2009 had doubled. Close to 1 per cent of all Israelis in the eighteen to forty age bracket admitted to having tried the drug. The proportion of cocaine seized by the authorities is estimated by the Israeli authorities to be in the 3–7 per cent bracket.

Neither is Israel immune to the impact of synthetic drugs. Other sources point to 2 per cent of the world volume of Ecstasy tablets being apprehended in Israel, a higher percentage than Italy, Spain or the UK.[12]

Cocaine Seizures by the Israeli Authorities

Year	Kilograms
2009	63
2010	71
2011	264
2012	171

Source: *Haaretz*, 19 October 2013.[11]

The Israeli government estimates that the total illicit drugs trade is worth in the region of NIS6 billion ($1.56 billion at 2012 forex prices). This figure is the equivalent of about 55 per cent of the annual military aid from the USA to Israel.[13] Echoing the sentiments of the former Prime Minister Ariel Sharon, speaking earlier in the decade, Mr Aharonovitch described the drug problem in Israel as posing 'a strategic existential threat on [*sic*] Israeli society'.[14]

Urban blight

The level and nature of the consumption of heroin in Israeli society is of rapidly rising concern. In the early 1990s injecting heroin was rare in Israel.[15] In the decade to 2005 the proportion of opiate abusers in Israel using intravenous (IV) methods of consumption rose from 19 to 63 per cent. Consuming heroin by the IV method is more likely to trigger drug dependency. Its related practices, such as needle-sharing, immediately expose the abuser to a range of secondary health problems. Of those regularly injecting, 5 per cent are estimated to be HIV positive, and half are carriers of viral hepatitis.[16] The fear is that both proportions are set to rise.

Parts of Israel's urban landscape have become blighted by the impact of hard-drug taking. An estimated three-quarters of property crime in Israel's largest city is committed by problem users.[17] In the mid-2000s around 150 homeless drug and alcohol abusers lived in and around the new Central Bus Station in Tel Aviv. They are still there, either on the streets or living in seedy apartments, their numbers swelled by prostitutes and foreign workers present illegally. After dark the place came popularly to be known as 'a junkie-occupied area', in a sardonic reference to the 'Palestinian Occupied Territories' of Gaza and the West Bank. Routine activities in the area, such as intravenous drug-taking and the buying and selling of drugs, constituted a serious nuisance for people living in the neighbourhood and a risk to public health more generally.

Since 2006 the area has been the focus of a concerted attempt at rehabilitation. But rehabilitation is difficult and expensive, and success far from guaranteed. In part this is because Israel is a small country, where finding drug suppliers is not difficult, purity levels are high, and prices tend to be modest ($22–$30 a gram for the time period 2002 through 2006).[18] Local reports indicate that only 20 per cent of those who complete a rehabilitation programme stay 'clean'.[19]

Institutional response

As the realities of such problems have become clear to state and society in Israel alike, responses have developed over time. Most visible among these has been the development of an institutional framework for the scrutiny and interdiction of drugs flows, and the social effects that such drugs have upon society. Israel's most important institution in this regard is the Israel Anti-Drug Authority (IADA), a quasi-governmental organisation. Created in December 1988, the IADA is Israel's dedicated body responsible for coordinating the activities of the numerous government agencies involved in different aspects of the issue.[20] The absence of clear and effective coordination has bedevilled any number of countries' responses to the growing use of narcotics, the likes of the UK included.

In Israel, the IADA possesses an authority born of the fact that it reports directly to the office of the prime minister. The IADA's primary responsibilities include: policy formulation; fostering research; developing services; improving expertise; and, somewhat incongruously, encouraging voluntarism. In recent years the IADA has focused its work on high-risk groups, notably the youth.[21] In June 2005 the Israeli cabinet decided to transfer responsibility for alcohol abuse to the IADA. This move came in recognition of the dangerous impact that licit substances can have on society, and the link between the social impact of drugs and spirits.

In spite of the central role the IADA has played over the last twenty-seven years or so, there continues to be a debate in Israel about what constitutes a reasonable budgetary allocation for it. In 2005 the IADA was faced with a drastic budget cut.[22] In 2009 the Knesset Committee on Drug Abuse complained about the inadequacy of the funding compared to that required.[23]

Israel has also developed its law-enforcement capabilities with the drugs problem in mind. Since 1993 a 180-strong branch of the Customs Authority has been in existence, established in order to increase the capacity of its successful drugs interdiction activities. In 2008 an elite police force, the Lebanon Border Special Drugs Unit, was established to develop specialist expertise to combat the illicit border trade. In fact the unit was the reincarnation of a force that used to operate in the so-called South Lebanon 'security zone', until Israel's withdrawal from the area in May 2000. Claims of the growing success of the newly constituted unit were given greater credence by the 2008 seizure figures. A total of 159 kilograms of heroin was apprehended in border operations during the year, and thirty-two traffickers arrested.[24] While these are impressive figures on paper, the trumpeting of such successes means that Israel runs the risk of falling back on to a military-oriented, supply-side solution to the challenge of illicit narcotics, as it does in many other areas of policy.

In Search of Enlightenment

In 2007 a feature-length documentary film was shown in Israel. Called *Flipping Out—Israel's Drug Generation (India)*, it told the story of the 'gap year' taken by a large number of Israel's conscripts after they complete their military service. At the end of conscription the demobilised soldiers receive a discharge bonus of some $4,300 each. It has become common practice for this money to be used to fund a year off, before entering higher education or looking for a job.

Around 50,000 men and women leave the Israeli army every year. Roughly, 30,000 leave for India. Of this figure, 90 per cent will try illegal drugs. The drug of choice is Indian hemp and its derivatives such as hashish and marijuana, though hard drugs are also present. There is a tendency towards experimentation and drug 'bingeing', an unstable pattern of consumption more typical of young people. Many of the rest head for Latin America, where their pursuit of oblivion is comparable. Those who travel but claim they do not touch drugs are said to be religious Jews interested in seeing something of the world, but determined to demonstrate, as they would see it, a greater mental and spiritual strength than their largely secular counterparts. Of the latter, some 2,000 are estimated to experience drug-induced mental breakdowns while abroad, literally to 'flip out'. Most of the rest tend to return to Israel, where they go on to live healthy adult lives, with soft drugs sometimes playing a recreational role, at least until they start a family, when drug use again declines.

The hippy recruits tend to move between the Himalayan mountain villages in the north of India, which are known as Kasol (sin or crime cities), and Goa in the south, depending on the time of year. There is certainly no difficulty in newly arrived Israelis making contact with their fellow citizens. There are said to be eight locations in India that 'everyone' goes to; one of the ex-soldiers states in the documentary: 'It's like summer camp in terms of meeting people.'

In spite of the spirit of adventure implied by a gap-year experience, many of these Israeli ex-soldier–backpackers tend to cluster together and move around little. Other nationalities are said to avoid the Israelis, for the somewhat improbable reason that they are regarded as being noisy, and late sleepers. This isolation from other travellers is perhaps better explained by a collective intro-spection, born of a prolonged and intense experience as soldiers, with which outsiders, especially from the West, cannot easily identify. Given their seden-tary existence, it is largely only in their engagement with illegal drugs that many such Israelis show a capacity for new experiences.

Neither does there appear to be any appreciable fraternisation between the Israeli visitors and their Indian hosts. Exchanges between the two communities are polite, but little more. The Israelis' Indian landlords and neighbours tend to show considerable indulgence towards these new arrivals. This is assumed to reflect the relative poverty of the local population, which is estimated to have an average annual income per head of about $500, and which expects to benefit from the shekel bubble economy in its midst. The local police also tend to ignore the drugs, in spite of the openness with which they are consumed. The local Indian police may possess sniffer dogs, but these appear to be deployed for other purposes, notably in the cause of VIP protection.

In the documentary interviews the former Israeli soldiers talk little about the politics of the Arab/Palestinian–Israeli conflict, save for a rather unfortu-nate comparison of Indians and Arabs. In relating their army experiences they tend to personalise rather than generalise them. For instance, a former soldier tells an anecdote in which his company commander was killed by a stray pistol shot. Though such an experience induces stress on the part of the soldier who tells it, the former soldiers are far from alienated from the army as a whole. Another interviewee praises the sense of comradeship and 'manliness' that military service has given its members. Another says that he believes he did little wrong during his three years in the Israel Defence Forces (IDF): bad things were the exception; we did what we had to do and life went on for both sides, he relates.

The most articulate *cri de coeur* comes from a young female former soldier, women serving for less time than men and usually not in combat zones. In fact, she was on her second trip to India. She describes her feelings while addressing one of the country's then deputy prime ministers, Eli Yishay, the leader of the

Mizrahi-dominated ultra-Orthodox political party Shas, and a former interior minister, who was visiting Goa at the instigation of the IADA. She says: 'Here [India] one can feel normal again, no bombings, no corruption, none of that pressure [faced] back in Israel ... one comes here and feels normal again.'

Aware of the licentiousness and turmoil that typifies the lives of these young ex-soldiers, both the Israeli state and civil society have attempted to respond to the predicament. The state, in the form of the IADA, has established a refuge or 'Warm House' in India, to dispense 'first aid' to those backpackers who have 'fallen victim' to narcotics. The drugs centre is peripatetic in that it moves seasonally between the small town of Manali in the north, some 155 miles beyond Shimla, and Goa in the south, thereby shadowing the seasonal migration of the former conscripts. The residential centre gives young Israelis a supervised setting within which to relax and distance themselves from the drug experiences. It is run by a couple, the man having retired from the Israeli military with the rank of colonel. His background undoubtedly creates empathy with some of the Israeli travellers. For others, presumably still wrestling with the psychological trauma of military service, it runs the risk of bringing them back to some of the experiences from which they are presumed to be trying to escape.

The counterpart of the Warm House, but firmly lodged in the private sector, are the Chabad Houses run by the Brooklyn-based Chabad Lubavitch, an ultra-Orthodox movement. They have a vast network of such centres across the world, though mainly in the USA, Australia and Israel itself. There are three Chabad Houses in India, located in Bangalore, Goa and Mumbai. The Chabad House in Mumbai was targeted by militant Islamist terrorists from Pakistan during the bloody attack on India's second city in November 2008, in which 166 people perished. The rabbi and his wife who ran the refuge, which housed among other things a drug-prevention clinic, were killed in the attacks, together with four Jewish visitors. With its strong religious ethos, the goal of the Chabad Houses is more far-reaching than that of its state equivalents, which are secular in orientation.

During his visit to Goa, Eli Yishay, himself an observant Jew, praised the activities of both state and ultra-Orthodox institutions. He described their activities as 'holy work', and said that they were doing nothing less than 'saving souls'. In the short speech that he gave to the Goa Warm House during his visit, he implored Israel to continue to fund these centres, finishing with a paternalistic, rhetorical flourish: 'These are our children, our boys and girls.'

On Duty

Concerns about drug-related effects are not confined to former soldiers. They affect serving soldiers too, whose potential performance on duty may jeopardise the safety of their fellow servicemen, and Israeli security more widely. This concern also relates to those men who have completed their three-year military service, as they are obliged to serve in their units for a month every year until middle age.

While there has probably been low-level usage of soft drugs in the Israeli army since its inception, concerns about such matters clearly increased after the 1990s. The Israeli authorities were able to detect trends in consumption because of the compulsory drug testing to which soldiers are required to submit, the only occupational group so randomly tested. According to a survey completed at the start of the 2000s, hashish was the drug of choice for eighteen- to twenty-one-year-olds in the army, with sedative-type drugs the next most commonly abused substances. The prevalence rate was estimated at 2.9 per cent.

The drug-abuse problem was regarded by the authorities as having worsened through the decade. A package of new measures were introduced to address this problem. These included billboard warnings on military bases about the dangers of drugs, and the adoption of tougher punishments for miscreants. A military police investigation that resulted in the arrest of members of the transport corps, operating close to Ben Gurion Airport, in December 2000, was an early sign of this clampdown in action.[25]

The punitive side of the strategy is complemented by a therapeutic approach. Soldiers found dealing or using drugs are certainly prosecuted and imprisoned. But, once incarcerated, concerted attempts are made to alleviate their drug 'habits'. Entitled 'Back to Uniform', this push does not only seek to end drug dependence. It is a proud boast of the relevant authorities that some former soldiers who are 'drugs free', having been successfully rehabilitated under the programme, have even returned to active service in the military. This is revealing. As recently as the mid-1970s a young Israeli man would not have been accepted for military service if he had a history of delinquency,[26] a description that would have included the abuse of illegal drugs. The myth of the noble citizen-soldier, fighting to protect the Jewish homeland, would not have been well served by sitting directly alongside the active presence of 'deviant' behaviour.

Organised Crime

Organised crime began to emerge as a serious criminal problem in Israel in the 1960s—that is to say, before any of the major immigrations from the USSR. Drugs did not appear to feature high in the portfolio of illegal activities at the time. Only in the late 1970s did Israel begin to take such criminality seriously. An early academic study of the phenomenon focused on the Georgian Jewish community in the mid-1980s. Between 1988 and 1995 more than 650,000 Jews from the former Soviet Union entered Israel.

The early involvement of Russian-origin Jews in crime was initially played down, for fear that it might deter others from immigrating to Israel, which is marketed in Diaspora communities as a Jewish utopia. By January 1997 the chief of police intelligence in Israel had gone on record as stating that Russian organised crime now represented 'a strategic threat to Israel'. The Israeli criminal justice system was viewed as liberal and lax, and presenting no deterrent to serious, organised criminal activity. By the mid-1990s there were said to be around eleven Russian criminal syndicates operating in Israel,[27] together with six major domestic groups.[28]

One grouping, the Abergil crime family, who are not of Russian origin, were allegedly heavily involved in the smuggling of 'night club' drugs such as Ecstasy (MDMA) to the USA. The conduit for such trafficking was New York, and another reputed Israeli crime figure, Ilan Zarger. Indeed, such Israeli-affiliated crime groups are better understood as being 'middlemen' in terms of the role that they play. The March 2003 International Narcotics Control Strategy Report stated that Israelis resident in Europe are the largest traffickers of Ecstasy from its place of manufacture, notably the Netherlands and Belgium, to the rest of the world.[29] The international nature of Israeli criminal activity at the time was illustrated by the arrest of a gang in March 2001. With the arrest of three Israeli criminals after a jewellery store heist in Barcelona, 10 arrests were made and an ecstasy smuggling ring was broken up.[30] Another underworld figure, Ze'ev Rosenstein, was arrested in Israel and extradited to the USA in 2004. He was sentenced to twelve years in jail as a result of a plea bargain in a Miami court, and later allowed to return to Israel to serve out his sentence.

This points to the comparative advantage that many Israeli crime groups and their partners have, namely excellent networks in the most salient parts of the globe, such as Europe and North and South America. Container traffic also figures highly as far as the trafficking of contraband is concerned, notably cocaine, with the Mediterranean port city of Ashdod of particular significance. More recently, organised criminal connections have been established between Israel and South American countries, such as Brazil, Paraguay and Peru, based on the illicit cocaine trade.[31]

The magnitude and rapidity of the emergence of organised crime in Israel led to speculation about whether it would have any effect upon the rule of law, and the impartial functioning of Israel's institutions. The prevailing view over the last twenty years is that there has been no such significant impact. Not that there have not been worries to the contrary. In December 2002 Israel's national police chief warned of the ability of criminal groups to penetrate and influence government institutions.[32] In 1997 Transparency International put Israel in the top fifteen least corrupt countries, though twelve years later it was thirty-second on the list, just above Puerto Rico and Taiwan.[33] The arrest and extradition of at least some of Israel's most wanted appears to endorse the view of the continuing robustness of the system.

Nevertheless, such a bald statement cannot be accepted without nuance. There has been a marked general deterioration in the standard of public life in Israel over the last two decades. For example, Israel's seventh president, serving between 1993 and 2000, Ezer Weizman, was obliged to resign because of his conduct towards some of the female members of his staff. His successor, Moshe Katsav, was found guilty of rape and sentenced to imprisonment in November 2011. Of more direct concern to the issue of corruption was the conviction of one of Ariel Sharon's sons for financial impropriety. Former Finance Minister Abraham Hirshson was convicted of corruption. There have been a number of scandals involving police officers, one of whom was jailed for six years for passing on confidential material to criminals in Eilat.

Neither is it accurate to suggest that financial misdemeanours have been confined to indirect relations with those holding public office. Before his serious sexual assault, President Katsav was obliged to resign as head of state, having received donations for his 1996 election funds from someone known as the 'king of the "grey market"'. In December 2002 Prime Minister Sharon dismissed Deputy Infrastructure Minister Naomi Blumenthal, reportedly for her refusal to cooperate with a police investigation into vote-buying during his Likud party primaries.

Money Laundering

Israel quickly became a focus for secondary criminal action, in support of such activities as narcotics and people trafficking. Up to 2000 Israel was, according to the head of the criminal investigation department in the police ministry, Yossi Sedbon, 'a wonderful country for money laundering'. Israel had embraced international financial deregulation with gusto, especially in the banking sector. Up to that point it had no dedicated law against money laundering. Because of this, it fell foul of the main Western institution active in the area, the G-7's Financial Action Task Force (FATF). It named Israel in June 2000 as one of fifteen countries that were uncooperative in international efforts to combat money laundering.[34] It had emerged as a safe haven for illegally generated funds from such activities as drugs, diamonds, prostitution and intellectual property fraud. It was removed from a specifically US blacklist in June 2002, as it was perceived to be addressing such omissions. The real reason may well have been to appease Israel politically, mindful of the close relations between Israel and the USA.

A conference on Russian organised crime in Israel, with the participation of officials from the Russian Federation, tried to estimate the magnitude of money laundering in Israel by organised groupings. Such figures are inevitably sketchy and inconsistent. They give a sense of the scale, however. The educated guess that resulted was that such operations are involved to the value of $2.5–$4 billion each year in the banking sector, and around $0.6 billion per year in the real-estate sector.[35] By 2005 it was estimated that between $5 billion and $10 billion had been laundered in Israel over the fifteen years since the collapse of the Soviet Union.

The overall political situation did not help Israel to curb the effects of organised crime. Even during the entire span of the Oslo peace process, between 1993 and 2000, Israel still complained about the limited nature of cooperation from its weaker institutional neighbour, the Palestinian Authority, in the area of smuggling. One Palestinian official, working in the area of protecting antiquities, a favourite target of transnational organised crime in the region, described the mutual assistance that was supposed to take place as being at 'a minimal level'.[36] After 9/11, Israeli attempts to combat organised crime suffered from a different ailment: the impact of competing priorities. So dominant was the terrorism agenda after 2001 that it squeezed resources and political will previously available to combat mainstream criminal activities.

An excellent illustration of the connection between Israeli society and organised crime can be seen in the emergence of criminal syndicates and their most notorious figures as national celebrities, somewhat comparable to the period of Prohibition in the USA during the inter-war years. Posing as businessmen, such figures found it easy to go to Israel, where they were feted, and, initially at least, looked up to as role models. Arguably the best such example was Yaakov Alperon, a reputed Israeli crime boss, who was killed at the age of fifty-four. Known widely as 'Israel's Tony Soprano', Alperon had even welcomed an Israeli model Yael Goldman into his home, as part of *Once in a Lifetime*, an Israeli reality TV show.[37]

A second way of illustrating the profile and impact of organised crime on Israeli society is to look at the nature and extent of the public feuding between the various criminal groups. More than two dozen people had been killed in Israel by the end of the 2000s in mob-related violence, which became at one stage so intense that it even involved the use of anti-tank missiles. The second half of 2008 was particularly alarming, with at least five serious, and very public, attempts by gangs to weaken, intimidate or kill their rivals. Consider the following:

- On 11 July Yoram Haham, one of Israel's best-known criminal lawyers, was killed in a car bomb in Tel Aviv. Mr Haham had recently represented suspected mobster Asi Abutbul, a Jew of Moroccan origin.
- In a second case, just seventeen days later, a mother of two was killed on a beach in Bat Yam, having been caught in the cross-fire of an assassination attempt. The intended target was Rami Amira, an associate of the Abergil crime family.
- In the final such case that year a car bomb killed Yaakov Alperon, who had survived at least three earlier attempts to kill him.

Ominously, following five or six years when there had apparently been far less blood-letting on the scale of 2008, a man was killed in Ashdod in early 2014, in what appeared to be a gangland-style killing.

Sex trafficking

The upsurge in organised criminality in Israel was not only illustrated by heroin and Ecstasy smuggling. This increasing activity was also witnessed in the exploitation of women for the sex trade. Unscrupulous pimps groomed vulnerable local girls between twelve and fifteen years old in Israel, before tricking them into heroin dependence and forcing them to 'work the streets'.

These types of practice have acquired a political intensity in recent times through an increase in sexual relations mostly between Jewish girls and Palestinian men. Anecdotal evidence suggests that such practices are now more common in Israeli society, whereas in the past they would have been extremely rare, not least owing to the absence of opportunity. Nowadays there is a range of opportunities, at the social margins at very least, for younger Jews and Palestinians to meet and to get together, not least when they share social problems such as drugs, and frequent shelters for homeless people, notably those in the big cities of Israel such as Jerusalem. Such refuges accept young people of mixed ethnicities, and house them in close proximity, thereby offering opportunities for them to form relationships.

This essentially benign narrative is not how some in Israeli society see this trend. Questions have even been raised in the Knesset, the Israeli parliament, such is the emotive nature of these inter-ethnic relationships. Right-wing MPs have voiced such matters in salacious and exploitative terms, emphasising the contrasting ethnic backgrounds of those involved. Attention has settled on supposed Jewish girls who go off with Palestinian men. For many on the right, it is inconceivable that girls might do so voluntarily. Consequently, there is a tendency to view such developments as 'kidnappings'. Framing it thus evokes comparisons between these Palestinian gangs and the Asian gangs that preyed on young, disadvantaged white working-class girls in Rochdale and Rotherham in the UK.

More widely, Israeli police estimate that around 3,000 foreign sex workers are trafficked to Israel every year.[38] A significant number of these women, who came from the likes of Moldova, Russia and the Ukraine, were flown to Egypt before being trafficked over the border by bedouin. Women's rights groups initially found the police uncooperative in trying to curtail the trade, partly because of the difficulty of proving that trafficking was involved. By the end of the 2000s there was a more combative approach towards such crime. The issue of a wanted notice for the ringleader, Jacky Yazady of the Abutbul crime group, Moroccan in origin, and the arrest of twelve of his fellow nationals, prompted the police to claim that they had shut down the largest trafficking ring in Israel.[39]

BOX 1

THE CASE OF ELHANAN TANNENBAUM

Elhanan Tannenbaum was a colonel in the IDF reserve, who travelled to Dubai in October 2000, expecting to broker a drugs deal. He is alleged to have made more than $200,000 on the deal. To his surprise, he was held against his will, before being spirited away by the Lebanese radical Shia group Hizbollah, apparently because he had been double-crossed by an old Lebanese Shia contact. At first it was assumed in Israel that Tannenbaum was working for Mossad, the Israeli secret service, on some commission related to national security. Eventually, Mossad let it be known that this was not the case, and that Tannenbaum was a freelancer. Hizbollah kept Tannenbaum imprisoned until Israel decided to exchange him and the bodies of three Israeli soldiers in return for 435 Arab opponents of Israel. Though Israel is routinely content to participate in such exchanges, on this occasion there was much soul-searching in the country because of Tannenbaum's 'unsavoriness'.[40] In the end, the Israeli government accepted the prisoner swap, which took place in January 2004, as a result of the good offices of the German government. Following his release, Tannenbaum was briefly incarcerated in Israel. However, he was soon released, having negotiated a plea bargain, under which he came 'clean' about his criminal activities. He was not charged with any criminal offence in Israel. Even some ten years later, the prisoner swap for Tannenbaum remains controversial because of the number of Israelis apparently slain by those Arabs released to enable the freedom of Tannenbaum.

The 'Oriental' Experience

If the Ashkenazi Jews have 'flipping out', Israel's Arab community also has a film that speaks to them, though it is actually a joint production. The film is called *Ajami*, and was a hit at the 2010 Cannes Film Festival, where it won a Special Mention in the Camera d'Or category. Though it is a work of fiction, the grittiness of the story line and the authority with which the film unfolds suggests that the script has drawn heavily from daily experience. The scenario elaborated in the film is recognisable given the nature of press and other reports over recent years.

The film focuses on Arab Palestinian communities in Jaffa and the West Bank. It shows the constant backdrop of low-level criminality and lawlessness with which younger Palestinian males must contend, and features the crude, often casual violence of some bedouin gangs, looking for ways of generating illicit income. It depicts the easy criminalisation of younger Palestinian migrant workers when they fail to return home across the 'Green Line', the pre-1967 border, at the end of the working day, much more often for chaotic personal rather than political—let alone security-related—reasons. It portrays the vulnerability to indebtedness that families experience, especially where there is no patriarchal male to stand up for their interests, and their subsequent susceptibility to extortion by the large clan-dominated gangs.

Moreover, it shows the distance between the predominantly Jewish state in Israel and such street-level experiences, and the inability and lack of interest on the part of this state to defuse and deter the violence faced by much of its Palestinian Arab citizenry. And it charts the ubiquitous nature of narcotics, both as a commodity to be traded and as a tempting escape from the desperation of everyday life. Alarmingly, it also reveals people's ignorance of such narcotics and the impact that they can have on the human body if taken in the wrong way or in too concentrated a dose. The final salutory lesson is that for those Palestinians who see illegal drugs as a sort of *deus ex machina*, that at a stroke can rescue them from their desperate lives, the stakes are very high indeed, especially when they are dealing with hardened professionals, police or criminals, on either the Arab or the Jewish side of the line.

The Palestinian Arabs of Israel have long been associated with the trafficking and distribution of illegal drugs. Some sources go further and state unequivocally that Israeli Arab crime families control the heroin trade.[41] The Freij clan of Israeli Palestinians, from Taibe, is reported to have had a long history of involvement in illegal activity, including narcotics.[42] Some 67 per cent of all arrests for the crime of murder were from among Israeli Arabs, even though this demographic only accounts for 20 per cent of the total population.[43]

Such families have developed close relations with clans and groups across the border in south Lebanon. This reflects the importance of Lebanon as a hard-drugs gateway for Israel. The way in which illegal drugs cross the border is simple in its conception. At night, packages of heroin, often in half-kilogram measures, are lobbed over the border fence from north to south. Equivalent packages of dollar bills are lobbed back in exchange. 'Drops' are arranged in advance, either by phone or by written message. The geographical difficulty of the terrain makes interdiction of the exchange, without the benefit of accurate intelligence, highly problematic. The proximity of the Hizbollah militia, and its ability and occasional willingness to operate across the border in northern Israel proper, is an additional impediment to rigorous border control. Israeli Arabs tend to act as couriers for such trade.

The ATMs

The centre of the heroin trade in Israel are the mixed Arab and Jewish towns of Lod (formerly Lydda) and Ramle, which were incorporated into the state of Israel in 1947, following heavy fighting with the Jordanian army. Lod enjoys a particularly dubious reputation as a centre of crime and social distress. Narcotics from Israel's northern border are taken to the southern outskirts of Tel Aviv and to Lod, where they are broken up and made available in smaller amounts, ultimately for retailing. The suspicion prevails that they are taken as far south as Lod in order to avoid a social backlash from the more affluent parts of Israel's biggest conurbation, north Tel Aviv, notably Ramat Aviv.

Lod has been infamous for its so-called ATMs, holes in the wall into which the purchaser would lodge his money, together with a request for the drugs that he intends to purchase and the weight. A package of illicit drugs would then be returned to the 'punter' through the same means, without any possibility of identifying the source of the illegal drugs. Israeli police insist that by early 2009 they had closed down all of these conduits, as part of a concerted campaign to squeeze the drugs trade. Those accepting that the Israeli police had won a tactical success were equally certain that new devices for the speedy and safe distribution of narcotics would emerge before too long.

The economic inducements for drugs trafficking are clear. In 2009 a kilogram of heroin was worth around $25,000 on the Israeli border. It sells for four times that amount when the street value is aggregated. At that rate, the 5 tonnes of heroin estimated to enter Israel yearly would be worth $125 million on the border and some $500 million on the street.[44]

Ethnicity is no barrier to cooperation between Arab and Jewish criminal groups, whether in the movement of drugs or the 'fencing' of stolen goods.[45] At the lowest point of distribution—retailing—where sellers are often themselves users, drugs are distributed without consideration of ethnic background, as is the situation in other divided societies, whether, for example, Balkan or South African.

BOX 2

THE GREEN LEAF PARTY (ALE YAROK)

The Green Leaf Party (GLP) is originally a single-issue political party established in 1999, with the explicit objective of campaigning for the legalisation of cannabis.[46] Since then it has put up a slate of candidates in six national elections—1999, 2003, 2006, 2009, 2013 and 2015— and, despite optimistic predictions, without yet securing its first MP. Frustratingly for the party, its share of the popular vote has risen, but so has the national threshold which all parties must pass in order to be represented in the Knesset. In 2006, for example, it attracted 1.3 per cent of voters, making it the second most popular political group not to be represented in parliament. The party is led by a comedian and talk-show host, Gil Kopatch, who comes from a strongly secular background, and has courted controversy by lampooning Israel's religious right. This has elicited criticism from among Israel's religious parties, which have accused him of ridiculing the Torah. Over the course of its existence the GLP has sought to widen its appeal as an 'ultra-liberal movement', making it increasingly the political home for a range of youth and counter-culture dissidents. This radical agenda has included: strict limits on animal experimentation; subsidies for alternative forms of energy; and same-sex marriage. The party holds generally dovish views on the Israeli–Palestinian dispute, favouring the establishment of an independent, demilitarised Palestinian state. It supports the continued prohibition of narcotics more harmful than cannabis. A sure sign that the GLP was making inroads into the electorate came when its principal opponent on the liberal end of the political spectrum, Meretz-Yachad, felt compelled to steal at least part of its platform; Meretz promised to seek the decriminalisation of soft drugs. Nevertheless, it is the GLP that remains firmly identified as 'the light drugs party' within the Israeli political system, as epitomised by its party symbol: an Israeli flag, with the Star of David replaced by a cannabis leaf.

Conclusion

Despite the superior assumption of Israel's founding fathers that drugs would never catch on in Israel, they have in fact caught on exceedingly well. So much so that illicit drugs are widely available within Israeli society, whether in the form of cannabis-linked drugs, opiates, cocaine or synthetics. On one level this reflects the newly emerged laissez-faire nature of Israeli society, notably since the 1980s, which many Westerners find so attractive. On another, the ubiquitous nature of drugs in a society as small as 7 million points to the laxity of such a setting. When set alongside the multiple markers of a drugs society— from organised criminality through secondary diseases to signs of social failure—Israel is awash with many of the more chronic aspects of a drugs culture. It is perhaps little wonder that the likes of the Lebanese armed militia

Hizbollah are apparently so tempted to try to exploit Israel's social weaknesses, including drugs, in its struggle for regional supremacy. On the other hand, it is impressive that Israel has been able to develop such a widely successful economy with such intoxicants in its midst.

It is in the area of its national, ethnic introspection, and the role that drugs play as a signifier, that best help to expose Israel's deep internal divisions and hence its vulnerabilities. Wherever there is ethnic marginality in Israel, there are dangerous drugs: from the recently demobbed young soldiers attempting to make sense of the stress of army service, to what one might call the 'double oppression' of Israel's 'black Jews', to the growing drug and alcohol problems of Arabs resident in east Jerusalem, and on either side of the 'Green Line'. In these ways and others, the drugs phenomenon has come to help define what Israel is today.

6

SAUDI ARABIA

AN INEVITABLE PART OF MODERNISATION?

Towards the end of September 2011 the Saudi Ministry of Interior announced that it had foiled an audacious plan to smuggle drugs into the country.[1] The operation, which featured the use of a motorised glider, had begun its journey in Iraq, carrying some 700,000 amphetamine pills, marketed under the brand name of Captagon. The glider's presence had apparently been identified by the country's Interior Ministry's MIKSA security system in Riyadh.[2] This comprises a network of radar and thermal imaging devices, together with the presence of a razor-wire fence along the 900-kilometre Saudi–Iraq border. The enhanced security initiative was begun in the aftermath of the first Gulf War in 1991.[3]

Once the presence of the glider had been picked up, the Border Guard, which is part of the Ministry of Interior, moved swiftly to close down the threat, which they proved more than capable of doing. A total of ten people were subsequently arrested. The use of a simple yet potentially effective technology such as a motorised glider has raised concerns that such a device could be used in the future by terrorists. Riyadh has subsequently banned the use of gliders flying over its territory.

The glider case raises a clutch of issues as far as drugs smuggling and Saudi Arabia are concerned. First, it confirms the growing extent of the demand for illicit drugs in the kingdom, and in particular synthetic drugs with a stimulant effect. Second, it shows how this escalating demand has attracted the attention of relatively big players from the transnational organised criminal sector, incentivised by the potential pay-off of such activities. In addition to the cost of the motorised glider itself, the traffickers were taking a not inconsiderable personal risk in organising the scam, as capital punishment remains very much on the statute books in the kingdom for the cross-border trafficking of a range of illicit substances. The expected return on the operation must therefore have been sufficient to make the crime appear economically worthwhile. Third, the glider affair underlines the challenges posed to the security of Saudi Arabia, exacerbated both by the length of its border and the expanse of its terrain. The anti-drugs authorities, with the Interior Ministry in the vanguard, face a continuing challenge in defending their country against such hostile activity, narcotic drugs included.

The Saudi authorities ended the glider counter-operation by stating that it was the first time that a glider had been used for cross-border trafficking into the kingdom. This was a confident boast. The truth of the matter is that nobody knows whether this was the first flight of its kind, or simply the first of many clandestine operations already successfully completed without this or other gangs actually getting caught. Officials refused to be drawn on when glider flights might be resumed, stating that such a suspension would remain in place until specific mechanisms to monitor and control gliders could be put in place.[4] The inference of this was that such provisions had hitherto been lacking, in spite of the tremendous capital investment in border security made by the Interior Ministry over the last couple of decades.

The Dominance of the Interior Ministry

The centrepiece of a visit to Saudi Arabia to study illicit drugs is the Ministry of Interior.[5] This may not sound so unusual, as the supply side of the drugs equation normally features uppermost in patterns of state responses, and Interior is at its organisational and policy centre. In Saudi Arabia, however, with its large, powerful and well-resourced coercive ministries, often headed by a senior prince, Interior enjoys a profile that is seldom matched, and then only by the Ministry of Defence and the National Guard. As the formulation used by local journalists would have it, these are the country's 'powerful security organs'. The swaggering energy of its operational personnel, the casual contempt for the latest official guest, the unengaged disregard for any attempt at dialogue all point to an institution that feels supremely self-confident about its leading place in the system. Such characteristics remind those entering its orbit, even briefly, that this is a body that is not used to having its approaches questioned and its policy scrutinised.

The first port of call for the visitor and his minder is the audio-visual suite. A short film is shown by way of introduction, lasting for perhaps twenty minutes. The film is heavy on Qur'anic recitation, scenes of Mecca and other holy sites located in Saudi Arabia. It is the nearest that one will get to seeing a senior member of the ruling family speaking on the subject. The late king, Abdullah bin Abdul Aziz, who died in January 2015, features prominently. Sharing star billing is the interior minister himself, Prince Nayef bin Abdul Aziz, at the time briefly also holding the position of crown prince, but since deceased. There is nothing to suggest that the current monarch and successor to King Abdullah, King Salman, favours a more liberal approach to public diplomacy as far as illicit drugs are concerned.

King Abdullah puts on his sternest face for the video recording. Prince Nayef does not have to put on a stern face. He already enjoys a long-standing and apparently well-deserved reputation within Saudi politics for being a conservative and a hardliner, and not being quick to show mercy. Illicit drugs are just his kind of issue. No pretence of balance or understanding is otherwise required.

The film's commentary gets under way. It refers to 'a relentless war against drug smugglers'. Its graphics show drug smugglers and terrorists as literally different sides of the same coin. The film is intercut liberally with sayings from the two men. Nayef is the more vocal. But the king is authoritative too. Drugs are at least one policy area where the senior princes appear to share unanimity, and can put their otherwise perpetual bickering aside. King Abdullah's comments to the film's interviewer are trenchant and uncompromising. He focuses attention on the interlinkages between terror and drugs, this time bringing money laundering into the equation. The scourge of terrorism and drugs combined is a theme that will reoccur as the visit continues.

Prince Nayef, meanwhile, has much to say. He states, apparently without any sense of hyperbole, that 'drugs are more dangerous than any other thing facing society'. He affirms that 'we [whether he is speaking on behalf of the government, his faction or the regime is unclear] will absolutely support' those who stand up to drugs. Following such a recommitment, the florid rhetoric starts to take over. Reference is made to the 'awful raping of children and girls' by drug-crazed abusers. The lauding of martyrs, predominantly law-enforcement personnel who have been killed in their line of duty, then follows. The leading chanter invokes the audience not to mourn the fallen, for they have been killed in the service of Allah. All present are urged to give thanks to God for striking against the presence of drugs. So confident are those present that the Almighty plays an active role in drugs policy that a sudden firming in the price of Captagon tablets is ascribed to his intervention.

With the film transmitted, the briefing begins. Here there is little to report, as the spokesman fears that any lapse in confidentiality may be costly. One does not take the muted responses personally. The police are also loath to share their secrets with other state bodies working on drugs issues. This includes the National Committee for Narcotics Control (NCNC),[6] formally the 'umbrella' for drug control in Saudi Arabia. A visitor will have to work hard in order to eke out even one page of notes. Captagon, hashish and heroin, we are told, are the most challenging drugs for a police force to have to try to deal with. Cooperation among the three responsible agencies—the Police, the Border Guard (both under Interior) and Customs (under the Ministry of Finance)—does exist, facilitated by 'a hot line' as well as three to four annual meetings to evaluate cooperation. These are interspersed by monthly operational meetings.[7] The spokesman does not risk anything more specific. For example, he does not mention the increasing involvement of the religious police (*mutawa*) in investigating and apprehending the purveyors of illicit drugs and alcohol.[8] For statistics on seizures and the like we are referred again and again to UNODC. This is comical, as the specialist UN agency only derives its statistics from the declarations of national governments, in which the Interior Ministry in Saudi Arabia is the lead institution!

BOX 1

THE CUSTOMS[9]

Saudi Customs are officially the third branch of the state dealing directly with illicit drugs. They are also the poor relation of the Police and the Border Guard, partly because they are not part of the powerful Interior Ministry and partly because of their difference in executive powers: Customs is an 'enforcement agency' that is not permitted to open cases and take them to court. Their jurisdiction lies only in the formal customs area, unless specifically coordinated with other security agencies, but only on a case-by-case basis. Customs shares the aversion to figures and detailed explanations displayed by the narcotics police in the Ministry of Interior. Consequently, a Customs briefing in Saudi Arabia features a lengthy period of time spent at the main dog-training centre, together with the scrutiny of specialist equipment, such as the

---

latest 'container-searching systems'. There are about 400 dogs in use by Customs across the country, an irony indeed, if one is mindful of the Islamic religion's ambiguity towards canines. Each port has a sniffer-dog unit present. The dog programme began in 1976, in conjunction with US customs. Some 79 per cent of trained dogs are for use in drugs operations. There is a general lack of sentimentality about the dog centre. By the sound of the animals' barking, they do not appear to be over-fed. Around half of the dogs belong to the German shepherd breed. They do not go home with the handlers, but remain on site, housed individually in small cages. They are acquired from Europe at a cost of €1,000 each. Somewhat disappointingly, we are told that the dogs simply supplement the work of the experienced customs officers, who make the real judgement calls. Meanwhile, the Customs department search around half of all container traffic entering the kingdom. A total of seventy-three container-search systems have been installed in the country. We are informed that the sixteen X-ray systems used for cars succeeds in checking some ninety vehicles per hour. Though the authorities aspire to achieve 100 per cent coverage, at present they are struggling to maintain even present capacity.

Our visit culminates with the dedicated drugs laboratory. A small and functional space, it is hardly in keeping with the size and resources of the headquarters. It is a surprise to find out that the deputy head of the lab is relatively junior, and only possesses a first degree and a diploma, from Jeddah and Dammam respectively. The laboratory can break down drugs into their various component parts. But this is a fast-moving field, where new substances are being discovered and proscribed frequently around the world. News that the Interior Ministry has just commenced a construction binge which will see the erection of no fewer than 111 new buildings around the kingdom, including at HQ, makes one hopeful for the future. Surely there will be decent lab facilities in there somewhere. We leave the premises after being shown a collection of ingenious smuggling methods, revealed by Interior operatives in the recent past. These include: the hollowing out of Qur'ans, which are then filled with drugs; heroin hidden in pistachio nuts; Captagon pills secreted in the back of a barber's chair; and drugs hidden inside toothbrushes with Islamic insignia. With such imagination and large margins to be made, the Interior Ministry certainly has its work cut out.

From Denial to Acceptance

Saudi Arabia is the ultimate country of mixed messages and extreme positions. The threat from illicit drugs is no exception. In 1999 the government of Saudi Arabia confidently denied that the kingdom had a serious problem with the consumption of illicit drugs. Factors such as Saudi Arabia's position as the cradle of Islam, the nature of its citizenry and the purported nimble responses of the government, significantly comprising much of the senior echelons of the royal family, were all put forward as helping to explain this reality.

A crystal-clear illustration of this practical approach at that time can be seen in the coverage of an Arab-wide study, printed in one of the kingdom's national newspapers, the *Saudi Gazette*, operating in an environment of limited press freedom. Having carried some general data about aggregate seizure levels in the Arab countries, together with the number of cases opened, the article proceeded thus:

> In the Kingdom [of Saudi Arabia], drugs cannot be considered as a phenomenon due to the religious factors, awareness of people and efforts exerted by the government to prevent such interactions.
>
> The statistics showed that the number of cases have dropped recently despite the great expansion of the phenomenon internationally. During the Kingdom's history, this country never witnessed any drug cultivation or manufacturing within its borders.[10]

Though without specifically describing what it means by 'a phenomenon', the Saudi press would continue to reproduce such blandishments for some years to come. In an article on suicide in Saudi Arabia in 2005, the newspaper concerned, apparently without any sense of inconsistency, referred to drug abuse as being a 'big contributor' to the increasing suicide rate, even though, it went on, 'the Kingdom has a low rate of drug abuse'.[11]

The stance of public denial started to change in 2005, when it became harder to brush concerns about illicit drugs aside. Since then an anti-drugs policy has emerged, elaborated and implemented: the Majlis al-Shura, the kingdom's unelected, pretend parliament, was charged with some oversight responsibility for illegal drugs, scrutinising at least in principle some of the relevant activities of the Health, Interior and Social Affairs ministries.[12] The policy was being driven, not by the king or the cabinet, but by public concern. The Saudi decision makers were having to run in order to keep up.

The conviction with which this denial was expressed was even before the report's publication is somewhat belied by Saudi Arabia's responses in other areas. Capital punishment had been introduced in the mid-1980s for drug-trafficking offences, implying that the country already had a trafficking problem nearly a decade and a half earlier. Moreover, the dangers of a drugs retail threat was already evident a couple of years prior to the report in the *Saudi Gazette*. As early as 1997 the kingdom had drafted and implemented a drug-awareness programme. One might quibble about the traction of a programme that ended up by quaintly giving school students rulers and pens bearing anti-drugs slogans as a reward for attentiveness (arguably, it is the inattentive ones who need the incentives to engage). But at least, as regards anti-drugs education, a start had been made.

Nor did the policy denial extend as far as public health. In 1985 Saudi Arabia had already opened the first of its initial four al-Amal hospitals, state-run bodies named for the word 'hope', and specialising in the effects of substance abuse and related matters.[13]

BOX 2

A SAUDI RECOVERING ADDICT

In the early to mid-1970s the first generation of Saudi youth influenced by the impact of the resources of 'the first oil age' (1973–86) was beginning to experiment with a lifestyle previously unknown to all but a very small number of the privileged caste. One recovering drug addict at the 'Half Way House' at Dreyeh,[14] in the old part of Riyadh city, described his experience of this period. He visited Thailand in the 1970s, where he began taking hashish and amphetamines. For him these proved to be 'gateway' drugs, giving him the inclination and the practical ability to access a wide range of illicit drugs. He married a Thai woman and fathered a son. He also started taking heroin. He would subsequently be hospitalised no less than twenty-two times in an effort to end his dependency on the drug. Though now in his sixties, and with his wife back in Thailand, he continues to fight his addiction, and was in the second part of a three-phase recovery plan, when interviewed in December 2011. His ambition for the future was a mild one: to remain 'clean', to stay at home and to get a modest job in Riyadh.

Even if the authorities had genuinely believed that the country was experiencing a negligible drugs problem in the late 1990s, they arguably should have worked harder to keep Saudi Arabia free from such developments, rather than simply taking succour from sweeping protestations of their version of reality. With such signs of growing addiction already beginning to emerge as far back as four decades ago, some Saudis are critical of the failure in imagination of a government that did not foresee the social side-effects of the country's rapid, oil-driven 'modernisation', in the drugs domain as in others. Saudi Arabia today is regarded as 'a big social workshop'.[15] This laboratory consists of: a large and increasingly educated population; the freedom to discuss matters relatively openly (compared to the closed restrictions of the pre-1990 period); and an overall context characterised by a series of national dialogues,[16] introduced from the top by King Abdullah in August 2003.

Despite the willingness of the protagonists to initiate a national conversation today, even on such a sensitive subject as illicit drugs, Saudi Arabia, like many other countries in the region, lacks even the basic raw material on which to base such a discussion. The first problem for Saudi Arabia has been not having an accurate idea of the illicit drugs problem that it faces, either in terms of the range of specific drugs or the volume of consumption.[17] Consequently, drugs policy in Saudi Arabia has to be based on the rough-and-ready intuition of those long engaged in combating the problem, and should therefore be taken with a pinch of salt.

The best guesstimate on such matters comes from the NCNC. It believes that Saudi Arabia has approximately 300,000 nationals who are drug dependent out of a total national population estimated to be roughly 18 million. Drug dependency in Saudi Arabia is described by sectoral professionals as being where behaviour and suffering resembles a disease. If one considers that around 15 per cent of Saudis are under the age of ten, below which few would yet be experimenting with drugs, and just over half of the national total are women (and hence much less affected than males), 300,000 as a proportion of the total male population would amount to around the 3.4 or 3.5 per cent mark. Rough calculations apportion more of the affliction to those based in the main cities of Dhahran, Jeddah and Riyadh. Those studying abroad will inflate the percentage.

Current Trends

Whatever the plausibility of figures on drugs use today, the trends in the emergence of consumption over the last three decades seem clear enough. There was a big surge in the use of heroin and other opiates in the kingdom between the early 1980s and the early 1990s. This trend subsequently flat-lined from the end of the 1990s onwards. Saudi drugs experts tend to cleave into two groups in trying to explain this more constant level of drugs demand: those who look to the impact of the introduction of capital punishment for drugs traffickers in the middle of the 1980s; and those who put their faith in the adoption of a drugs-awareness programme deemed to be a success. Though execution remains the ultimate punishment for any smuggling of illicit drugs, it was originally introduced because of the particular medical and social threat from heroin and the secondary impact of the spread of HIV.[18] It should be noted that of the recovering addicts in the kingdom's four currently constituted al-Amal hospitals, some 35 per cent are also suffering from a major disease, such as HIV/AIDS or hepatitis B (mental illness excluded).[19] Of the existing cohort, between 25 and 30 per cent would be suffering, separately from or as well as these major diseases, from mental illness.

By the new millennium concern at the widespread availability of amphetamines had to a great extent replaced the enduring concern with opiates, experienced above. This was mainly because young people were more likely to consume synthetic drugs than opiates. For the youth of Saudi Arabia, the attractions of 'uppers' have proved to be multiple and compelling. School and university students saw it as an effective way of studying when fatigued; youngsters from poor backgrounds embraced it as a way of achieving a 'high', which had been scarcely available and mostly unaffordable before; even the athletic were attracted to it because it was claimed to bolster physical stamina; and young and old took it as a way of achieving enhanced pleasure during sexual intercourse. By 2009 an estimated 700,000 Captagon pills were being consumed on average in the kingdom every day.[20]

An insight into the sheer volume of the pills trafficked can be seen in the magnitude of the seizures of the drug. In 2009, after the first of a series of big anti-drugs clampdowns, it was claimed that the volume of synthetic drugs seized in the kingdom exceeded that of China and the USA combined.[21] An aggregate total of 14 million pills were seized in various raids over a two-month period.[22] In spite of such revelations, a senior Saudi spokesman robustly rejected the description of Saudi Arabia as having assimilated a 'Captagon Culture', a defence that has proved increasingly difficult to sustain.[23]

Fifteen and more years ago, the market for synthetic drugs such as Captagon in Saudi Arabia was relatively stable.[24] The early illicit supplies of the pills seem to have been manufactured in South and South-East Asia, notably in places such as India and Thailand.[25] As the market has expanded in Saudi Arabia, it has caught the eye of other would-be producers. Brazil and China are notable recent entrants into the Saudi market, their product appearing in significant volumes over the last five or so years. Eastern European countries, notably Bulgaria and Serbia, are significant producers for the Saudi market,[26] with supplies moving through Bulgaria and Turkey before entering the Middle East. Close police cooperation at the operational level between Bulgaria and Saudi Arabia helps explain the rising seizure levels in the late 2000s.[27] Syria, at least before the advent of the 'Arab Spring', and other countries in the Middle East have also been growing in importance as producers of Captagon.[28]

The level of adulteration of such products, together with the indifferent quality of production, raises the question whether such pills can still meaningfully be referred to as 'Captagon'. It goes without saying that such pills entering Saudi Arabia are not subject to any meaningful quality control. The growing diversification of supply has also led to increasing variation in the levels of safety of such drugs. For example, poorly manufactured Captagon can even include a dangerous heavy metals content, such as lead and mercury. The abuse of rogue Captagon supplies tends to be roughly comparable: addiction, degradation of the nervous system and, *in extremis*, organ failure.[29]

In addition to the increasing prevalence of Captagon, the Saudi drugs market also seems to be travelling in a more eclectic direction. High-purity 'night club' drugs, such as Ecstasy, have been seen in quantity since 2011. In 2013 there was a big seizure of cocaine in the kingdom, although this does not seem to have presaged the emergence of a significant and stable market for the drug. There has also been a big increase in the consumption of qat, resulting from an increase in the plant being trafficked across the border with Yemen. Meanwhile, the heroin market seems to have become more volatile. A decade ago there was a ready supply of the drug with high purity levels. Then the volume and quality of supply both declined. Since 2012 the quantity available has increased again, but with lower purity, such adulterants as crushed glass and talcum powder being mixed with the drug. Drug professionals find such changes difficult adequately to explain, especially in the absence of any discernible trend.

'Classic Vulnerability'

Saudi Arabia is a classically vulnerable state as far as its susceptibility to the trafficking of illicit drugs is concerned. The country has a big land mass, the interior of which is difficult to police. It has a long land border, in excess of 4,500 kilometres in length. It has two very long sea borders, totalling 2,400 kilometres on its eastern side facing the Persian Gulf, and 1,100 kilometres on the Red Sea or western side. Added together, Saudi Arabia has a colossal 9,000 kilometres of borders. It is located relatively close to the centre of drug production in the form of opiates and hashish in Afghanistan, and close to its western supply routes. Moreover, much of the expatriate workforce in Saudi Arabia comes from countries that are themselves vulnerable to the impact of drugs, notably Pakistan, many of whose nationals are active in the opiates sector in Saudi Arabia. In the words of a senior member of the Border Guard, one of the three agencies that police the country's borders, the kingdom has 'very sensitive borders'.[30]

Table 1: Saudi Arabia's Land Borders

Land neighbour	Border length (km)
Yemen	1,326
Iraq	811
Jordan	745
UAE	684
Oman	657
Kuwait	228
Qatar	86
Grand Total	4,538

The geo-narcotic vulnerability of Saudi Arabia to drugs trafficking is reflected in the routes of entry into the kingdom for Captagon, and their subsequent patterns of distribution. According to the Saudi anti-drugs authorities the kingdom's sea ports have a reputation for being difficult to smuggle drugs through, especially for Captagon, in contrast to the ports in Dubai. The land borders are therefore the natural routes of choice. The most favoured access from a Saudi perspective in descending order are as follows:

1. The North–South-West Route. The pills are concealed in motor vehicles and imported equipment.[31] They are transported from Turkey via Syria and Jordan, or from Syria via Jordan direct to the Saudi border. Local bedouin tribes in Jordan in particular are enlisted to transport this contraband across international boundaries.[32] With the Customs required to remain at the border crossings and the police unfamiliar with much of the country's

inhospitable terrain, it falls to the Border Guard to try to interdict such smuggling. The contraband is taken to the nearby cities of Tabuk and al-Jawf, where they are broken up and distributed through much of the rest of the country.

When they arrive in Riyadh, for instance, the drugs gravitate to the parts of the city that already have high rates of criminality and a relatively transient population. With this in mind, the favoured entry point into the city is the south side, notably Manfuhah. This is where much of the low-cost housing is occupied by migrant workers from abroad, together with tribesmen without papers, the *bidoun*—literally 'without'—who originally tended to come from Iraq. This is the part of the capital where illicit drugs are most prevalent, and where there are relatively high rates of crime. In mid-November 2013 the Saudi authorities launched a campaign to rid the capital of its illegal workers. This was followed by a brief but intense period of social protest, before a large number of migrant workers were expelled.

Other parts of the capital are home to smaller pockets of drugs-related criminality, such as al-Nadim district in the east of the city.

2. The North–South-East Route. This route sees Captagon pills smuggled across the Jordanian border into Saudi Arabia, but instead of being directed for use on the western side of the kingdom they are moved to the eastern side instead. From there they are either distributed to regional towns and cities, including most importantly Riyadh, or they are transported to the smaller Gulf states, for which a market in Captagon appears rapidly to be emerging. Dubai is a favoured regional hub, with the emirate's free zones being well set up for secondary distribution. This again comes from Turkey in the north and flows south-easterly to the eastern part of the kingdom.

3. The Yemeni Route. Owing to the mountainous terrain alone, Yemen could hardly be the favoured route for the transportation of illicit drugs into Saudi Arabia. Distance too would seem to mitigate the feasibility of this route. These drawbacks are to some extent compensated for by the open and largely lawless mutual border that characterises the states of Saudi Arabia and Yemen, as further exacerbated by the current Yemeni civil war.[33]

It is not only supplies of Captagon that are finding their way into Saudi Arabia from across the border with Yemen. The smuggling of both qat, which is illegal in the kingdom, unlike in Yemen, and alcohol, which is also illegal, have benefited from the porous nature of the border, as indeed has the illicit trade in weapons. The city of Jizan is important as a focal point for such illicit trade. Saudi Arabia has seen a steep increase in the consumption of qat in the country, especially between 2007 and 2010, reflecting strong demand at home for the narcotic. The fact that the inhabitants of Saudi Arabia's Asir province in the south-east of the kingdom are mainly ethnically Yemeni virtually guarantees a high demand for the narcotic in the country. The strong tribal ties across the boundary make the disruption, let alone the ending, of the smuggling, whether qat or firearms, very difficult to effect. To date, efforts to establish an impermeable barrier on the Saudi–Yemen border have not achieved a rate of success anywhere near comparable with the hi-tech regime established on the Saudi–Iraq border.

Qat

For those caught selling qat, punishment is more nominal than punitive. If apprehended in possession of qat in Saudi Arabia, one is likely only to face something in the vicinity of a SR15 fine, the equivalent of about £3. The aim behind the lightness of the fine is to symbolically insist on respect for the law, but to do so in a way that does not irreparably alienate qat chewers from the Saudi state. This finely judged response reflects the continued concerns that the Saudi authorities have about the re-emergence of home-grown al-Qaeda terrorism.

In spite of the threat that each poses in its own way, Saudi drug sources perceive only a 'weak' connection between drugs and terrorism. Their simple but unequivocal view is that drug smugglers tend to be motivated by money, terrorists by ideology.[34]

Apart from ethnic Yemenis, the Saudi–Yemeni smuggling route is also attractive to African nationals, especially those from Ethiopia. They smuggle both drugs and alcohol into Saudi Arabia, having crossed the Red Sea with their contraband. One of the main types of alcohol being smuggled into the Arabian Peninsula is the aniseed spirit arak. Its clear liquid is often disguised for efficient trafficking by being transported in water bottles. Ethiopian nationals were disproportionately represented in those illegal workers expelled from Manfuhah in the south of Riyadh in late 2013.

Risks at Home

If the political geography of the Saudi state is classically vulnerable to illicit drugs, the same may be said as far as Saudi society is concerned. Saudi society consists of a young and relatively wealthy population that travels abroad frequently, and has an absence of varied leisure pursuits at home. Currently, between 110,000 and 130,000 young Saudis are enrolled in higher education, living and studying abroad. The initial use of stimulants begins with children in the ten- to twelve-year age bracket. The real 'risk period' in the kingdom for the escalating consumption of drugs is between thirteen and seventeen years of age.

Young people in Saudi Arabia are initially at their most vulnerable when away from the authority of both school and family. The space within which such authority is located tends to be very specific: the school during lesson time, and the family premises at meal- and bedtime. There are no after-school clubs in Saudi Arabia, operating from schools. The only facilities offered by neighbourhood mosques to local children are Qur'anic memorising and recitation classes, rather than offering havens for social protection.

This leaves school students with a potentially lengthy period of time between the end of the school day and their arrival time at home,[35] in which responsible authority is effectively absent. During the journey home from school, youngsters are susceptible to attempts by young adults, themselves often only between eighteen and twenty-two years old, often driving motor vehicles intended to impress, to 'groom' them as part of the creation of new markets for drugs. The young 'market makers' give cigarettes to the younger children, and even Captagon pills. With their energising effects on the brain and body, these are often attractive to youngsters.

Responses from Society

Independently, so it seems, both of Saudi Arabia's leading anti-drug NGOs have come to the same conclusion. As far as adopting a strategy for combating drugs is concerned, both profess a clear focus for prevention. In doing so, they seem to have arrived at the same conclusion for largely the same reasons: other areas of the drug sector, especially rehabilitation, are too costly, too uncertain in terms of outcome and hence too risky in terms of helping to raise future funding from their membership base to be viable alternatives. Having accepted that drugs are dangerous and are entrenched in Saudi society, potential funders do not want to be confronted by a future where there is little other than frustration and indifferent success rates at best.

Wiqaya

Like so many others progressive activities involved in social affairs in the kingdom, responding to illicit drugs in Saudi Arabia, the National Association for

Drugs Prevention, Wiqaya, is a new institution, barely some nine years old. Its board is made up mainly of ageing businessmen, but congenial types, men who want to put something back into society. They are intent on ensuring that their grandchildren's generation does not succumb to illicit drugs. The association is described by its leaders as being 100 per cent an NGO. It is registered with the government because this is the law. It receives what is described as being 'a little money' from the Ministry of Social Affairs.

Wiqaya fully accepts the dangers that drugs present to society, adapting an Arabic proverb to state that 'drugs are in every house'. Mindful of how politics in Saudi Arabia works, representatives of the society visited Crown Prince Sultan before his death in 2011, who was supportive of their activities. They also visited Prince Nayef the Ministry of Interior, before his death. Nayef urged the society to establish a presence in every city, town and village, with preventative action in mind. Despite such access, it seems that Wiqaya was less than entirely happy with the latter visit; it is expensive opening new offices in the kingdom. The organisation is nevertheless happy to parrot the official rhetoric. Referencing the country's leaders, they repeat the mantra that 'narcotics are worse than terrorism': it is coming from all directions and is very difficult to stop.

The association has identified two priority areas of activity to date. First, it is in the process of setting up and funding a research chair at the Nayef University, specialising in security affairs. The brief of the person appointed will be prevention in its widest and most integrated form. This will involve bringing together such differing policy disciplines as defence studies and psychology. Second, it is cooperating with the Ministry of Education and the NCNC, state body and quango respectively, to take a professional prevention campaign into Saudi Arabia's high schools. The organisation has learned that it can be more effective if it divides school students into differing 'segments', depending upon their vulnerability, and deals with them accordingly. For example, Wiqaya has learned that more must be done to help nurture children with bad home conditions, as a major component of the task of containing the spread of drugs.

In all of these activities, and indeed other complementary areas too, the organisation is convinced that as an NGO it can be an effective bridge to the local community. Cooperation, it is pointed out, is much more likely with the NGO sector. This approach is contrasted positively with that of the state, and by inference the Ministry of Interior. Many local people are fearful of the police, especially those who have had a previous brush with the law. People are generally afraid of the government, which they associate with punishment and, *in extremis*, imprisonment for assumed infringements of the law.

al-Anood Foundation

Named after King Fahd's favourite wife, the al-Anood Foundation was set up when she gave away one-third of her wealth for philanthropic reasons on her thirty-seventh birthday.[36] The Foundation soon established its position as a focal point for social responsibility programmes, of which women's affairs has been a long-standing priority. Moving into the realm of anti-drugs activity therefore seemed like a logical progression. At first, its profile in the anti-drugs sector was rather tame. For example, the Foundation is responsible for sponsoring the Saudi component of the International Day against Drug Abuse and Illicit Drug Trafficking.

Activity of a more substantive nature, focusing on complementarities with existing social campaigning, has proved to be more popular and viable of late. One example of this sort of cross-over work may be seen in the area entitled 'heal the families', which dove-tails with the Foundation's continuing involvement of women. This activity is based on a concern for the growing level of family breakdown and attendant dysfunction in Saudi Arabia. Other aspects of individual and social behaviour, which may aggravate this tendency, such as substance dependence, have been brought into the orbit of such activism in order to manage the social consequences. The Foundation would like to empower what it refers to as 'civil community' to identify aggravating circumstances, which may in turn leave families and neighbourhoods susceptible to drug abuse. Echoing Wiqaya, the al-Anood Foundation believes in the importance of getting 'close to the people', holding to the view that civil community groups of all kinds prove more effective in such activities than as the state.

At this point, the parallels between al-Anood and Wiqaya begin to diverge. One only has to begin a cursory count of the number of princes (though not princesses) whose photographs adorn the wall of the Foundation's honours board to see that despite Wiqaya's connections to the well-heeled business community, it is al-Anood that enjoys direct political connections to that most rarefied of ranking figures in Saudi Arabia, the senior princes. Even here, however, there is a difference of status between those princes whose patriarch is a serving king or a king in waiting, and those, such as the Al-Fahd (sons of Fahd), whose king is deceased, with all his powers behind him. For all of his formal connections, the head of the Foundation spends a surprising amount of his time railing against 'the bureaucracy'. This translates into 'the lack of a central strategy' for drugs and the absence of figures from civil society represented in the top echelons of illicit drugs decision making.[37] In the absence of the active patronage of King Fahd and Queen al-Anood, only by manipulating the political system can the Foundation hope to prosper.

The best current illustration of this frustration with the system relates to the Foundation's attempts to establish a national network of anti-drugs training centres. It would like the centres to be able to make a profit from this activity, allowing them to be free standing and self-funding, with extensive coverage across the cities and rural towns of the kingdom. The alternative to the proposed profit centres would be non-profit centres. These would still be designed to attain a high standard of care, but would not have the resources to spread the coverage of such organisations across the kingdom.

The frustration of the Foundation is exacerbated by the knowledge that the framework of such an initiative is already in place, as are the personnel to manage it. To date, however, the Foundation has only been given a temporary licence, meaning that it can only plan ahead one year at a time. Only one such training centre has so far been opened hitherto in the Kingdom. The application for permission has been issued, but no response has yet been received. The responsibility for the hold-up in approval has come from the anti-narcotics police, which was established and nurtured by one of the former King Fahd's full younger brothers and former heir apparent, Prince Nayef, to whom we were introduced at the beginning of this chapter. Though now also deceased, Nayef dominated the ministry for five decades. It is his police culture, with its emphasis on conservative values, the use of force and, in the drugs field, an obsession with supply-side interdiction, that still prevails within the organisation today.

The most plausible reason for Nayef not having approved the next stage of the training-centre proposal is not any particular animus towards the Al-Fahd, or even a lukewarm position on the issue; on the contrary, Nayef is identified with florid rhetoric on the subject. The most likely explanation for the bureaucratic stasis is the existence of a policy bottleneck, in which the training centres are vying for the political will of the topmost leadership, in rivalry with many other public-policy issues.

BOX 3

PRINCE SAUD BIN FAHD BIN ABDUL AZIZ AL-SAUD

Prince Saud, one of the most prominent sons of the former King Fahd and, as a direct descendant of the founder of the kingdom, notionally eligible (though unlikely) to accede, is the vice-chairman of al-Anood

Foundation, a charitable body dedicated to alleviating a range of social problems. Anti-drugs activism is a central part of its remit. The sixty-seven-year-old Prince Saud, who regularly goes into his office in the Foundation, appears well briefed on the subject, contrasting the absence of drugs in the kingdom thirty years ago with today. He also sticks to the princely script by quoting the now-deceased hardliner Prince Nayef, on this occasion saying that 'drugs are worse than terrorism' in their wide-ranging effects on society. Taking advantage of his reputation for being easy-going and accessible, senior Foundation officials attempt to prompt and encourage Prince Saud to channel their concerns and ideas about drugs to the highest level of the Saud family. Even a foreign researcher on illicit drugs may find himself primed and pushed forward to make a short pitch to the prince in favour of some aspect of policy.[38] Appointed as deputy head of Saudi intelligence in 1985, Prince Saud's connections clearly extend beyond the kingdom, and lean more to the supply side of the equation, especially given the profile of drugs in Saudi Arabia's relations with Afghanistan and neighbouring countries. The fact that he served in intelligence under the leadership of his cousin, the more assertive and ambitious Prince Turki bin Faisal bin Abdul Aziz, means that it is doubtful that Prince Saud would directly have the connections that would allow him to play a role commensurate with the position previously held.

Responses by the State

Until recently, regulations governing the treatment of public-sector workers reflected the strong disapproval of the state towards drugs. Thus, any public-sector employee caught with illicit drugs was summarily dismissed from their post. This changed as the state realised the need to win the confidence of drug abusers, and to view drug takers more as victims than as criminals. Consequently, a 'three strikes and you're out' of work was introduced instead. This has now evolved into more of a 'two strikes' approach, a reflection of the continuing social disapproval that illicit drugs still generate.

The various branches of law enforcement and the military in Saudi Arabia have also been subject to change as far as the use of drugs are concerned. As is the case in Israel, the military in the kingdom is now subject to random samplings for illegal drugs. As with so many areas of social policy in the country, no figures are available to illustrate how serious is the failure rate. It may be assumed to be significant because those failing are not automatically dismissed, although dismissal may be the end point of the process. Those found to be regularly taking drugs are just as likely to be channelled into detoxification (if relevant) and rehabilitation as made subject to a punitive decision. The real reason for treating the various security bodies in this way is the fear that, if alienated, their personnel may drift into radical political circles in the kingdom, namely al-Qaeda.

BOX 4

THE KING'S NEPHEW, THE DRUGS RUNNER

Nayef bin Sultan bin Fawwaz al-Shaalan, the maternal grandson of Saudi Arabia's first king, and husband of one of the alleged fifteen daughters of King Abdullah bin Abdul Aziz, was convicted in absentia in 2005 in a French court for smuggling cocaine with a street value of $36 million in his private jet. The court sentenced him to a ten-year prison term and a fine of $100 million. In reality, he has never served any of this time, his case having been conducted entirely *in absentia*. The cocaine came from Colombia and was flown to France via Miami. Nayef studied at the University of Miami, and lived in the city between the late 1970s and the mid-1980s. He has an earlier prosecution for the possession of drugs in Mississippi in 1984. Nayef al-Shaalan has insisted that his aircraft was transporting plastic pipes. He further insists that he has been cleared of cocaine trafficking by the Saudi authorities. The Saudi government made no official comment on the case. Needless to say, there has been no question of capital punishment being applied in this case. According to French police, Prince Nayef bin Abdul Aziz, until his death in 2012 the kingdom's crown prince, threatened to cancel contracts to the value of $6 billion in the event of the prosecution proceeding; the French state went ahead with the prosecution regardless. Nayef al-Shaalan is understood to own Kranz Bank in Switzerland, an institution that has come under suspicion of money laundering. Since the affair Nayef al-Shaalan and his wife are said to be kept under close supervision by the Saudi king, now deceased, in one of the senior princes' palaces in Riyadh.

Conclusion

Of all of the states in the Middle East, Saudi Arabia was arguably the last to recognise and accept that it had a serious and persistent drugs problem. This has notably taken the form of the stimulant Captagon, which is popular among Saudi youth and, increasingly, young people in the wider Arab Gulf. The cause of this reticence has been the embarrassment felt by the Saudi regime, which hosts the most important sites of Islam, and mobilises religion for its own legitimacy, while at the same time presiding over the burgeoning consumption of drugs. This helps to explain why the Ministry of the Interior insists on dominating the anti-drugs sector, even to the extent of depriving the country's coordinating body of essential statistics. It also helps explain why the Saudi authorities so instinctively employ capital punishment to deal with what they regard as heinous and persistent offenders.

While the preoccupation of the Saudi regime is with religion and how it impacts upon the political order, it is to the realities of socio-economic change in the kingdom that one needs to turn in order to understand the increasing use of drugs. Saudi Arabia has been described as being 'a big social workshop', in which a rising youth demographic, with unprecedented levels of wealth at their disposal, has to address and reconcile itself with a range of social problems, such as family breakdown and domestic violence, in which drugs are more of a symptom than a cause. If one then takes into account the long, deserted and difficult-to-police frontiers of the state, then the choking off of drugs supplies is never likely to be entirely successful.

The Saudi ruling family have not really taken this on board, although it too has lost senior clan members to the ravages of hard drugs. They see drugs as a strategic threat, as the product of other states that would seek to undermine and weaken the Saudi state from within. The consent of the Saudi authorities to grant a visa for the research visit on which this chapter is based was eventually forthcoming on the basis that the security threat from drugs would be a central focus of the research and analysis. After giving due consideration to such dynamics, it is the impact and consequences of 'modernisation' that are judged here to be the most important in explaining the profile and distribution of drugs in the kingdom.

7

IRAN

GRAPPLING WITH ADDICTION

Contemporary Iran is based upon a paradox. The Islamic Republic of Iran claims to be a paragon of political and social virtue. Its very existence as a political system, as its formal name reveals, is justified on religious grounds. It has been dominated by Shia clerics for the three-and-a-half decades of its existence. The innovative basis of its system, rule by the righteous jurist, was crafted by Ayatollah Ruhollah Khomeini, its founder and inspiration. Intrinsic to the political order of the revolutionary period has been a set of norms that have rigorously and conservatively governed the way Iranians are permitted to conduct themselves: no alcohol; no courting couples; little or no music; modest dress for women. By establishing such benchmarks from the outset, and by so rigorously policing them, it is by its social values that the Islamic Republic has invited evaluation.

Yet, in spite of these apparently comforting realities, contemporary Iran is a country that has been addled by the social blight of narcotic drugs. True, old men in rural Iran have since time immemorial imbibed opium while they reminisce about their younger days, as they used to puff on tobacco in briar pipes and sip a half pint of warm bitter in nostalgic reflection in an England long past. But Iran has experienced something quite different over the last thirty years. A heroin epidemic and an epidemic of crystal meth have swept through Iran's cities, Tehran included, blighting many of its poorer neighbourhoods. Increasingly, consumption has been based upon intravenous usage. An associated AIDS and hepatitis wave has followed, as needles are regularly shared among drug users, in spite of the pursuit of admittedly uneven policies of 'harm reduction'.[1] New intoxicants flow into the country, deepening the range and complexity of the problem. Prostitution is rife within Iran, partially driven by the demands of addiction and an associated sense of hopelessness.

This coexistence of pious values and rampant drug abuse is a reminder of the difficulties of trying to build a utopia on earth, whether of the religious kind or some other. Though Shiite Islam is the long-established, dominant religion in Iran, it is one that has to coexist with other experiences and values. In Iran today that includes: poverty and unemployment; a desire on the part of the educated young to travel and engage with a wider world of cultural experience; and a flirtation with pre-Islamic forms of religion. For Iranians without the means to emigrate or the qualifications to get a job, there is little choice but the oblivion that is on offer within.

Opiates, the 'Opium of the People'

The Iranian narcotics profile is unusual among the illicit, drugs-consuming countries of the world. Whereas the 'typical' country consumes a broader base of 'soft' drugs, such as tobacco and, among illegal drugs, cannabis or hashish, tapering in number when 'hard' or 'problem' drugs are included, in Iran it is opiates (extending from opium to morphine to heroin), usually identified as more addictive and less desirable, that are by far the largest category of abused drugs. It may be a bit of an exaggeration to say that Iran simply has no taste for cannabis and its derivatives. After all, in 2011 the Iranian authorities did successfully seize more than 57,000 kilograms of the commodity (see Table 1). Nevertheless, this figure paled when set alongside the figure for seizures of opiates, which stood at roughly seven times this amount.

As with narcotics debates elsewhere, figures for consumption, trafficking and rehabilitation remain frustratingly elusive or contested. All one can do is to give banded approximations of the presence and impact of illegal drugs. In Iran, there are always three different answers to the key question regarding the level of abuse, the product of a range of factors from ignorance to regime self-interest to inconsistent criteria for addiction.

- The first figure, coming from official sources, places the number of problem users at around the 1.2 million mark, with another 700,000 classified as recreational users.
- A second figure, born of the exaggeration that is a byproduct of strict information control, especially as far as such sensitive issues are concerned, places the total number of users at around the 9 million mark.

- The third figure, still frustratingly imprecise, is that which circulates among experts and parliamentarians. It places the number of addicts at 4 million, with 2.5 million recreational users.

If we assume for a moment that the mean figure is closer to the truth, it would be the case that around 26 million Iranians out of a population of 73 million would have a family member in their midst who was a regular user of narcotics.[2] Wild fluctuations in estimation are not just a contemporary phenomenon: in the mid-1920s official sources placed consumption at 5–10 per cent of the population, while contrary views estimated the problem at between 20 and 50 per cent.[3] An estimated 130,000 new abusers join this number every year.[4] The number of drug-related deaths grew to 2,106 in 2001.[5] Research conducted by the Ministry of Health in the early 2000s found that in six cities in Tehran Province many problem users were female sex workers.[6]

The reason for the dominance of opiates among Iran's national drugs profile is straightforwardly geographical and economic. Iran is located adjacent to Afghanistan, the biggest purveyor of raw opium in the world, and a country that, as the 2000s have unfolded, has refined increasing levels of heroin within its own borders, as heroin production has moved 'upstream'. Moreover, the two countries have long borders, characterised by difficult terrain, which are hard to police effectively. This is also the case for the border with Pakistan, significant flows from which also enter Iran. The total length of Iran's borders with these two neighbours is 1,125 miles. According to the specialist UN agency, UNODC, around 40 per cent of Afghanistan's narcotics exports, overwhelmingly in the form of raw opium, morphine base and heroin, are smuggled into Iran. It is further claimed that of this figure an estimated 30 per cent of the drugs entering Iran will remain in the country, to be used for domestic consumption.[7]

If geography makes Iran especially vulnerable to the supply of opiates, it also has a decisive bearing on the economics of illegal drugs. The value of narcotics roughly doubles every time a consignment crosses an international boundary. This is because of the vulnerability of the trade to interdiction and the need for the services of specialist traffickers to circumvent the pitfalls of the borders, which tend to be heavily policed. Consequently, in Iran prices tend to be modest and drug-purity rates high. For example, in Iran in 2005 a gram of heroin with 50 per cent purity sold for approximately $5. This helps to explain why Ali Nariman, a poor inhabitant of Tehran interviewed at the time, said with resignation that he would drink beer if he could afford it,[8] before disappearing to consume a small grey ball of opium.[9] In Iran narcotics have a pronounced socio-economic class base to them. As in the rundown areas of Glasgow and Edinburgh in Scotland, the heroin in south Tehran is identified most closely with people at the margins of society.

The Tehran authorities claim that they have been active in trying to stem the flow of drugs. Iran routinely posts 30,000 law-enforcement personnel along its eastern border.[10] The most striking figure in support of this view is that 3,600 Iranians working in law enforcement have been killed in the line of duty over a three-decade period, primarily in the border areas. One factor in explaining this extraordinary figure is that local clans in border provinces such as Sistan–Baluchistan, where much of the smuggling takes place, have long derived significant income from the cross-border movement of contraband. For example, in one small town near the provincial capital, Zahedan, between 40 and 65 per cent of residents are estimated to earn their livelihood by smuggling goods between Iran and Pakistan or facilitating those who do.[11] They are familiar with the border terrain in a way that the younger conscripts serving for relatively brief periods, and drawn from across Iran, can never be. These tribesmen's long-accrued local knowledge of the borderlands that divide them also exceeds that of Iran's border police, who enjoy more of an elite reputation.

A second factor contributing to the disadvantage of border law enforcement is the relative balance of military materiel on the two sides. Instead of the familiar story of the forces of the state having the upper hand in an asymmetrical struggle against localised criminals engaged in drug trafficking, the smugglers regularly out-gun the Iranian authorities. From four-wheel drive vehicles and night-vision equipment through the possession of heavy ordinance even extending to anti-tank missiles, the smugglers are often in a position to give at least as good as they get from the state's law-enforcement sector. Even when border patrols have been able to summon helicopter support, they have on occasion been faced by deadly American-made Stinger shoulder-launch missiles in the hands of their foes on the ground.[12] Consequently, helicopters have been brought down. Sometimes the smugglers adopt very different tactics and, in order to limit their risk, send unaccompanied camel caravans across the border. Female 'junkie camels' may be relied upon unerringly to travel great distances for a further shot of opium or to be reunited with their offspring.

The Tehran authorities routinely claim that Iran spends the annual equivalent of between $250 million and $800 million on trying to prevent illegal drugs crossing its eastern borders. These resources, no doubt exaggerated but still substantial,[13] have helped to fund an impressive list of anti-trafficking measures. These have included: the doubling of Iran's frontier force in three years; the construction of an 80 kilometre cement wall—Iran's own 'separation barrier'—3 metres high and with barbed wire atop; the building of 160 watch-towers; and the excavation of a 460 kilometre canal, 4 metres wide and 5 metres deep, although these ditches tend to silt up again quickly, as a result of the ravages of the desert winds.[14] When the authorities do feel that they are getting the upper hand the traffickers can resort to other methods of exercising leverage, such as the kidnap and murder of local people in order to discourage their fraternisation with Tehran and to secure and retain their logistical assistance.[15]

BOX 1

IRAN'S MOST EFFECTIVE BORDER CONTROL

Iran's most effective anti-narcotics operation on the border with Afghanistan came in late summer 1998. It was not the result of the acquisition of new weapons systems, nor was it the implementation of a new strategy. In fact, it was not even the product of a narcotics-oriented policy, but the consequence of other issues. The situation came about as a result of a bloody development in domestic Afghan affairs, when the Taliban first took over the north-western city of Mazhar-e Sharif. In the course of the conflict eleven Iranian nationals, including diplomatic staff, were killed, as were a large number of people from ethnic and religious minorities. The authorities in Tehran mobilised the military and deployed it in force to their mutual border as one of a package of measures to emphasise the gravity with which the development was viewed. At the height of the tensions as many as 300,000 Iranian troops were reported to be in the vicinity of the border, a tenfold increase over routine deployments. Iran laid down a series of conditions for the defusing of the border tension, including an apology for the loss of life, the return of the bodies and the bringing to trial of the perpetrators. War was implied in the event of non-compliance. Such was the size, profile and potentially aggressive intent of the Iranian military that the professional smugglers on the joint border greatly scaled down their activities, for fear that the big build-up could easily be redeployed to undermine their livelihood. Once the source of the tension itself had dissipated, Tehran had little to justify the continued presence

---

of such a force on its eastern border, or indeed its expense. To have done so might have left Iran open to accusations of war-mongering or even territorial expansionism, and could have had wider regional ramifications. Men and materiel were therefore gradually scaled down. In turn, the traffickers returned to their cross-border trade. Once again it was business as usual for the drugs smugglers.

In spite of these major impediments, Iran's drug-seizure rates are impressive, though again very much a function of geography and proximity. In the Iranian year to 20 March 2009, Iran made 85 per cent of the world's seizures of opiates.[16]

Table 1: Drugs Seizures in Iran (kg)

	2010	2011
Heroin	27,141	23,096
Morphine	8,098	6,811
Opiates (opium etc.)	400,032	373,818
Cannabis	60,378	57,096
Methamphetamines	1,371	3,917
Cocaine	16,000	1,000

Source: Drug Control Headquarters, *Drug Control in 2011*.

The narcotics that are not successfully interdicted tend to traverse Iran in one of three different ways. The 'northern route' takes the opiates through Khorasan Province into Turkmenistan, down to Tehran and then to the Turkish border, from where they head primarily into the Balkans and then onwards to Europe. The 'southern route', historically the most important, sees the trafficked drugs heading more or less straight to Tehran, from where they continue direct to Turkey. The third route, 'the Hormuzgan', involves drugs consignments heading further south to the Persian Gulf's most important seaport, Bandar Abbas, from where they move out of the Gulf by small boat or speedboat. The Straits of Hormuz have been an important focus of the interdiction of drug-carrying dhows since 2003, with hashish and heroin the main cargoes. The dhows are loaded in one of a number of the small ports that exist on the Iranian side of the Gulf.[17]

The port of Bandar Abbas is also an important entry point for precursors, notably acetic anhydride (AA), the chemical essential for the processing of morphine base into heroin. With its underdeveloped economy, there is nowhere in Afghanistan that produces such a chemical, and no industry that makes use of it for licit purposes. AA therefore has to be brought in from countries with a reasonable level of industrialisation. In this case, the chemical is trafficked 'the wrong way', that is to say from west to east, in contrast to the flow of opiates, before heading to the sites of the heroin labs in Afghanistan.[18]

Smoke and Mirrors

In spite of the impressive sacrifices that many Iranians have made in trying to defend the integrity of their borders from smugglers, it is doubtful if this simple narrative is, as things rarely are in Iran, all there is to it. First, there are bound to be examples of small-scale, low-level bribery at and around the border. The non-specialist police force in Iran, as is the case in other regional countries such as Afghanistan, Iraq and Turkey, is well known for being poorly paid, indifferently trained and suffering from low morale. Many policemen supplement their incomes through bribes. In the Iranian case especially, given the volume and value of the narcotics involved, these temptations are likely for some to be irresistible. The fact that local police raids on apartments in Tehran used to be a regular occurrence, but, by the end of the 2000s, had become rare, can almost entirely be put down to bribery, or 'coordination',[19] as the cynically well-to-do of the northern suburbs euphemistically put it. In 2004 alone, some 500 members of the Iranian police were sacked for corruption. Narcotics are estimated to be responsible for 70 per cent of the bribery cases in Iran.[20]

Drugs and Politics

Iran is a country where corruption and smuggling in general is rife. Because of its endemic nature, and the overall political context of authoritarianism, it is unthinkable that parts of the political establishment are not involved. There has been persistent speculation over time that the Iranian Revolutionary Guard Corps (IRGC), a parallel military force set up by the Islamic regime at the inception of the revolution, is implicated in such activities. The organisation is opaque, and is not subject to routine safeguards, making abuse of position and power relatively easy. The reliance of the Iranian regime on the IRGC for its very survival makes disciplining it all the harder. The IRGC has gradually expanded its activities into the commercial sector, a direction in which it was encouraged by the presidency of Mahmoud Ahmadinejad. An expansion of activities into the realm of illegal drugs is therefore quite conceivable.

Some Iranian critics even go so far as to say that regime involvement in the supply and trafficking of illegal drugs is more sinister than simply being a lucrative source of income. They point to the availability of narcotics as being part of the regime's strategy to maintain overall political control of the country, of which a docile younger population is a *sine qua non*.[21] While the charge is perhaps an extraordinary one to Western ears, its proponents claim that they have evidence in their favour. They claim, for example, that after the student rioting on the Tehran University campus in 1999, drug dealers were given privileged access to the campus and permitted to distribute narcotics for free.[22] Regime spokesmen hit back with their own extraordinary claims of anaesthetising the young. In the early years of the revolution the clerical establishment saw the spread of addiction as part of a Western strategy to 'annihilate the revolutionary youth of Iran'. Under Ahmadinejad, a similar refrain was heard again. The association of the spread of narcotics with 'global imperialism' had been made anew.[23]

The overall context of a thriving black economy with smuggling at its heart cannot be denied. Foodstuffs, luxury goods, cement and asphalt were among goods trafficked via Basra, through Iran, during the Saddamist domination of Iraq. This helped Iraq to evade the international sanctions regime which was in place at the time.[24] There are many other examples, with some even confirmed from regime sources. Ahmad Seifkaran, a Construction Jihad official, stated in November 1999 that more than 1.2 million cattle are smuggled out of Iran annually. Nearly 50 per cent of Iran's saffron production leaves the country illegally. Petroleum products are shipped illicitly to Afghanistan and Pakistan. Such is the big business of Iranian smuggling that there are an estimated 2,000 companies based in Dubai alone, which are engaged in some form of illicit trade with Iran. Inadequately implemented sanctions and state subsidies distributed in Iran, especially on such mass-consumption commodities as petrol,[25] which exacerbates the price differential with neighbouring countries, best explains the profligate nature of the black-market trade.

The Iranian regime has long been accused of executing political opponents as 'drug dealers',[26] on the grounds that such justification is more likely to appear to be viewed as legitimate at home and abroad. During the period between 1991 and 2001, well after the excesses of the Khalkhali period (see Box 2), an estimated 5,000 people were executed in Iran, ostensibly for narcotics-related offences.[27] Likewise, the suspicion exists that the Iranian regime has used counter-narcotics activity as at least a partial smokescreen for counter-insurgency operations against local communities.[28]

Sistan–Baluchistan

Iran's ethnic minorities are generally found to be located along the underdeveloped periphery of the country. Sistan–Baluchistan is routinely seen as the poorest of Iran's provinces, with its vast desert scapes, a 350,000 Afghan refugee community and 20,000 local nomads. Many aspects of existence are grim, with life expectancy standing at sixty-one, compared to seventy in Tehran.[29] Periodic political disquiet among the Baluchis mean that far fewer military engagements can be reduced to the simple level of drugs trafficking than might appear at face value to be the case.

A Sunni insurgent group, Jundollah (God's soldiers), or the Iranian People's Resistance Movement, launched a campaign of violence against the IRGC following its creation in 2002/3. It expanded its campaign in 2005,[30] its most audacious act being an attempted assassination of President Ahmadinejad in December 2005 in Baluchistan. Much damage was done to the organisation when its leader, Abdolmalik Rigi, was arrested in February 2010, after his plane was forced down by Iran en route between Dubai and Kyrgyzstan. It appears that Tehran's success against Jundollah followed the withdrawal of support for the group by the Pakistani state.[31] A brother of the Jundollah leader, Abdulhamid Rigi, had previously been arrested by the Iranian authorities, having been extradited by Pakistan. He was tried in 2008 for among other things, according to Iran's Press TV, drug offences.[32] His Jundollah organisation was better known for a campaign of violence in favour of autonomy for Sistan–Baluchistan. Abdulhamid Rigi was executed in May 2010, after the arrest of his brother, when concerns regarding a retaliatory outbreak of violence had subsided.[33] The Iranians then pressed their advantage, a Revolutionary Court convicting Abdolmalik on a range of charges including armed robbery, kidnapping, drug smuggling, assassination attempts and murder.[34] He was executed a month later, in an Iranian state attempt to roll up the organisation.

Narco-Diplomacy: The West and Beyond

For the first decade of the new regime Iran was largely out of bounds for Western visitors. Obtaining a visa to travel there was enormously difficult. For much of this time countries such as the USA and the UK went largely unrepresented in Tehran. Formal relations were often frosty and unforthcoming. Infamous experiences such as the 444-day US hostage crisis hardly encouraged travel to Iran, even where it remained possible. Bilateral relations between countries like Iran and the USA were characterised by an antipathy born of Iran's radical international agenda and American support for Tehran's adversaries during the eight-year Iran–Iraq war. The bilateral agenda between Iran and the West remained almost uniformly negative during this time. Issues such as human rights abuses at home, the sponsorship of terrorism abroad, radically polarised differences over the Arab–Israeli peace process and, during the latter stages of the war, Iranian attacks on commercial shipping using the Gulf waterway, all reinforced a strongly pejorative stance among the Atlantic countries towards Iran.

BOX 2

NARCOTICS AND REVOLUTIONARY TERROR

The most notorious figure of the early months of the post-Shah political order, and there were plenty to choose from, was an uncouth minor cleric named Sadeq Khalkhali. In February 1979 he was appointed head of the Islamic Revolutionary Court. More importantly for our purposes, he also served as the head of the Anti-Drugs Revolutionary Court, which was a subsidiary of the main revolutionary court, during the so-called Kerensky period equivalent, between May and December 1979, before a decisively Islamic regime emerged from the revolutionary turmoil. Khalkhali spent much of his time moving around the country, dispensing revolutionary justice as he went. This invariably meant capital punishment at the outcome of short and peremptory court hearings. Khalkhali is the name most closely associated with Iran's period of revolutionary terror. He was, in short, Iran's Robespierre, though with sweaty black turban rather than white powdered wig.

Khalkhali interpreted his brief as heading a concerted campaign to eradicate hard and soft drugs from revolutionary Iran. In Iran at the time there were estimated to be between 500,000 and 800,000 heroin addicts. In order to reduce this number Khalkhali set about targeting drug dealers. At least 582 persons were executed under his direction during the eleven months of his tenure. During this time Ayatollah Khomeini, who had described as 'inhuman' the executions of drugs traffickers under the Shah (though this number had proved to be much smaller than Khalkhali's), was mute. Generally, Iran's clerics had seemed relatively uninterested in the issue of narcotics, with no fatwas on the subject issued prior to the revolution.

In spite of the punitive nature of Khalkhali's *modus operandi*, his actions did impact drugs trends on the ground, at least in the short run. Like Mao's campaign against drug dealers in late 1940s China, Khalkhali's draconian approach had a discernible impact on consumption levels in Iran. In the longer run, however, opium abuse 'became increasingly rampant'. Iranians, imprisoned in their homes during the revolutionary turmoil, and then bored by the contraction of the public cultural space, looked for a respite. During the 1980–8 Iran–Iraq war those in various branches of the military found easy access to a broad range of drugs, apparently provided by the authorities in order to ameliorate the fear felt on the battle fronts before Iran's 'human waves' were sent into action. After the revolution of 1979, locally grown opium was cheaper and more accessible than alcohol, which had to be smuggled in from Turkey or distilled by Iran's small Armenian population illicitly. Despite the risks, Iranians faced an economic incentive for its purchase.

Khalkhali's career was brought to an abrupt end when he was forced to resign. The ostensible reason for this move was that $14 million, the proceeds of drugs raids and fines over the previous months, had gone astray. Khalkhali claimed that the missing funds had been spent on the operations and activities of his office. In reality, such corruption alone would have been unlikely to bring down such a figure, especially if one considers the institutionalised corruption that would typify later periods of the regime. Rather, his time had passed. Iranians no longer had the stomach for his violent ways.

With the end of the war in 1988 and the death of the first leader of the revolution, Ayatollah Ruhollah Khomeini, in June 1989, the atmosphere between Iran and its foes appeared to soften. The environment seemed ripe for pursuing a thaw in relations. In the end, this proved to be illusory. But of the long list of problems that cluttered the agenda of bilateral relations, only illegal drugs emerged as a factor that was not perceived to be a zero-sum exercise.

The Khatami Phenomenon

The real improvement in relations began with the election of President Mohammed Khatami in 1995, which enabled the European Union to draw a line under such infamous events as the Mykonos affair, when Iranian opposition emigres were murdered in a Greek restaurant in Austria, allegedly at the instigation of the regime. By November 1997 the Iranian deputy foreign minister, Morteza Sarmadi, was a visitor to Brussels, where he met senior EU officials and discussed such issues as refugees and illicit drugs. While Brussels stressed Iran's constructive policies with the EU and praised its anti-drug campaign, Sarmadi urged the Europeans to do more by way of cooperation, viewing current levels as 'inadequate'.[35] Flushed with the success of such a breakthrough with the EU, high-level Iranian representatives sought to build bilateral relations elsewhere, leveraging the narcotics issue; for example, deputy speaker Hassan Rouhani, who in 2014 would go on to be elected Iranian president, led such a delegation to Moscow.[36]

Declaratory diplomacy could only generate a finite amount of momentum for rapprochement. Further means had to be identified in order to carry the process forward. Again, cooperation over illicit drugs was the only practical topic for cooperation. In November 1998 the UK sent a high-level delegation from Customs & Excise to explore ways of future cooperation with Iran. In responding to this approach, the Iranian side was not viewed as being coy.[37] Soon after, the British took further advantage of Tehran's newly minted interest in limiting drug demand-side pressures domestically. A delegation of demand-reduction experts from the UK visited Tehran in February 2001.[38] At their head was Mo Mowlam, the cabinet office minister and arguably the most popular British politician of the day, though sadly already terminally ill with cancer. She was the first British cabinet minister to visit Iran since the revolution. Her presence was a powerful statement that Britain was willing to recognise the ruling Islamic regime in Tehran. The focus on the practical nature of the demand-side problem allayed Iranian fears that British motives were exclusively narrow and self-centred.[39] In the words of one British diplomat engaged in the process at the time, there was 'a real synergy' in Anglo-Iranian relations in the early 2000s, driven by the narcotics issue.[40]

But it was in relation to ties with the USA that the fortunes of an anti-drugs-led rapprochement would be measured. Iran and the USA had worked together under the umbrella of the UN-sponsored Six Plus Two group on the future of Afghanistan.[41] Tehran even nominated the USA to be the coordinator of the group's counter-narcotics initiative. In contrast to the UK, the USA adopted a more rigid approach to the issue of cooperation with Iran at a bilateral level during this time.[42] Pro-Israeli think tanks discouraged such an initiative in Washington DC, arguing that Iran endorses drugs smuggling by terrorist organisations when convenient, and that its anti-drugs campaign was 'sometimes a cover' for suppressing dissidents.[43]

President Khatami seized the initiative in bringing about a thaw in bilateral relations with the USA. His appointment of Ata'ollah Mohajerani as minister of culture and Islamic guidance 'made room for a vocal, daring, agenda-setting press'.[44] Khatami himself reached out to the American people through a wide-ranging interview with CNN in January 1998. The Clinton administration belatedly responded to Khatami's overtures. Clinton was persuaded to use drugs policy as a relatively safe device through which to reach out to Tehran. Washington made a reciprocal gesture by removing Iran from an official black-list of drug-problem countries at the end of 1998.[45] The momentum sub-sequently spread to the plane of political relations. But by the time the Clinton administration and his secretary of state, Madeleine Albright, had cut through their domestic constraints, there was simply too little time in which to contemplate the restoration of full bilateral relations.

George W. Bush was elected president in November 2000, by which time hopes for a breakthrough in relations were receding. By the time of his state of the union address in January 2002 Bush had unexpectedly added Iran to his list of rogue states, uninterested in the narcotics issue and its potential for conversation. The US invasion of Iraq in March 2003 unleashed a new list of bilateral problems that more than cancelled out any influence towards coop-eration that the more technically oriented narcotics issue might hitherto have generated. With the issue of suspected Iranian nuclear-weapons proliferation dominating relations between Iran and the Atlantic community from 2003/4 until the Vienna nuclear agreement in July 2015, all else paled.

Energetic Multilateralism

Iran was left able to do little more than two things. First, it has embraced the various multilateral initiatives that notionally took off during the 2000s, with this activity not entirely confined to that of a paper exercise. These included breakthrough cooperation brokered by the UN between Iran, Afghanistan and Pakistan, in spite of their individually frosty bilateral relations.[46] In just two years this Triangular Initiative had grown to include the establishment of a joint planning cell and an intelligence-exchange cell, upon which the first ever joint operation against drug traffickers was made possible on 8 March 2009.[47] This cooperation included Iranian training for specialist Afghan anti-drugs police. Within five years regular high-level political and technical meetings had been introduced.

Tehran is active within the Paris Pact, a multilateral initiative for countries affected by the Afghan opium economy, with its main focus on border control and law enforcement along the trafficking routes. Regional organisations that have proliferated since the end of the Cold War, and in which Iran is a member, from the Economic Cooperation Organisation (ECO) and the Caspian Sea Initiative to the Shanghai Cooperation Organisation, all have joint anti-narcotics activities. Though bilateral relations were strained prior to Vienna, the EU has continued to keep the anti-drugs portfolio active for the sake of keeping channels of communication open, albeit through small, lower-level and sometimes indirect cooperation.[48] Meanwhile, Iran has signed memoranda of understanding with more than twenty-one countries, further evidence of narcotics cooperation as a bridge to generally cooperative relations.

Second, Iran has periodically bemoaned the absence of resources forthcoming from countries situated further along the supply line into Europe, which have effectively enjoyed a 'free ride' at the expense of costly Iranian efforts. 'These men are fighting their version of the Colombian war on drugs', says one sympathetic foreign voice: but they have not received anything like the resources of which Bogotá has been the recipient.[49] From time to time Iranian frustration boils over with caustic comments such as that Iran is fighting a bloody battle for 'all the youth in the world'. So cumulative and frustrating was the Iranian experience that in 2006 it even briefly dallied with the idea of allowing drugs freely to transit its territory pending significant financial assistance from the demand-oriented countries downstream. Using the UNODC as its post box, in 2005 the Drug Control Headquarters (DCHQ) supremo even went so far as formally to deliver a bill to the value of $500 million to compensate it for the magnitude of the resources spent on anti-drugs activities.[50] It was of course a political gesture with no hope of payment. It was aimed at making a reasonable point about the unreasonable absence of financial burden sharing. It is unlikely that Iran would ever see through such a threat. Such action would entail the abandonment of supply-side action in the home market. One possible consequence of such action might be to stimulate further drugs consumption internally.

A Kinder Place?

In spite of the ideological and geo-political distance between Iran and the Atlantic countries, many of the debates over anti-drugs policy have been reassuringly comparable. One such area of tension, exposed by the stance of successive governments, is whether or not to take a punitive approach to drug abusers; in short, whether to criminalise or medicalise their predicament. A second area of disputation, and every bit as contentious as it has proved to be in different parts of Europe and North America, is whether or not to adopt a list of measures, such as needle-exchanges and the distribution of condoms, that fit under the umbrella of 'harm reduction'. Iranian experiences are comparable to the West in terms of the role being played by NGOs, especially in trying to provide support for drugs abusers and their families. There are currently some 600 NGOs in Iran,[51] active in the area of drugs campaigning. If debating and adopting harm-reduction measures is more advanced in Iran than it is in the USA, for example, and that is a matter of surprise to us, it may be an argument for revisiting preconceived ideas about Iran as much as it may justify a re-examination of American drugs policy.

There is no better illustration of the contradictory positions of different parts of the regime than what was witnessed in the Khak-i Sefid district of Tehran in 2001, the epitome of the intensification of the campaign against drug trafficking that had been taking place in Iran over the previous few months. Khak-i Sefid is a neighbourhood of Tehran known as a haven for car thieves and petty criminals, where different kinds of illegal drugs can easily be purchased. At the end of February that year the security forces initiated a crackdown against drug sellers, in order to make an example of them.[52] As a result, around a thousand alleged dealers were apprehended. Five of those arrested at that time were subsequently executed in public on 19 March—including a woman, the execution of women being comparatively rare in Iran. The five were hanged from tall cranes, a typical method of execution in revolutionary Iran, with the crowd baying for their blood. They seemed to have taken about ten minutes to die, with the crowd chanting 'death to dealers'. That the hardliners in the system were unrepentant towards this action could be seen in the subsequent remarks of Iran's chief justice, Ayatollah Mahmoud Hashemi-Shahrudi, who used the 2001 celebrations of the International Day against Drug Abuse and Illicit Drug Trafficking to state that 'drug traffickers and sellers must no longer benefit from any amnesty—on the contrary, they must be severely repressed'. The deputy interior minister, Gholam Hussein

Bolandian, did what aspirant interior ministers do, he 'complained that not enough of the people on death row [in Iran] are executed'.[53]

In 2000, 60 per cent of the prison population in Iran was formally incarcerated for drugs offences.[54] A further 30 per cent of the prison population were found to reoffend as a result of narcotics abuse. Most convicts at that time served sentences of forty-five days to six months for drugs offences.[55] The first HIV case was identified in Iran in 1987. In 1996, 146 inmates in an Iranian jail, out of a sample of 400 tested, were found to be HIV positive.

Against such a grim backdrop, Mohammad Fallah, the head of the DCHQ, set up to coordinate the efforts of Iran's internal and external agencies, ridiculed the hardliners for their crude attempts to end the drugs problem. He pointed out that drugs are still widely distributed on the streets of Tehran, it later being confirmed that they had even returned to the Khak-i Sefid district. Within a year it became clear that Fallah had won the debate, at least for the time being. About 50 per cent of the anti-drugs budget for 2002/3 was to be made available for harm reduction.[56] This included free syringes, clean needles and condoms—a controversial list given the unimpeachable morals that were claimed by the Islamic Republic. The focus of policy had shifted towards a new emphasis on trying to curb the demand for drugs, while keeping up the continuing effort against supply. This new approach included sponsoring a hard-hitting series of television advertisements.[57] It also included the launching of an information strategy in schools and universities against the impact of illegal drugs. In 2001 the government relented to allow HIV/AIDS-related issues to be included in school textbooks.[58]

Further political will was galvanised behind this more liberal approach by the executive head of the government, President Khatami himself, who increasingly took an interest in the problem as his two-term presidency progressed.[59] Khatami was particularly reliant on the youth vote—the young being enfranchised from the age of sixteen—for his election and re-election, making him more sensitised to the views of the young in the country.

Initially, this recalibrated strategy seemed to go well. Iran was applauded for its new emphasis by the head of the United Nations International Drug Control Programme (UNDCP) office in Tehran, Antonio Mazzitelli, who expressed cautious optimism that the country's drugs crisis could be turned around. Indeed, the UNODC, its successor, even went as far as to turn the Islamic Republic into 'the flagbearer of the global campaign against illicit drugs'.[60]

NGO Activism

It also made it easier for Iran's anti-drugs NGOs to work with government.[61] It became easier for organisations such as Anti-Addiction Anonymous, established by a female MP, Soheila Jelodarzadeh, and the Aftab, or Sunshine, Society, set up by a former abuser, Hossein Dejakam, to offer a humane and enlightened refuge in which long-term addicts could be weaned off drugs.[62] Yet another NGO, Persepolis, named after the ancient Persian capital, began life as a drop-in centre attached to a primary care facility, in order to normalise the idea that drug abusers should be entitled to medical treatment routinely. By 2005 Persepolis had a full harm-reduction programme in place, including a team of outreach workers, and had become the country's first NGO to offer a methadone service.[63] In 2009 a total of 130,000 Iranians were in methadone treatment, placing Iran in the top two countries in the world for dispensing such care.[64]

Arguably, Iran's most successful anti-drugs NGO has been Narcotics Anonymous (NA), which in the mid-2000s had a membership of 30,000, and held some 2,200 weekly meetings in 183 towns and cities. Interestingly, NA believes that prayer as well as advice and group therapy is a necessary part of the drug counsellor's kit, thereby giving it a culturally sympathetic orientation in religiously conservative Iran.[65] The work of the NA has not, however, been controversy free. It has attracted criticism because of its advocacy of spirituality, some of the more conservative elements of the regime suspecting it of proselytising because of its use of confessions and admissions of guilt in group sessions.

It was not only the private sector that was responsive to the new circumstances. The Ministry of Health, which enjoys a general reputation for being liberal in orientation and dedicated to patient care,[66] also took on an increasing burden as far as narcotics-related problems were concerned. The establishment of 'triangle clinics', located in hospitals and prisons, was especially controversial. They concentrated on a three-pronged approach, treating AIDS, sexually transmitted diseases and drug addiction simultaneously in a holistic way. By 2005 there were sixty-five such clinics established in Iran—inadequate given the scale of the problem, but an improvement on the provision that had existed before.[67] The agency estimates the number of Iranians that were treated and rehabilitated between 2003 and 2009 at 500,000, a suspiciously round number. It is difficult to have confidence in such a figure, given the high failure rates in rehabilitation programmes across the globe.

By the middle of the decade, however, it looked as if the more flexible, liberal approach was beginning to wane. The outspoken Fallah was replaced in 2005 by Ali Hashemi, who himself lasted only a matter of weeks, becoming a victim of the changeover in government when the gentle but ineffectual Khatami was succeeded as executive president by the abrasive and illiberal Mahmoud Ahmadinejad. The new anti-drugs head, Fada-Hossein Maleki, lost no time in reversing the emphasis on demand reduction. With the approval of the new president,[68] he announced a renewed emphasis on supply interdiction, with his second priority being cooperation with governments and multilateral organisations to pressure governments of drug-producing states. Demand reduction came only third on the new list of priorities,[69] although its retention as an objective suggested that the previous priorities had not been thrown entirely into reverse. Predictably, though, these sentiments were followed by promises of a 'relentless campaign' against drug dealers and traffickers on the part of the Tehran prosecutor. This approach found a favourable macro-policy home, for instance in the Ahmadinejad government's curtailment of all NGO funding.[70]

By the end of the first decade of the 2000s, however, there was every sign that the hardline leadership of Ahmadinejad had waned under the weight of the realities of the problem. There was a new head of the DCHQ, the fourth in less than a decade. NGOs were once again being encouraged, as the state struggled to take the slack. Most importantly, the slavish emphasis on the supply side strategy had waned, with harm reduction once again at the centre of government policy.

Conclusion

Drugs, mainly in the form of opiates and more recently heroin, have had a major impact on society in Iran, through the current century and the one before. Iran has seen a ready supply of such drugs regardless of the many efforts to try to curtail such sources. Over the last two decades the origin of this supply has been Afghanistan. Iran has invested heavily in law-enforcement attempts to stem these flows. Though laudable enough, such efforts have little to show, if we use the benchmarks of availability and price as the measurement of success. Iran may be the most successful country in the world at seizing smuggled opiates and heroin (89 and 32 per cent respectively in 2011), but this has made little difference to consumption, either in Iran or downstream in the continent of Europe.

These cold realities have prompted Tehran to re-evaluate its strategy. It did so initially under the administration of the benign President Khatami, who saw the narcotics issue as a way of drawing Iran close to 'East and West'. It was under his leadership that Iran overturned its drug policy, introducing a more demand-side orientation, and warmly embracing such controversial elements of policy such as a harm-reduction agenda, largely imported from Western Europe. The Ahmadinejad aberration saw the policy pendulum swing back against the liberal reformers. But Ahmadinejad and his team were realistic enough to see that a more combative line would only increase harm, and, more pointedly, undermine the standing of the Islamic Republic, such as it is. Even the Islamic regime's most implacable beneficiaries and supporters have felt unable or been unwilling to implement an entirely hardline and uncompromising position on the issue of illicit drugs.

Despite Rouhani's flexibility towards the nuclear issue, his policies have not so far been as liberal in other areas. We await future developments before assessing his legacy to social reform.

TRANSIT SPACES

8

TURKEY

FROM CULTIVATOR TO CONDUIT

In February 2010 it was announced that Turkey's best-known pop star, Tarkan, had been arrested in Istanbul for the possession of illegal drugs.[1] The arrest caused a sensation, as Tarkan was a world-renowned artist who had scooped many global music awards, and had sold some 29 million albums and singles since his initial rise to fame in 1994. The story was sensational in part because of the singer's heart-throb popularity; the *Washington Post*, in a fit of hyperbole, had declared his impact on Turkey to be comparable to that of Elvis in the USA. Comparisons with Ricky Martin, or, for UK aficionados, Peter Andre, might be more accurate.

The arrest was also eye-catching because Turkey is widely regarded as a country where it is routinely claimed there are no appreciable signs of the large-scale consumption of narcotics. Tarkan's arrest in Istanbul was deliberate, following a lengthy investigation by the city's drugs squad. If the Tarkan drugs bust was a gesture by the police to warn Turks of the growing threat from drugs it seems to have been a failure. In spite of such high-level attention, the singer was only found to be in possession of 12.5 grams of hashish. He was held in custody for a few days. The charge sheet initially asked for two years in prison for the use, purchase, storage and marketing of drugs.[2] Upon his release, Tarkan was the picture of contrition, apologising publicly to his fans for his dalliance with drugs. All was apparently quickly forgiven by the Turkish public, and Tarkan was the star of the show staged in Taksim Square later that year to celebrate Istanbul's year as Europe's 2010 Capital of Culture.

Turkey has often been described as a bridge between Europe and the Middle East: a bridge for merchandise exports; a bridge for the diffusion of the norms of good governance; and, one might add, a bridge for the supply of both precursor chemicals in the manufacture of heroin and synthetic drugs heading for Turkey's nightspots. Bridges, however, tend to be open for traffic in more than one direction. Since the 1970s Turkey has emerged as the primary land bridge for the export of heroin to Europe. The export of Turkish *Gastarbeiter* labour to Germany from the early 1960s, of which Tarkan's parents were for a time a part, complemented by the surge in migrants in the aftermath of the 1980 military coup, has fuelled this. It has put in place the human networks necessary to transport and distribute hard drugs across the continent. The arrangements could not have been made more efficiently if this had been the stated goal from the outset.

The emerging importance of Turkey as a transit space for hard drugs coincided with the expansion in the heroin markets in the Atlantic countries from the late 1960s onwards. It also coincided with the effective curtailment of Turkey as a territory for the illicit cultivation of opium poppy. Only Afghanistan remained as a major source of opium and heroin for countries to its west. Moreover, unlike Iran, in Turkey there has to date been no significant emergence of a domestic drugs market to undermine the country's youth and distort the local economy. Turkey's role, though changing, was to remain a relatively specialist one: moving from being a cultivator and an exporter to a refiner and a trans-shipper.

Turkey's limited involvement did not make it immune to the secondary impact of narcotics-related criminality, especially once the issue of drugs had been conflated with radical Kurdish politics, and the insurgency of the Kurdistan Workers' Party (PKK). The Turkish state allied with established tribes in the traditional periphery of the country, setting up the Village Guards as militia allies against the PKK, even though these groups were involved in the black and grey economy. It marked a period of official ambivalence towards key aspects of criminality. With the PKK gaining ground, in the early 1990s the state hired ultra-nationalist hoodlums to undermine the infrastructure of the PKK insurgency through violence and intimidation. But once lodged in the state, the gangs expanded their operations to include a takeover of the criminal networks already in place, narcotics included. It was only after a sustained and painful act of collective will that the state succeeded in purging itself of most of the organised crime involved, and institutionalised corruption was—at least partially—squeezed out of the system.

Drugs from the East

The lateral routes which see opiates traverse northern Iran continue on into and across Turkey, whence they are trafficked onwards mostly through the Balkans and into Europe. Once they have entered and been brought across Iranian territory little concerted effort is made by the Tehran government to seize them. They end up exiting Iran in the west of the country with minimum difficulty on the Iranian side. After all, in view of its own chronic drug-abuse problem, why would the Iranian authorities deploy resources to keep illicit drugs inside their country?

This ease of departure is felt most acutely in Turkey, the next destination for the majority of the opiates leaving Iran. The border terrain between Iran and Turkey is extremely difficult for the defending side, both in terms of altitude and ruggedness. The border area is said to be home to thirteen mountains of between 3,500 and 4,500 metres in height. In winter the challenging nature of the terrain is accentuated by inhospitable climatic conditions. Local tribes, with active branches on both sides of the border and regular contacts between them, undertake most of the cross-border smuggling. This involves a range of commodities, such as sugar and tea, and is not limited to illegal drugs.[3]

The Turkish side of the border is patrolled by the Gendarmerie. In Turkey this body is organised as a branch of the armed forces rather than the rural police force that the name would tend to suggest. Even for other branches of the Turkish state, coordination with the Gendarmerie is markedly more limited than it is with the police and customs. It is widely viewed as a military organisation operating 'under the radar'.[4] Its foot-soldiers are national servicemen; their overriding aim is not to die while in uniform, far away from home. This tends to make them cautious and reluctant to fight. They are drawn from across the country, making them uniquely ill-suited to play any military role in the difficult conditions of the south-east. The force is also known for its poor discipline and general lack of expertise. It was not until the completion of a first round of the reorganisation of the force in 2001 that the Gendarmerie acquired specific, standing, in-house expertise on narcotics.[5]

There are twenty-one security posts on the Turkish side of the border with Iran. Authoritative Turkish sources admit that this is an inadequate number, given the inhospitable physical conditions on the ground.[6] This may well explain why the Turkish authorities have, until very recently,[7] been so reluctant to allow even drugs liaison officers from Western Europe to visit the country's eastern borders, established crossing-points included, though it has long permitted access to other customs posts located across the country, such as Edirne in western Turkey.

Like the tribesmen who traffic drugs into Iran, the 'crime tribes'[8] involved in smuggling contraband into Turkey from Iran are well organised and familiar with the mountainous terrain, though they do not pack the firepower of those smugglers straddling the eastern Iranian border. They are, however, ruthless in the pursuit of their lucrative livelihood. They use both the carrot and the stick in their dealings with the outposts of the Turkish state. On the one hand, they will offer large financial inducements to Gendarmerie officers and senior policemen in the region.[9] Such bribes are usually offered to encourage these officials to turn a blind eye to the favoured smuggling routes, or at least to ensure that their men are not patrolling in the vicinity of a likely drugs delivery. They are also used to bring about the swift release of fellow tribesmen, apprehended during normal military activities. If an officer or police chief refuses to cooperate, tribesmen involved in criminality can easily resort to intimidation. This is likely to be difficult to resist, especially if the senior officer has his family living and attending school in the jurisdiction for which he has professional responsibility.

The illegal drug consignments tend to arrive in Turkey using any of a number of entry points, with the otherwise impoverished governorates of Hakkari and in particular Van, in the far east of the country, at its centre. The drugs are then moved on to ethnic Kurds and Turks on the Turkish side of the border with wider contacts. Before moving their contraband away from the east of the country, these drugs networks may still have had to pay a 'tax' to cover 'security services', levied by any grouping that has a predominance of power in the area. In the 1980s and 1990s, until the arrest of its leader, Abdullah Öcalan,[10] this was most likely to be the PKK, which was strongly embedded in south-east Turkey. Once the consignment has left the vicinity of the border, it is possible to move it around the country more easily, with a minimum risk of interdiction. The contraband tends to be transported by land vehicle, secreted inside the engines, oil tanks and even headlights of trucks.

If the drugs arrive in Turkey in the form of morphine base the merchandise will be taken to a heroin laboratory, where it will be processed using the essential precursor of acetic anhydride (AA). The heroin labs tend to be located in one of two areas: near to the smuggling entry points in the east of Turkey; or in the greater Istanbul area to the west. The preference for these two locations is explained by the weakness of the state relative to the tribal-cum-criminal networks of the former, and the reality that Istanbul is such a large and sprawling city that policing certain neighbourhoods is difficult and uneven at best.

Corroborating this, evidence of hard-drugs consumption in Turkey, admittedly inadequate, suggests that Diyarbakir, the main Kurdish city in the southeast of the country, and Istanbul are the two centres where recorded heroin consumption in Turkey is at its greatest.[11] The Turkish cities with the largest proportion of heroin seizures in 2005 were Istanbul and Van, with 59 and 11.5 per cent respectively.[12] Since the early to mid-2000s, however, the processing labs for heroin have increasingly moved 'upstream' in location, notably to Afghanistan, so that a greater proportion of the opiates entering Turkey do so already in the form of heroin. This may well in part be a reflection of the successes of Turkish law enforcement, as traffickers seek to reduce the risk to their merchandise on Turkish soil, morphine base being bulkier than heroin, and the static labs more vulnerable to police raids.

Table 1: Heroin Seizures in Turkey by Volume: Official Figures

Year	Weight (kg)	Percentage Change
1995	2,409	
1996	3,065	27.23%
1997	2,484	−5.90%
1998	3,738	50.48%
1999	2,249	−39.83%
2000	5,230	132.54%
2001	3,033	−42.00%
2002	2,124	−29.97%
2003	3,546	66.94%
2004	6,515	83.72%
2005	6,664	2.28%
2006	7,380	10.74%
2007	9,078	23.00%
2008	10,332	13.81%
2009	12,234	18.40%
2010	9,053	−26.00%

Source: KOM Report, 2005 and 2009.

Most of the heroin passing through Turkey departs via Istanbul, either through the city's extensive port facilities, or by road through Eastern Thrace. The bulk of the latter used to be smuggled by TIR trucks driven by Turks, until the authorities in Britain and other countries became wise to the practice and the profile of the drivers. More recently, traffickers have tended to use a variety of smuggling methods, often involving smaller vehicles, while drivers are more likely to be European nationals, in order to make the lines of supply less obvious.

The majority of the Turkish-controlled heroin then joins the 'Balkans Route', consistently the main conduit into Europe.[13] It does so using some combination of the land-based northern trafficking branch through Bulgaria, Romania, Hungary and Austria, with large quantities of heroin being 'warehoused' in the states of Eastern Europe, where they are safer from law enforcement interdiction than they would be in Western Europe. In these countries the quantities of heroin sold on are reduced in size in order to manage the exposure of the traffickers in case of seizure.

The southern branch of the smuggling route goes through Bulgaria, Greece, Macedonia, Albania and Italy to Western Europe, and is sometime referred to as the 'Mediterranean Sea Route'. The drugs are then transported into the lucrative markets of Britain, Germany and Holland in particular, from where they are distributed through a network of small businesses, such as cafes and kebab shops, many of them run by Turks and Kurds of Turkish origin.[14] At the street level, drug retailers tend to be heroin abusers themselves, eager to make a small margin on sales in order to finance their own addiction, and therefore, more often than not, of local nationality.

Political Will?

An enduring question posed to the Turkish authorities has been how committed they are to the cause of the eradication of illegal drugs. As recently as 1997 the anti-narcotics bureau of the Turkish National Police only had 173 officers. In Istanbul the specialist police could only deploy a single four-man team to cover three of the metropolis's most populous districts, one of which, Beyoğlu, had acquired a reputation as a centre of criminality, including for illegal drugs. The chief of the Istanbul bureau at the time, Ferruh Tankuş, publicly expressed the view that the drugs squad was 'stretched way too thin'.

Other, more material factors hindered the ability of specialist officers to get the job done. The Turkish budget for anti-drugs law enforcement in 1997 was just $30 million a year, a modest amount compared to Iranian levels of spending of more than ten times that amount. Monthly wages of $300 for members of the anti-drugs teams invited poor morale, especially for a job that requires long and unpredictable hours. The deployment of bottom-of-the-range, locally made Renault cars hardly raises team spirit, especially as drug dealers often drive expensive, top-range models,[15] and were easy to spot. Corruption too was a serious risk, and the Istanbul bureau was subject to periodic personnel purges, even at the highest level.

The recent history of an indifferent response towards drugs smuggling has at heart been a question of political will. Some have argued that if Turkey does not have a domestic problem with drug taking why should the issue enjoy a priority either in terms of the attention span of government or the deployment of state resources? Narcotics-related aid, it is regularly pointed out by Ankara, is modest in volume from the Western countries. The situation in Turkey is certainly different to that of Iran, where chronic domestic addiction problems drive political will. It is often pointed out that the problem of consumption exists in Europe and North America. It is simply not Turkey's problem.

A second argument regularly put forward relates to the fortunes of the Turkish economy. Historically, Turkey has suffered from a shortage of liquidity, inward investment and foreign exchange. Consequently, Ankara has built up a large foreign debt, the origins of which lie in the mid-1970s, and the rocketing cost of oil imports and its refined derivatives. The flow of drugs-related money back into Turkey, not least because of the national connections of those involved in the drugs business, has helped to regenerate the country economically, with the informal economy providing a social-cum-economic safety net, greatly supplementing the limited performance of the formal economy. This has been facilitated by the opportunities for laundering criminal funds in Turkey. The rapid expansion of the construction, real-estate and tourist sectors—three traditionally 'soft' sectors for money launderers—over the last three decades has turned these resources into increasingly bankable assets. Those with criminally generated capital have also bought small businesses and retail premises, and, more recently, football and sports clubs. Until they were banned in 1998, casinos were a sleazy and occasionally violent focus for the movement of black money. It was not until 1997 that Turkey adopted specialist anti-money-laundering legislation.[16] Prior to that, there were few constraints upon criminal investment.

A final obstacle to the galvanising of the political will necessary to confront the narcotics issue was the controversial problem of the PKK. Over the course of a Kurdish nationalist insurgency that began in 1984, an estimated 45,000 people have been killed. Moreover, the PKK has had at times avowed, and is still believed to harbour, ambitions to divide Turkey and create a separate Kurdish state. A PKK–Ankara ceasefire of November 2012, brokered by the national intelligence organisation, the MIT, followed by what many at the time felt to be a genuine peace process, has failed to persuade many, especially among the Turkish public. Given the Turkish people's nineteenth-century-style attachment to sovereignty, this has drawn a forceful and dismissive response from the Turkish state and a large majority of its people. The deployment of extensive military force in the south-east of Turkey for much of the duration of the PKK's insurgency has been directed at undermining this political challenge, rather than preventing the flow of hard drugs from Iran into and across Turkey. For the Turkish national security state, it has been difficult to look much beyond the presence and the threat of the PKK, even if there is a general sense that narcotics are undesirable.

The preoccupation with the PKK has spilt over into Turkey's relations with the leading states of Europe, where most of the hard drugs transiting Turkey are distributed and consumed. The growing realisation that the need to constrain the PKK converges as a policy strategy with the restraining of the trafficking of illegal drugs helps explain why Turkish political will towards the latter has increased over the last decade. The second and more immediately pressing driver of renewed reserves of political will was the threat to the Turkish state that emerged over the course of the early to mid-1990s.

Corrupting the State

The volume and value of narcotics traversing Turkey, together with the ability of criminal organisations to corrode the standing of the state, at least at its geographical periphery, indicates the vulnerability of the state in Turkey to the corrupting influences of illegal drugs. In this way Turkey was no different to other states in the world, which faced a challenge from narco-corruption. Indeed, for an extended period during the 1990s, arguably stretching from 1992 to 1998, the Turkish state, ever opaque at the best of times, teetered on the edge of a Colombian-style descent into failure.[17]

As we have seen, the driver of such decline was not illegal drugs as such, but the growing insurgency of the PKK, and its partial control of the south-east of Turkey, adjacent to the entry points for drugs coming into the country. Frustrated by the PKK's guerrilla warfare, and its relative success through the period 1989–94, the Turkish state looked increasingly desperate. In order to remedy the situation, it did what it had done a decade earlier when faced by a campaign of assassination by an armed nationalist Armenian group, the Armenian Secret Army for the Liberation of Armenia (ASALA). The Turkish state turned to a network of ultra-nationalists (Ülkücüler), who had come to prominence in the 1970s, as part of the armed wing of the far-right movement of the time. Its expectation was that the Ülkücüler would unleash a campaign of extra-judicial killings against those who were guilty of helping the PKK, including those Kurdish 'businessmen' who paid informal taxes to the organisation, and hence were seen as complicit in its activities. In order to facilitate this operation, the Turkish state effectively gave the Ülkücüler immunity from prosecution.

In adopting such a strategy, the Turkish state miscalculated the effects of its decision. First, a campaign against the PKK necessitated a much greater level of violence than that perpetrated against ASALA, partly because the latter was much smaller in size, and partly because the PKK had the benefit of a widely sympathetic constituency on the ground in the south-east. Second, that part of the Turkish state that was complicit in unleashing the Ülkücüler failed to take into account the nature of their activity over the intervening decade. During that time the Ülkücüler had morphed from a violent, primarily ideologically oriented gang into a violent criminal network, with no intrinsic political function. The loyalty of the group was no longer to a body of ideas, or even to the state as such, but to itself and its generation of illicit income. It was to this group that some of the most powerful arms of the state, such as the Turkish National Police, the Ministry of Interior more widely, and the MIT, Turkey's main intelligence body, which was split in its attitude towards the Ülkücüler, now made their resources available. The Ülkücüler were the recipients of a range of services provided by the national security state in Turkey, from false (including diplomatic) passports,[18] to safe passage abroad and help in evading arrest.

The ultra-nationalist gangs, some of which had been recruited into elite forces within the police and the Gendarmerie, were quickly successful in their mission as death squads. Among their victims were those Kurdish businessmen who had been identified as bankrolling the PKK. The Ülkücüler moved on to target moderate Kurdish nationalists, such as intellectuals and journalists, in the south-east of Turkey.[19] Rather than simply closing down illegal activities, the ultra-nationalists moved in and took them over. Given the climate of illegality, the general suspension of liberal rights in the south-east,[20] and the help rendered by various parts of the state, it was some time before it became clear what had happened. Initial attempts to marginalise or close down the gangs foundered, as the groups demonstrated that they possessed significant leverage over parts of the Turkish political class as well as the elements of the state that had assisted them. This included incriminating audio tapes of politicians fraternising with known gang leaders. By the mid-1990s it had become clear that a major challenge to the integrity of the Turkish state had emerged, one that would require serious medicine to rectify.

Cleansing the State

Turkey's secret world of criminality and protection exploded into public view with a two-vehicle accident in the town of Süsürlük in November 1996. The male occupants of one of the vehicles, a Mercedes, were a microcosm of Turkey's broader problems. They comprised: Hüseyin Kocadağ, a senior police chief; Abdullah Çatlı, an infamous Ülkücü, who was officially on the run; Sedat Bucak, the head of the large Bucak clan, based around the south-eastern town of Siverek, and whose men had been armed by the state as Village Guards. With Kocadağ and Çatlı perishing in the crash and Bucak surviving, though pleading amnesia, the evidence was never any more than strongly circumstantial. But the apparently cosy relationship among such disparate figures did at least free the Turkish media, hitherto intimidated by what had infamously become known as the 'deep state' (*derin devlet*), to pursue an investigation into such relationships, something that they did with vim. The second vehicle involved was a truck with a trailer, and speculation grew that the crash had been deliberately staged by reform-minded state insiders in order to expose the extent of the state-organised criminal alliance.

Though the issue has still to be conclusively proven, and perhaps will never fully be resolved one way or another, the case for conspiracy is persuasive. There is evidence that the state had been trying to clean itself up prior to Süsürlük. Where the outcome of such cleansing seemed uncertain, action began to be taken in complementary areas. So, for example, in April 1996 the National Security Council (NSC) drove forward a process for the adoption of a narcotics demand-side strategy, where little impetus had hitherto existed for such a change, and Turkey was not adjudged to suffer from the domestic consumption of hard drugs.[21]

Though it may be viewed as the trigger for change, Süsürlük alone was not a turning point for the Ülkücüler gangs within the state. The precise outcome of the internal struggle was not clear until summer 1998. In May of that year the NSC formally asked the government to step up the fight against organised crime 'which aims to destroy stability in Turkey'.[22] At its August meeting the NSC further defined the ultra-nationalist mafia not simply as a national security threat, but as the '*primary* threat',[23] designating it as more important than the recurrent threats from either Islamic fundamentalism[24] or the PKK insurgency itself. It finally became clear that unequivocal, official policy now existed: that there should be no gangs operating autonomously within the state.

Certainly, it was a clean-up: à la Turca. There were at least three formal enquiries set up, though each was given only limited access to the case history. Few were arrested. Even fewer went to court. Very few indeed were found guilty and sentenced. Among them was İbrahim Şahin, who had led the police's Special Teams (Özel Timler) in the south-east. Though carefully and pragmatically calibrated, the attitude of the state was by now quite clear. An expression of this was the arrest of one of the most notorious Ülkücü crime bosses, Alaattin Çakıcı. He was a particularly egregious example of the type. He had had his wife, who was herself the daughter of another mafia clan head, murdered in a contract killing. Though he had been apprehended a number of times before, but then mysteriously released, on this occasion it was for real. He went to prison rather than being allowed to escape or to negotiate a cosy deal with the authorities.

Within the state, officials were more likely to be quietly retired on full pensions than brought to book. Some of the more infamous figures had already been killed. These included the head of JITEM, Gendarmerie intelligence, Cem Ersever, and the main advocate within MIT for the relationship with the CIA, Hiram Abas, who enjoyed the rank of deputy under-secretary. There was the odd exception, where profiles were too high to ignore. Some fifteen years later Mehmet Ağar—the interior minister when the Süsürlük crash took place and a former chief of police, former MP and opposition leader in Turkey—was still being pursued by the country's cumbersome judicial machine.

Drugs at Home: The Dog that Hasn't Barked (Yet)

Apart from some solvent and cocaine abuse at opposite ends of the social continuum, Turkey has never suffered from a significant drugs problem. This has for some time been a source of pride for Turks. By contrast, it has been a cause of puzzlement to narcotics experts, used to seeing societies awash with drugs, like Afghanistan and Pakistan, succumb eventually to their influence. In short, it has seemed to defy prevailing wisdom within drugs theory.

When pressed to explain the absence of a significant local market in drugs, Turks tend to fall back on one of two arguments: Islam, and family solidarity. Neither are particularly satisfactory as explanations. If being collectively clean was simply a matter of religious faith, then presumably Iran and Pakistan would not have experienced such social devastation. With pluralism tending to characterise Turkey's religious landscape—Sunni Islam v. Alevism (a form of Shiism),[25] and multiple religious orders within the former—diversity rather than simplicity and homogeneity seems to militate against such easy explanations.

The tight hierarchical and patriarchal nature of most Turkish families may be a more persuasive factor, not least because families make it their business to know the affairs of their individual—and notably the younger—members. But if family solidarity is key, then one should face the future with some trepidation. Mass rural-to-urban migration over the last three generations, the haphazard growth of sprawling cities, expanding consumerism and persistently high levels of unemployment all place the traditional, rural model of family solidarity under sustained stress in a newly urbanised society.

There is a third explanation that many Turks believe, even if they are reticent about sharing it with foreigners. It is the nationalist argument, which lies just beneath the top-soil of just about everything in Turkey. Turks are less likely to 'do drugs' because they are stronger, nobler and more resilient than their feckless, pusillanimous counterparts anywhere else, but particularly in the West. Not to consume heroin becomes a sign of strength and a badge of honour.

There is a fourth possible reason. It is a more down-to-earth explanation for the absence of hard drugs across the interior cities of Anatolia, and, for all its prosaic nature, may have some veracity to it. Perhaps the drugs networks have no interest in trying to build up a consumer base in the most conservative parts of the interior of the country. To do so simply slows down the speedy transportation of hard drugs to Istanbul, and onwards towards an assured and lucrative market. Once the merchandise has crossed the border into Europe proper, its mark-up can be doubled to the benefit of the networks concerned.

Clearly, one arrest does not make an epidemic. An arrest like that of Tarkan can always be dismissed as the antics of the privileged and the indulged. Certainly, Turkey is not publicly blighted by the widespread and open taking of drugs and their consequences, as is the case in both Iran and Israel, where municipal parks and open spaces have been taken over by drug abusers and their paraphernalia. But there is evidence to suggest that neither is Turkey entirely drugs-free. Perhaps as importantly, Turks are deep-down somewhat preoccupied about their future vulnerability to domestic drug consumption. With large volumes of drugs in transit across Turkey at any time, and with income levels growing rapidly to deliver significant consumer prosperity to its emerging affluent middle classes, complacency is a luxury best avoided.

At present there are four factors that warn against excessive expressions of smugness over the issue of drugs consumption at home. The first is that drug taking in Turkish society is already an established and growing phenomenon. This is certainly the case as far as the sub-sector of hemp-related drugs is concerned, making cannabis 'the most extensively produced, used and seized drug in Turkey'.[26] In four years from 2006 to 2010 seizures of cannabis and its derivatives in the jurisdiction of the drugs police increased more than threefold. Hemp drugs were either produced in Turkey, solely for internal consumption, or were imported into the country, primarily from Iran and Syria (implying that they originated in Afghanistan and Lebanon).

Table 2: Hemp-Related Seizures in Turkey (kg): Annual Percentage Increases

2006	9,787	–
2007	13,349	36.4%
2008	20,575	54.1%
2009	25,778	25.3%
2010	31,197	21.0%

Source: KOM, Annual Report, 2010.

If soft-drug abuse is arguably already a reality in Turkey, the second factor also relates to current consumption, in this case there being plenty of evidence to suggest that solvent abuse in particular has been growing in Turkish society among the young over the last decade. This is a blight that has long been associated with the street urchins of Turkey's big cities, notably Istanbul, a phenomenon stretching back to the 1940s. These children live off their wits, indulge in petty crime, and work in low-income areas such as shoe-shining. Evidence generated by a younger generation of doctors involved in treating those suffering from addiction through the AMATEM network of hospitals has more recently indicated the prevalence of solvent abuse in ordinary schools in the big cities of Turkey. If glue-sniffing and its ilk emerge to play the role of a 'gateway' drug, that is to say a drug that points its user in the direction of more dangerous drugs, then we may see the ill-effects of such activity upon Turkish society in the medium-term future.

The third reason for being concerned about the dangers of illicit drugs in Turkey is that in spite of enduring assumptions that no significant problem exists, that which does exist seems to have a higher profile and a wider geographical sweep than is widely assumed. For example, April 2010 saw a major police operation in the southern city of Adana against a local criminal group known as the Cono clan, whose illicit activities are alleged to include drug dealing. The fact that the police operation is reported to have included 1,000 officers, with a police helicopter giving aerial support,[27] indicates how powerful local groups can become on the back of a portfolio of criminal activity, with narcotics potentially forming a part.

The Cono clan story coincided with reports that a young Turkish man, himself a drug abuser, had been gunned down by a policeman in the Aegean resort town of Kuşadası. Shooting in broad daylight and, according to some witnesses, without provocation, the policeman concerned attempted to coerce onlookers into supporting his version of the event. While the police narrative labelled the young man a drug dealer, his family rallied to his defence, saying only that he was a drug user.[28] The local community's sympathy seemed to be squarely with the young man and his family, based on the perceptions of the incident, and no doubt a generally shared, widespread suspicion of 'beat' policemen in Turkey.

The fourth reason for concern is that, beneath the surface, Turkish society too is anxious about the increasingly proximate dangers of illegal drugs. This collective social stress can be observed in the creative arts, notably film, the edgy sophistication of contemporary Turkish cinema contrasting with the crude Hollywood representation of it, as epitomised by *Midnight Express*.

BOX 1

MIDNIGHT EXPRESS

Though only a Hollywood movie, few things have done as much damage to Turkey's reputation internationally as *Midnight Express*. Made in 1978, with the screenplay by a young Oliver Stone, the film tells the story of a preppy young American man, who tries to smuggle hashish into Europe from Turkey, strapped to his body. Apprehended by the authorities, he is locked up in a squalid jail and subjected to systematic violence from and violation by his jailers. His only friend is a blond Scandinavian, the contrast with the swarthy Turks appearing to portray a crude distinction between good and evil. The film ends with an improbable escape to freedom. Though extremely popular at the time, with six Academy Awards (including for script and music), the movie has been frequently criticised over the years for its racist overtones. Less remarked upon has been the disconnect between the context of

American government pressure on Turkey to clamp down on illegal drugs and the sympathetic portrayal of the drugs trafficker. Made during a period of weak government, rising domestic instability and the imminent deployment of military power in a *coup d'état*, Turkey was susceptible to sustained attack from both the conservative establishment in the USA and its own liberal intelligentsia.

In the 2008 movie thriller *Kabadayı*, the plot begins with a criminal gang that sells drugs, such as cocaine, and extorts protection money from local bars. The plot thickens with news of the imminent arrival of a new consignment from Afghanistan, presumably heroin. The local police, who have been bought off, don't want to get involved. Enter the *kabadayı*, traditionally a neighbourhood 'tough', who dispenses rough-and-ready justice within the community,[29] when the state is too distant or venal to get involved. In the film, the *kabadayı* is played more like a salt-of-the-earth uncle, who by the end of the film has stepped in to thwart the ambitions of the gang leader, and restore order, much to the relief of the local population.[30]

By contrast, the movie *Can*, named after its heroin(e), is a searing portrayal of a young woman's failing attempt to break into the professional world of high fashion, tipping over instead into a drug-fuelled downward spiral,[31] egged on by her directionless boyfriend. The film contrasts the glitzy glamour of the Istanbul-based fashion industry with the sordid tawdriness of the drugs world, where Can binges on marijuana, cocaine and injected heroin. Neither are the possible consequences of drug dependency ducked in this very honest film. It is implied that Can steals from her mother, prostitutes herself and acquiesces in group sex in order to get the money to buy drugs. The film ends with her barely conscious, lying on rocks by the water's edge, implying an imminent death. The film's director, Oğuz Eruzun, is didactic in the explicit warnings he delivers to the younger generation, a reflection of his intense social concern, notably through the use of captions displayed periodically on the screen, such as:

Cigarettes start aged 10
Alcohol starts aged 11
Drugs start aged 12

Conclusion

Turkey is a central part of the 'northern tier' of Middle Eastern states, also including Iran, which connects the drug-producing country of Afghanistan with the main drug entry point into Europe, through the 'Balkans Route'. At different times the role of such countries has changed, Turkey included. Gone are the days when Turkey was a significant cultivator of opium, with large-scale leakage into the black economy—although it does still supply morphine for the licit pharmaceuticals sector. Largely gone too is its role as a venue for the refining of heroin at the hands of criminal gangs. And gone too is the rampant complicity of the Turkish state with organised criminal elements, especially with the ultra-nationalists, that lasted from the 1970s through the 1990s. Bilateral cooperation may still have to be pursued with care, but in the anti-narcotics arm of the Turkish National Police, the drugs squads of Europe have an institution that they can work with and trust.

BOX 2

HÜSEYIN BAYBAŞIN[32]

The most notorious drug dealing clan in Turkey is the Baybaşin clan, a Kurdish family from eastern Turkey, whose head, Hüseyin, has enjoyed the florid acclamations 'Europe's Pablo Escobar'[33] and 'the Heroin Emperor'. Baybaşin, aka the 'godfather', was jailed for life in Holland in the early 2000s, for conspiracy to commit murder, kidnapping and drug trafficking, having amassed a large fortune from heroin smuggling.[34] Yet fifty-six-year-old Baybaşin came from humble origins in the town of Lice, one of the least developed parts of Turkey, and a hotbed of Kurdish ethno-nationalist politics. He started as a low-level drugs operative. He was arrested in London for heroin smuggling in 1984. Sentenced to twelve years, he was sent back to Turkey after serving three, whereupon he was immediately released. Posing as a business-man,[35] Baybaşin rapidly worked his way up the fluid criminal hierarchy. By the mid-1990s he had been offered 'sanctuary' in the UK, in exchange for cooperating with Britain's Customs & Excise. He was accused of donating some of the proceeds from the narcotics trade to the PKK. In particular, he is alleged to have given money to the PKK television channel MED-TV. He was arrested in 1998 by Dutch police and prosecuted. His defence included some extraordinary though not totally implausible claims: he was surreptitiously working for the Turkish government; had strong connections with MI5; and had been approached by Russian intelligence to help assassinate Chechen leaders in Istanbul.[36] He claimed to have become the head of one of the world's top crime syndicates with the help of Turkish politicians, policemen and the Turkish security service.[37] In spite of such claims, he was still found guilty and jailed for twenty years. Since Hüseyin Baybaşin's incarceration, other members of the clan are said to be continuing to run its narcotics operations, though others too have been arrested. One of these was thought to control the criminal network from the Green Lanes area of Haringey in North London, with the help of a small army of thugs known as the *Bombacilar* (bombers).

That does not mean that Turkey is no longer a key country as far as the entry of hard drugs into Europe is concerned. Over the last three decades it has emerged as a pivotal transit space as far as the routing of illicit hard drugs is concerned. Kurds and Turks from Turkey have a profile in the trafficking and sale of heroin in the likes of Britain, Holland and Germany wholly disproportionate to their size and profile. This twin demographic group is extensively involved in the trafficking of opiates from the border with Iran all the way to their outlets in kebab shops and cafes, where wraps of heroin sell in Western Europe. The widespread knowledge of these trends has tended not to be translated into effective interdiction, probably due to the impenetrability of what are still largely closed networks based on clan and provincial solidarities.

In spite of the high-volume spread of such drugs across the Anatolian landmass, relatively few of the Turkish people have succumbed to the allures of such addictive substances. The worst of the drugs problem to afflict Turkey is that of solvents and the like among street children. There has also been a significant growth in the consumption of cannabis-related drugs, much of it home grown, noticeably since the mid-2000s. Why the rest of the country has bucked the trend of significant hard-drugs use at home has been the focus of much debate within Turkey. In part, this may be because the entry and exit points are in the far east of Van and the far west of Istanbul/Edirne, with traffickers having little interest in anything other than shifting the drug consignments as swiftly and as securely across the country as they can. Such a grounded explanation sounds more convincing than dubious notions of group solidarity based on nationalism or religion, and contrasted with the godlessness of the West.

9

DUBAI

THE DRUGS HUB

As Grooverider in one half of BBC Radio One's clubbing DJs Fabio and Grooverider, Raymond Bingham visited Dubai in November 2007 on what he expected to be a short trip to play a Drum-'n'-Bass set at a local nightclub. With Dubai enjoying a reputation in the West for being liberal and laid back, he probably did not consider the trip to be any different to those he had made before to the likes of Ibiza and Ayia Napa. He entered the emirate with 2.16 grams of cannabis in his pocket, a modest £10 worth, an amount that in Britain would have been regarded as being exclusively for personal use. This was a serious mistake. With a minimum automatic prison sentence of four years for the possession of even the most modest of volumes of the allegedly least dangerous of narcotics, Dubai's legal regime was anything but liberal. Moreover, the Dubai airport authorities had recently installed new, highly sensitive equipment with which to undertake thorough searches. Being black may not have helped Bingham's cause, as any form of profiling by airport security, which is overseen by British police officers, would have drawn attention to him as a prime drugs-trafficking suspect.

Bingham was duly arrested and subsequently imprisoned. Four months later his case came to court. He was convicted and sentenced to four years in jail.[1] His was simply the most high profile of a spate of cases that saw fifty-nine British people arrested for drugs offences in the UAE in 2007. This even rivalled Thailand, which at the time had forty-five British men in jail for various drugs-related crimes. Other celebrities had been caught in the Dubai net.[2]

An American R&B performer, Dallas Austin, received the same sentence for possession of Ecstasy. A *Big Brother* television executive of German nationality, Cat Le-Huy, was arrested on arrival for possession of a very small amount of cannabis, together with the health supplement Melatonin.[3]

In the end, Bingham served just under a quarter of his sentence. Once the media attention had faded, the British authorities were able quietly to prevail upon their counterparts in Dubai. Bingham was released, immediately deported and subsequently blacklisted.

The Grooverider case illustrates much about the drugs issue in Dubai today. Its draconian laws are a tough—some might say desperate—response to the spread of narcotic drugs within the original Emirati community. They also reflect organised crime's use of Dubai as a major drugs-transit space, bound for their final destinations in Europe and the Far East. The law-enforcement and judicial regimes addressing the drugs issue arguably managed to achieve the worst of both worlds. Arrests are made for the possession of minuscule amounts of drugs, resulting in a reputation for rigidity and unreasonableness, while those convicted may be released early if sufficient external pressure can be galvanised, throwing into doubt any claims made that Dubai operates according to the rule of law. The case of Pakistani international cricketer Muhammad Asef also illustrates this point. He was deported after two weeks in custody rather than jeopardise Dubai's relations with his home government, 0.24 grams of opium having been found on his person.[4] Attempts by Dubai to increase its attraction as a tourist destination to younger people through staging such events as 'Desert Rock Fest' and 'Dubai Musik Week' have uneasily bumped up against Western counter-culture, notably the application of the law in drugs-related cases.[5]

Ethnicity and Drugs

Dubai is a micro-state of around 1.8 million inhabitants, with a small indigenous population of 300,000,[6] about one-quarter of whom are of Iranian origin.[7] It has a large expatriate workforce drawn from up to 140 nationalities, comprising around 85 per cent of the overall total. This makes Dubai comparable in its vulnerability to other Gulf emirates, Abu Dhabi and its four other partners in the loose federation of the United Arab Emirates, together with independent Gulf Arab principalities, such as Kuwait and Qatar.

The coastal emirates have a tradition of smuggling on north–south and east–west axes, along and across the Persian Gulf waterway, and beyond into the Indian subcontinent.[8] It was the challenge reputedly posed by piracy that gave Britain the excuse to bring the coastal emirates under its control in the late eighteenth and early to mid-nineteenth centuries, though smuggling activity in a more clandestine form remained. In recent times Dubai has exploited its location, its liberal trade regime and the large number of small cargo vessels that make up the bulk of the merchant fleet that uses its ports to make money in the face of international sanctions boycotts.

Smuggling has remained an active part of Dubai's economy. Gold dominated smuggling to India, especially after the dredging of the Creek, the natural harbour located in the centre of the emirate, in 1963. Arab crafts would take on the gold in Dubai, hiding it with their cargoes, or secreting it in the hollowed-out timbers of their boats.[9] Iran too was always a major destination. Goods could be delivered easily and quickly by launch, with a good chance of evading duties levied on the Iranian side. The smuggling of arms caused the British authorities particular concern in the 1930s.[10] Rifles and sugar were the smugglers' commodities of choice bound for Iran during the Second World War.[11] Traders using Dubai have flouted international sanctions imposed against Iran since the Islamic revolution of 1979. Cigarette and other smuggling via Dubai helped to erode the international sanctions against Iraq, in the aftermath of its invasion of Kuwait on 2 August 1990.

Given this long history of trafficking, it is hardly surprising that narcotic drugs, with their big profit margins, have proved to be, among other things, favoured commodities that are traded in the Dubai black economy. Typically, there are three directions of travel for such merchandise.

- Hashish and heroin originating in Afghanistan enters the country by sea from Iran or Pakistan, reflecting the close proximity and high volume of traffic between these countries.
- A wider range, though lower volume per trip, of illicit drugs enters the country by drug 'mules' or couriers, mostly using the international airport.
- A third route sees predominantly synthetic drugs flow into the country from across the long and sparsely populated land border with Saudi Arabia. Among Emiratis, heroin was the most commonly used drug in the early 1990s, mostly consumed by smoking.[12]

The overwhelming majority of illicit drugs entering Dubai do so as a result of the actions of non-nationals. This reflects such factors as opportunity and the existence of supply and distribution networks in exporting and importing countries respectively. The role of subcontinent migrant workers in the importation and distribution of illicit drugs in Dubai is analogous with that of Mexicans in the USA, or Turks and Kurds in Western Europe. The traditional practice of drugs being consumed by Indian, Iranian and Pakistani expatriates stretches back prior to the 1980s. Only a relatively small number of older UAE nationals used drugs before this. As in Egypt and Morocco, the consumption of drugs was not perceived as being a problem, or anything out of the ordinary, during this earlier period. It was only in June 1969 that this changed, with Dubai registering its first prosecution for drugs offences. In that case a Pakistani national was arrested for possessing 25 grams of hashish. In 1971, ironically the year that Britain formally relinquished its control of the lower Arab Gulf, Dubai adopted its first Dangerous Drugs Act, thereby criminalising such a recreation overnight.

Dr Hashim Sarhan, for twelve years the head of the anti-drugs unit in one of the UAE's seven emirates, Fujairah, has identified the 1980s as the threshold period for increased prevalence in the UAE. After that drug abuse spread faster among nationals than non-nationals, with consumption affecting a broader range of social groups.[13] An early illustration of growing concern among the political leadership at the increasing drugs use was the creation in 1987 of a national coordinating body. The National Committee for Combating the Illegal Use of Drugs and Alcohol was created as a result of a decree adopted at the federal level of government in the UAE.[14]

'At-Risk' Groups

Emiratis would appear to be a particularly 'at-risk' group within Dubai. Theirs is a social stratum which is strong on the practice of private consumption, but weak on collective and individual self-esteem. They are culturally swamped in their own country because of its demographic lopsidedness. This is having serious consequences in the realm of identity politics, with, for example, younger Emiratis feared to be losing their proficiency in Arabic. The widespread consensus among professionals is that the education sector is poor. It is under intense pressure, with an estimated 50 per cent of nationals leaving high school effectively illiterate.[15]

But Emiratis do not have to be able to read and write in order to enjoy high levels of consumption. This is not the ruling bargain. Land in Dubai, which is owned by the ruler, is parcelled out to nationals, who then use it to build and rent out apartments and villas, thereby creating an opportunity for a further private income stream. The military, the police and parts of the public sector are used as repositories of employment for Emirati nationals, though under-employment is rampant in such sectors, and any real job satisfaction is presumed to be scarce, except among the most talented members of the elite. Boredom among younger males is a particular problem. This helps explain the popularity of other potentially escapist activities, such as dune racing, and reckless, F-1 style driving practices at night on the emirate's main thorough fares, notably the Shaikh Zayid Highway. As Dr Sarhan has observed, drug use among UAE nationals correlates with high salaries, low education attainment and young age.

A tradition of secrecy, which characterises the *modus operandi* of Dubai's governance in general, has dominated the area of illicit drugs. Zero tolerance of foreigners who are found to be consumers or traffickers of illegal drugs provides a powerful disincentive to cooperation with officialdom. The authorities have consequently been left with only such intrusive techniques as snooping as a way of trying to gather intelligence. The opaque and separate existence of Emirati society exacerbates this difficulty, as does the overall economics of the problem. For example, Emirati drug abusers are more likely to fund their consumption of drugs through their high level of disposable income, or through retailing drugs themselves. Such revenue strategies are more practical and socially less problematic than potential alternatives such as crimes against property.[16] The fact that Dubai is a heavily policed, surveillance society would make burglary or muggings difficult to sustain as a source of income through which to fund drug consumption.[17]

Nevertheless, the warning signs are there to be read. The Sarhan study referred to above indicates an early initiation into the consumption of illegal drugs. Over one-third of respondents named their age of initiation at between nine and fifteen years, while almost half of those interviewed identified the sixteen-to-twenty-two-year bracket.

Criminal Justice

Evidence gathered from the criminal justice system, notably courts and prisons, has been revealing too. At the end of 2012 journalist sources in Dubai estimated that of the cases coming to the emirate's criminal court, between 50 and 80 per cent were for drugs offences.[18] This compared consistently with the recent historical record. In the mid- to late 1980s half of those incarcerated in the UAE's prisons were inside for drugs-related offences. Indeed, the courts were so clogged up from the drugs-related business that the creation of a dedicated drugs chamber was widely expected. This would mean cases being heard on a functional rather than a geographical basis, the practice at the time, as was the case with commercial prosecutions.

Though Saudi Arabia tends to attract the opprobrium of the international community for doling out death sentences, Dubai too carries the death sentence as the maximum penalty for drug dealing, together with terrorism, rape, murder, espionage and apostasy. In June 2012 a Syrian and a British national were condemned to death for selling Dh1,500 worth of marijuana to an undercover policeman.[19] The authorities in Dubai were keen to emphasise that it was unlikely that the two men would actually be subject to capital punishment, as none of those sentenced to death for drugs crimes over the previous five years had been executed. A final plea for clemency would in any case be referred to the ruler of the country. Though this procedure may be true enough, such a statement masks the protracted nature of the appellate system in Dubai and the stress that accompanies the uncertainty.[20] Moreover, there is no guarantee of a favourable outcome. In February 2010 death sentences were handed down by a court in Ras al-Khaimah, one of the northern emirates, to five traffickers. They had attempted to sell 5 kilograms of heroin and hashish to the value of Dh50,000. With the sentence being described as a 'strong' warning to others, it was far from assured that it would be commuted.

In the prisons too, one finds evidence of the free circulation of drugs. In January 2009 an unnamed twenty-three-year-old Emirati man died of a heroin overdose in a holding cell while in police custody. This tragedy prompted the chief of the Dubai police to draw attention to the persistent attempts to smuggle drugs into prison.[21] X-ray machines have been introduced into Dubai's prisons in order to try to prevent inmates gaining access to such substances. Everyone entering the prison is subject to checks, including prison warders and the police. Manual searches have not hitherto proven to be particularly successful.

Trans-shipment

Before it became carried away with the development of its high-end-value real estate, Dubai's main economic comparative advantage was as a hub for regional trade. It intentionally put itself forward as a low-tax, generally lax regulatory environment in order to attract a disproportionate part of the region's business.[22] In this, Dubai has been startlingly effective, with some 65 per cent of the goods entering the emirate either in transit or for re-export.[23]

In 2006 Dubai was still the world's third-largest re-exporter, after Hong Kong and Singapore. Indeed, it has proved to be adept at offering itself to various sides in the games of regional power politics, with minimum questions asked. It has, for example, acted as a staging post through which Iran can import those goods whose manufacturers would rather not ship direct to the country. This effectively immunises third-party companies from the fear of provoking the ire of the US government, which has enthusiastically and repeatedly sanctioned Iran since the revolution. The risk of retaliation is therefore greatly reduced. Intelligence sources state that much of the freelance work of the Pakistani nuclear maverick A. Q. Khan, who used Dubai as a base of operations, was done there because the authorities looked the other way.

At the same time the USA has routinely used Dubai's port facilities to service the warships it has posted to patrol in the Gulf. Dubai has also emerged as a centre for the provision of rest and recreation to its servicemen. If Dubai could function so effectively in the field of largely licit trade, there was nothing to prevent such successes being extended to the illicit, and more particularly the narcotic drugs market, with a consequent adjustment in margins to reflect the additional risk involved. And this has indeed been the case. Take three examples of Dubai and its major drug-importing neighbours.

- The Saudi authorities have identified al-Batha on its border with the UAE as a particularly vulnerable entry point for illicit drugs. It was concerns about drugs flows that explain the slow implementation of border-entry procedures in 2007 and 2008, during which 900,000 and 1 million trucks respectively used the two formal border crossings.[24] Rough figures for border checks suggest that around 400,000 trucks a year cross the border without being properly scrutinised for illicit drugs.
- Egyptian authorities have pointed to the trend of the last five years, during which there has been a sharp rise in the trafficking of psychotropic drugs. This has mainly affected the inflow of illicit trafficking in Tramadol from India. The drug is moved from India in container traffic to Dubai, where it is routed through Jebel Ali port, in order to remove its association with the subcontinent. The drugs are then shipped onwards to the sea ports of Egypt, from where they are unloaded and distributed.[25]
- Turkey's anti-narcotics police, among the best and most experienced in the Middle East, have identified Lagos–Dubai and Accra–Dubai as routes that have been extensively used in order to smuggle cocaine into Turkey.[26]

These and other developments proved to be so commonplace that at the beginning of 2010 no less a personage than the head of the Dubai anti-narcotics department, Major-General Abdul Jalil Mahdi, went as far as to admit on the record that Dubai had emerged as 'a hub' for drugs traffic.[27]

The main attractions of Dubai for illicit drug smugglers have been twofold. First, the high volume of cargo and passenger traffic using the facilities has made it easier to hide the transfer of illicit materials. Second, breaking the relationship between the commencement and the end-point of drug-trafficking journeys makes it much less likely that the contraband will be identified and intercepted, especially by destination countries. Just consider some of the statistics. By the end of the first decade of the new millennium Dubai airport was a hub for over 100 foreign airlines, seeing nearly 25 million passengers per year passing through its facilities and travelling to more than 150 destinations. Emirates Airlines alone, which had only been established in 1985, had a fleet of 137 aircraft, with 700 flights departing from Dubai every week.[28]

If anything, Dubai's role as a conduit for trade is expected to expand even further. A new airport, Al-Maktoum International Airport, located at Jebel Ali, was completed in July 2010. The new airport was built in order to cater for volumes of traffic estimated for 2050. It was projected, for example, to have an annual cargo-handling capacity of 12 million tonnes per year.[29]

In the last few years Dubai has emerged as an important hub for the distribution of cocaine from Latin America. The success in the early 2000s of the US authorities in reducing the importance of the Caribbean distribution lines has resulted in new routes being opened via West Africa. However, sending West African 'mules' to Europe or to South-East Asia on flights from South America would, to say the least, be unlikely to result in a large number of such consignments evading detection. In order to ensure that this is not the case, such contraband is now routed to Europe and Asia via Dubai or, with an even greater chance of success, via a third destination as well as Dubai and then onwards into Europe or Asia. It is therefore not at all surprising that in summer 2010 Dubai customs officials twice broke their record for the volume of an individual seizure, with 5.5 kilograms found in the luggage of a man travelling from Brazil being superseded by the arrest in June of a Nigerian woman with 7.3 kilograms in her luggage, though in both cases Dubai was actually believed to have been the destination for the drugs.[30]

Jebel Ali port

It is not solely through the individual that drug trafficking takes place through the emirate. The region's oldest and largest port, Jebel Ali, which is home to over 6,000 commercial units, is used for the smuggling of contraband, notably in container shipping. Jebel Ali is big business. It accounts for 21 per cent of Dubai's GDP,[31] and is the gateway for most of the 9 million containers that enter Dubai every year. Container trafficking involves a complex formula of shell companies, false paperwork and repackaging. Customs officials are in any case disinclined to go looking for such activities, as it is their primary responsibility to keep the merchandise trade flowing, not to hold it up, especially during times of recession. Dubai's attractiveness is built precisely on the low regulatory regime that it administers.

The UNODC has documented examples of goods being trafficked which help to illustrate the nature and direction of some of the re-shipping. Neither involves the movement of illegal drugs, as such, the smuggling of illegally produced but licit goods being easier to track. Much of the annual bootleg trade of 32 billion cigarettes, bound for North and West Africa, having been produced in China and Vietnam, is routed through Jebel Ali port.[32] The value of the fake cigarette business has been estimated at some $775 million per annum. There is also a trade in fake medication, along similar trade lines. The unlicensed anti-malaria medication alone is estimated by the UN to be worth an annual $438 million.

Money Laundering

In addition to the trafficking of narcotic drugs for domestic use and trans-shipment purposes, Dubai has also experienced the related problem of money laundering. According to Dr Christopher Davidson, a leading academic expert on the UAE, money laundering has been 'for many years' a component of Dubai's informal economy.[33] Black money was attracted to Dubai because of the permissive atmosphere created by a convergence of hands-off supervision, loosely regulated free zones and a myriad of foreign trading connections. In Davidson's view 'every major [Dubai real estate project] has been, in part, financed with laundered cash'.[34]

In describing this permissive atmosphere, it is useful to think in terms of analogies that might illustrate what is otherwise an opaque practice. One insightful analogy referenced by those who know the two cases well are that of the Republic of Cyprus, effectively limited in jurisdiction to the south of the island, under President Tassos Papadopoulas.[35] Serving as head of state between February 2003 and February 2008, he positively welcomed the proceeds of Serbian organised criminality. These were then cleaned up by being recycled through the Cypriot economy, with real estate, hotels and construction the favoured outlets.

This situation was exacerbated after March 2002, when the Dubai authorities introduced freehold ownership for expatriates to the property sector. This move was immediately identified as a step that would increase the volume of dirty money entering Dubai. One well-established research group at the time estimated that the volume of money being laundered in Dubai could grow by as much as $1 billion as a result of this policy change.[36] Business people and lawyers involved in property purchases say that once the policy was implemented the figure very likely exceeded this estimate. Stories became legion during the first decade of the 2000s of prospective property purchasers turning up at sales and investment brokers with large volumes of cash literally in hand.

Concern at the role being played by Dubai in money laundering grew after the terrorist outrages in New York and Washington DC on 9/11. Funds to the tune of six figures were moved through the Dubai banking system to banks in the USA in order to help finance the operation. In moving such funds around, the hijackers utilised the *hawala* system, a trust-based approach to banking that promotes informality and speed of transaction, to the detriment of scrutiny and the tracking of such funds. US officials, driven by the political fallout from 9/11, subjected Dubai to a hitherto unknown level of scrutiny. The Dubai authorities have had little choice but to fall in line with the demands made by the USA. They have taken active steps to tighten up the regulatory framework. Anti-money-laundering legislation was introduced in Dubai in the early 2000s. At the federal level an Anti-Money Laundering and Suspicious Cases Unit was created in the UAE Central Bank. Newer ventures, such as the establishment of Dubai's financial free zone in 2004, have apparently been subject to a more rigorous level of supervision. The Dubai Financial Services Authority (DFSA), the regulatory body in charge, has drawn attention to the importance of its role in order to maintain credibility.

In spite of such institutional changes, there is an enduring sense that Dubai's financial-sector reforms have amounted to a case of too little and from too low a base. Moreover, they seem to be taking considerable time to bed in. The Financial Action Task Force (FATF), the international organisation responsible for combating money laundering, has criticised the UAE's anti-money-laundering unit for being understaffed and for operating an inadequate legal framework, for example as far as the implementation and monitoring of customer due diligence is concerned. It expressed concern at the lack of effectiveness in the identification of the true owners and beneficiaries of companies in the UAE. FATF has also expressed concern at the operation of the securities and insurance sub-sectors in the UAE,[37] and the absence of any real scrutiny of vulnerable professions, notably lawyers and accountants.

There is evidence to suggest that the authorities in Dubai turned a blind eye to the activities of many of the money-laundering operations in the emirate. One private-sector lawyer, Hamdan Abdullah al-Sayyah, recounts how a purported businessman from Russia sank $10 million into a land deal in the emirate. He did so by presenting a sales contract and then making a large number of smaller transactions, in order to stay beneath capital thresholds that would act as trip-wires for regulatory investigation.[38]

BOX 1

JAMES IBORI

In spite of such tightening, the periodic emergence of sensational cases gives a glimpse into the continuing situation on the ground in Dubai. Such a case was that of James Ibori, a former Nigerian state governor of the oil rich Delta State. He was arrested in Dubai in May 2010 at the prompting of London's Metropolitan Police on charges of money laundering and fraud. In August 2007 the UK had frozen assets to the value of $35 million, more than 100 times his annual salary. He was held in connection with charges that he allegedly stole $85 million during his governorship. In December 2009 a Nigerian court subsequently threw out 170 counts against him. But Mr Ibori's position soon deteriorated once again with the death of his ally, Nigeria's President Yar'Adua, and the announcement by his successor, Goodluck Jonathan, that he would reinvigorate the anti-corruption drive. The fact that Mr Ibori fled to Dubai is instructive, both with regard to the presumed location of a significant proportion of his asset base and the perception of where he would be most secure. Mr Ibori's detention was triggered by Nigeria's main anti-corruption agency, which was pursuing him over allegations that $290 million had been looted from the state's coffers. In April 2012 he was jailed for fraud and money laundering in the UK for thirteen years, where he remains.

Dubai therefore remains a large, predominantly cash economy, with little transparency, and only an embryonic legislative infrastructure. For example, since 2002 all foreigners entering Dubai through the airport have had to declare the cash that they carry in excess of $11,000. In the first two quarters of 2010 the aggregate figure for this movement of cash topped a colossal $6.4 billion, a rough average of $5,000 per person using the airport during that time.

The Afghan Connection

The principal axis for the laundering of illegal money, much of it drugs related, exists between Afghanistan, the primary producer of opium in the world, and Dubai, the main centre for financial services in West Asia. Before the war in Afghanistan there was comparatively little smuggling between the two countries, according to a senior source in Dubai. That has all since changed.[39]

A rare insight into the murky world of this connection came in October 2009, when one of Afghanistan's then vice-presidents, Ahmad Zia Massoud, was stopped and questioned on his way into Dubai. In his possession that day was some $52 million in cash. UAE law permits the export or import of any amount of currency, provided cash and travellers' cheques to the value of $10,800 are declared, which in this case they had patently not been. Massoud was grilled by officials from both the USA and Dubai. Eventually the vice-president was allowed to go on his way, retaining most of the money. One may presume that this outcome was driven on the American side by a reluctant desire not to exacerbate its mercurial relations with the Afghan regime led by President Hamid Karzai in Kabul. The Dubai authorities, on the other hand, were keen to cover up what was otherwise embarrassing evidence of their role as a destination for cleaning money. Massoud did not in the end provide a satisfactory explanation for the origins or the destination of the cash.

An incident that might have been dismissed as 'an outlier' and an aberration began to look more typical of the *modus operandi* of part of the state with the release of US government cables by the Wikileaks organisation. A second notorious incident that came to light was that of Sher Khan Farnood, the former chairman of Kabul Bank,[40] who was disgraced in summer 2010 after corrupt loans made by the bank almost brought down Afghanistan's fragile financial system. Farnood, who was reputed to have a weakness for high-stakes international poker tournaments, was reported by Wikileaks to own thirty-nine properties in Dubai on the Palm Jumeirah, one of the artificial island developments on its coast.[41] Clearly, asset wealth on such a scale could not have been purchased on the regular salary even of the head of a bank.

Massoud and Farnood were clearly not exceptions as far as cash-smuggling operations between Afghanistan and Dubai were concerned. Even senior figures from the Dubai authorities have been obliged to accept the realities of the black-money relationship between the two. Bryan Stirewalt, the director of supervision at the DFSA, has accepted that he cannot disagree with such an assessment. The best spin that Dubai officials can put on such a practice is to say that Dubai is not the only jurisdiction internationally in which such criminal practices take place.[42]

The impoverished nature of the Afghan economy means that it is a fact of life that there is a strong economic incentive for capital flight in search of higher value assets, whether among criminals or those acting legitimately. One Wikileaks cable, for instance, recalls that 'drug traffickers, corrupt officials and to a large extent licit business owners do not benefit from keeping their millions of dollars in Afghanistan'. The vehicle of preference for Afghanistan's cash couriers was, until Farnood's disgrace, Pamir Airlines, a private carrier, which is jointly owned by Kabul Bank and influential Afghans, such as the president's brother, Mahmood Karzai, and the Tajik warlord Mohammad Fahim, a vice-presidential running mate in the 2009 election.[43] It regularly plied routes between Afghanistan and the Gulf, and its unregulated journeys contributed to the phenomenon of capital flight. In one day in July 2009 alone, just prior to the general election, a minimum of $75 million worth of Afghan cash transited to Dubai, as those previously in senior government positions hedged their bets against defeat for their side in the outcome of the poll.

Other senior regime figures alleged to be involved in cash-trafficking activity included a governor of Ghazni in south-east Afghanistan and a governor of the neighbouring province of Paktiya. Both have been accused of embezzling public funds and extorting money from construction contractors. Corruption is believed to be endemic in Ghazni in particular. Paktiya's former governor is alleged to have had a wide range of contacts, including with Afghan insurgents in Parwan, Kunar and Kabul provinces, as well as the controversial Pakistani intelligence service the ISI, and Iranian regime elements.[44] The Wikileaks cable also describes the governor as being a business partner in Dubai with the son of Gulbuddin Hekmatyar, the head of Afghan opposition party the Hizb-i Islami, one of the most ruthless and unscrupulous of all the Afghan warlords of the last twenty-five years.[45]

When Afghan cash is not being physically smuggled out via Dubai, it is being wired out, using the *hawala* system operated especially in the money-changing sub-sector. The most favoured conduit is the New Ansari Money Exchange. According to a cable signed off by the US ambassador, Karl Eikenberry, criminals work through an array of front companies both in

Afghanistan and the Gulf. The process offers a wide range of 'illicit financial services for narco-traffickers, insurgents, and criminals'.[46] The US authorities named Azizullah Alizai, a drugs kingpin, trafficking heroin in south-west Asia and the Middle East, and the Haji Juma Khan Organisation, which moves opium, morphine and heroin, and operates on and across the borders of Afghanistan, Iran and Pakistan, as two prominent criminal gangs utilising the services of New Ansari. In response to these and comparable activities, in February 2011 the US Treasury adopted a range of sanctions against key figures within New Ansari, including its founder, Haji Abdullah Barakzai, its Dubai manager, Mohammed Noor, and Rahmatullah Mohammad Afzal, described as a key cash courier for the organisation, which was accused of moving $94 million from Afghanistan to Dubai.[47]

Governance and Responsibility

The political authorities in Dubai have a long history of acting boldly, opportunistically and pragmatically as far as the management of the emirate is concerned, and, in so doing, generally making good judgement calls. Such a *modus operandi* has become part of the founding narrative of the emirate of Dubai. The original 1833 migration led by Maktoum bin Butti of 800 members of the Bu Falasal clan of the Bani Yas to Bur Dubai on the Creek, the very heart of the present location of the city-state, was the foundational example. Bin Butti is the acknowledged founder of the Maktoum dynasty. It was his decisive leadership that laid the basis for the establishment of Dubai.

A second illustration of Maktoum canniness came at the turn of the nineteenth and twentieth centuries, when Shaikh Maktoum al-Maktoum undercut the rising taxation regime being imposed on the Iranian side of the Gulf. By offering a lower tax environment, and attracting the relocation of Iranian merchants, Dubai was able to secure for itself a pivotal position as a trading centre in the lower Gulf, and as a regional entrepôt for the Iranian market. In short, the ability to spot a favourable opportunity and to exploit it on a grand scale has been central to the story of growth and prosperity of Dubai over the years.

Such nimble-footedness has served the interests of the emirate more recently, as this chapter has shown. Dubai has been happy to cooperate with the governments of both Iran and the USA, even while they have politically been at one another's throats, if the perception of commercial advantage in its relationship with both has accompanied such practice. Issues of morality do not enter into it. This is international politics. For a non-oil state, amidst larger and wealthier powers, located in a historically unstable sub-system over the last forty years, Dubai has done whatever it must in order to increase the chances not only of survival but also of achieving a level of prosperity commensurate with its aspiration, determined by the oil-rich neighbouring emirates. That it has succeeded in the goal of domestic wealth creation without jeopardising internal stability may be taken as justification alone.

The same may be said of the area of narcotic drugs, and its associated ills of money laundering and the existence of a black economy. The hagiography of the emirate is full of references to the swift and wise decision making of Dubai's political leadership, with the country's economic-development model shorn of the red tape of countries operating elsewhere. If Dubai is going to personalise its decision making to the degree that it does, then the structural presence of criminality prospering within the system is also likely to accrue to the man at the top.

Shaikh Mohammad is an absolute monarch. Danish researcher Martin Hvindt notes that Shaikh Mohammad 'runs Dubai as if it were a corporation: Dubai Inc.'. There is widespread agreement that the decision-making structure in Dubai is 'extremely centralised'. Moreover, Hvindt observes that 'the leadership in Dubai identifies itself with the Asian model of development in general and the Singapore model in particular'. Shaikh Mohammad sits astride this lofty oligarchy. He concludes that one should conceive of Dubai in terms of 'ruler involvement' rather than state involvement.

Listed by *Forbes Magazine* in 2005 as the world's fourth-richest man, Shaikh Mohammad's estimated fortune of $14 billion was presumably based on in part a paper estimate of the worth of land prices in the emirate. That figure has clearly declined over the last six years, especially with the halving of residential property prices in Dubai since the 2008 global credit crunch. With the Dubai economy ailing of late, the continued buoyancy given to it through the transfer of black money and funds from Afghanistan in particular would have been extremely welcome. It would presumably not have been lost on the asset and portfolio managers of such capital that Dubai would have been poorly placed to dictate terms, given the overall global backdrop of recession and the persistent rumours in 2008 and 2009 that it was effectively bankrupt.

While one may debate whether Shaikh Mohammad would actively have welcomed the proceeds of drug transactions, and criminality more widely, or just practised a form of passive complicity, it is surely inconceivable that he would have been unaware of their existence or their impact on the emirate's economic or political fortunes. Just consider the political context in which the leadership of Dubai functions. In spite of its generally liberal reputation,

Shaikh Mohammad is unencumbered by even the most meagre of checks and balances in place elsewhere in the Gulf. For in Dubai there is no separation of powers between the executive and legislative branches of government, no effective scrutiny of decision making, and no formal structures for the political representation of Emiratis, let alone expatriates. Shaikh Mohammad appoints the body that approximates to being Dubai's cabinet, he hires and fires the country's leading economic managers, and he has designated his own successor, his second son, Prince Hamdan bin Mohammad bin Maktoum, whom he has made crown prince.

BOX 2

CLASSIC-CAR SMUGGLING

One of the most effective ways of smuggling hard drugs into Dubai is to hide volumes of it in the engine compartments of classic cars being imported into the emirate through the free zone at Jebel Ali. Because of the high price of such vehicles, they are carefully and elaborately cocooned in a high-grade version of bubble wrap. Customs officials from Dubai are extremely wary of stripping off such protection in case the car is damaged in the process. By definition, anyone ordering a classic car is going to be wealthy and from an influential family. Customs officials fear that they will be held personally responsible for any resulting damage. Knowing the aversion to interdiction on the part of state employees, smugglers will literally take out the whole of an engine and replace it with tens of kilograms of drugs before attempting to transport it into the emirate.

While such a strategy of benefiting from external capital transfers—even those with an uncertain provenance—may be described as a success, it has nevertheless been a high-risk one. As Joe Bennett has written, 'Nothing frightens Dubai like a threat to its reputation.'[48] To date, Dubai has succeeded in keeping its overall reputation as a top-line brand intact. This is in spite of its links with drugs trans-shipments and the laundering of black money, largely because those who approve of the former are largely ignorant of the latter. But for how much longer can this ignorance be relied upon as an integral part of this strategy?

Conclusion

Dubai may be a small entity, with a status significantly less than a state, but its role in the movement of drugs and the perpetuation of criminality remains a large and significant one. The biggest role played by Dubai as far as illicit drugs are concerned is as a functioning physical hub, with large volumes of heroin and cannabis in particular being shipped through its space. The swift pace and diverse directional nature of its transport links means that drug routes can be switched around rapidly, thereby keeping law enforcement on the back foot. The potential for changing the identity of contraband using the massive Jebel Ali port means that illicit goods more generally can easily be repackaged and dispatched before being subject to official scrutiny. Dubai's connections with money laundering and with the unregulated economies of places such as Afghanistan well illustrate its international vulnerabilities.

But Dubai's drugs challenge is not simply one that profoundly affects the international political economy of drugs. There exists a very significant level of drugs usage within the emirate itself, notably among the Emirati population. A vantage point from the courts and prisons of Dubai brings home the widespread nature of usage internally. Given this pattern of consumption, it is a surprise that the government of Dubai has not been more assiduous in making provision for the treatment and rehabilitation of problem drugs consumers inside the emirate.

10

IRAQ

INSURGENCY AND STATE COLLAPSE

Introduction

As recently as the 1980s, Iraq was a strong and confident player in the international politics of the Middle East. It had a massive arsenal of conventional weapons; it had deployed non-conventional weapons in its 1980–8 war against Iran; it had used chemical weapons against the Iraqi Kurds at Halabja in March 1988. Baghdad had concluded a friendship and non-aggression pact with the Soviet Union in 1972. It had a despotic leader, with ambitions of regional hegemony, who was unafraid to resort to violence, internally and externally, to realise his goals. Since the defection of Egypt from the 'rejectionist' camp in the late 1970s, following Cairo's peace agreement with Israel, Iraq had fleetingly held the leadership of the Arab world, as indicated by the staging of the 1978 and 1979 Arab summits in Baghdad. In hard-power terms, Saddam's Iraq was the most feared in the Middle East. For regime supporters as a whole, Iraqi national self-esteem was at its zenith.

Within two decades the power of Iraq had been broken. The country had been exhausted by two wars and the rigorous application of a wide range of international sanctions. Iraq's weapons of mass destruction had been largely dismantled during the intrusive visits of UN weapons inspectors in the 1990s. Its jails had been emptied of common criminals. It had been subject to a US-led invasion and occupation. Its former leader had been apprehended and executed. The Iraqi state had largely collapsed, torn apart during the invasion and dissolved by decree. Society had fractured. There had been an extensive movement of populations in a desperate quest for security.

Of course there had been some winners as a result of regime collapse in Iraq, notably the poorer, urban Shia neighbourhoods and their largely religious leadership. But even the Shiite communities had been convulsed by violent internal power struggles. The country's borders were suddenly wide open and permeable to neighbours. National self-esteem was at an extremely low ebb. Only the likes of the Soviet Union had experienced a collective collapse of power and self-confidence comparable to that in Iraq. And the consequences for the former Soviet space had been an explosion in hard-drug taking and prostitution.

Empirical experience indicates that organised criminality is attracted by state collapse. Criminal activity can then be organised free from the intrusion of state processes, such as justice systems and external defence, whose *raison d'être* is to regulate and restrain. Where such institutions still exist in a disabled form they can be paid off or brought into the criminal activity on the basis of a division of labour. Conflict and competition among the new bodies created in an attempt to rebuild the state but as yet uninstitutionalised are susceptible to exploitation by newly organised criminal activity. In both psychological and organisational terms, Iraq from 2003 onwards was vulnerable to a surge in the supply and use of narcotic drugs as a result of the extraordinary circumstances that had afflicted the country over the previous twenty years.

Surviving Saddam

Stigmatising Hard Drugs

In its final phase, Saddam Hussein's Iraq has been described as 'a thoroughly criminal enterprise masquerading as a nation-state'.[1] Saddam and his associates took advantage of the international sanctions regime, which came into place in August 1990, in the aftermath of the Iraqi invasion of Kuwait, in order to make super-profits from the smuggling of goods such as alcohol and cigarettes.[2] In 2000, it was estimated that the Iraqi regime alone earned around $1 billion a year from smuggling, with $400–$500 million coming from a southerly direction, through Iranian territorial waters.[3]

Meanwhile, on one of Iraq's most commercially lucrative borders, the Jordanian authorities seemed to be as much concerned at the smuggling of small arms as of hard drugs. In 1991 the Jordanians moved the border post to the actual frontier in order to try to stymie the flow of such weapons.[4] A decade later smugglers were still trying to move weapons through Jordan.[5] There is less evidence to suggest that their activities extended into the realm of hard drugs.[6]

The absence of hard-drugs smuggling in part reflects the considerable social stigma in the Iraq of the 1990s over the consumption of such drugs. A regime-inspired 'Faith Campaign', which emphasised religious observance and a return to conservative values combined with harsh penalties, notably for 'prostitutes', provided the normative backdrop to the conduct of affairs in Saddam's Iraq, during the last full decade of its existence. This seems to have influenced the overall policy environment in Iraq. For example, a 1999 decision by the top political body in Iraq, the Revolutionary Command Council, pardoning a range of different criminals in Iraqi jails, exempted just four categories of prisoner from such a gesture. These comprised those who had been found guilty of espionage; incest, rape, homosexuality and indecent assault; persistent recidivism; and drug trafficking.[7]

The declaratory diplomacy of the Saddamist regime on narcotics, expressed in the realm of regional affairs, further supports this view. In January 2001 the Iraqi cabinet agreed to sign up to an inter-Arab accord to confront the illegal trade in narcotics. Iraqi law-enforcement operations were encouraged to combat such smuggling. Specific rewards were prescribed for seizures of drugs that had been trafficked into Iraq. Additional, though unspecified, funding was allocated to the Ministry of Interior to increase at the very least the appearance of effectiveness in such matters.[8]

The seriousness of such threats is indicated by the difficulty of buying hard drugs inside Iraq during this period. Anyone caught selling them during the final years of the Saddam era risked the death penalty. Reflecting the general absence of narcotics, high-profile drugs 'busts' were simply something that did not take place in Iraq.[9] From a specialist UN agency perspective, the situation in Iraq before the 2003 invasion was reckoned 'not to be one of the hottest spots',[10] as far as the global movement of illicit drugs was concerned.

This negative overall view of narcotics on the part of regime and society alike provided the immediate post-Saddam era with a legacy of initial lack of interest. The Ministry of Interior, which controlled the relevant institutions dealing with smuggling, such as the Border Security Police, did not even bother to track narcotics-related arrests or seizures. Most of Iraq was deemed too arid to grow classic drug crops such as cannabis in commercial volumes. The Interior Ministry reported no known production of illicit drugs in Iraq. While corruption quickly re-emerged as a chronic affliction of governance in Iraq, the problem was not perceived as having a strong drugs dimension.

Money laundering was extensively resorted to in order to generate funding for sectarian militias and terrorist groups. The laundering of drugs-related monies was simply not an issue.[11]

In general, Iraq lacked a national anti-narcotics effort because on the whole it had not hitherto needed one.

'Prescription Drugs'

But this does not mean that Iraq was entirely free from problem drugs during the Saddam period. Starting in the early 1990s Iraqis increasingly began to manage the high levels of stress involved in living in a country under intense external pressure by taking cocktails of psychotropic or 'prescription' drugs, alongside alcohol. Favoured among the former were anti-depressants going by the commercial names of Artane, a muscle relaxant used extensively in the treatment of Parkinson's disease, and Artivan, which was used in the treatment of anxiety disorders. These were generally only available with a doctor's prescription.

A couple of years or so before the US-led invasion the source of such 'tablets' became more plentiful.[12] For the head of the Iraqi anti-drugs police, Omar Zahed, there was no doubt about what had transpired. He attributed this increase to 'a well-planned international criminal effort', an apparent allusion to an unspecified conspiracy. He notes that these substances sold for just a few US cents per strip. This was a modest amount even by Iraqi society's by then utterly impoverished standards. There had been periodic collapses in the exchange value of the Iraqi dinar before, presumably, according to this logic, as an economic device through which to weaken resilience and promote dependency.

Licit drugs were also being smuggled out of the country during this period, also taking them into the domain of the illegal. The source of the latter supplies may well have been in part Iraq's own pharmaceutical sector. Iraq had developed two factories during its previous attempts at industrial development. They produced a range of medicines, from amoxicillin to flu medicines, under international licence and to an internationally recognised very high standard. Those responsible for moving these medicines clandestinely out of the country were undoubtedly regime figures and their attendant networks. These medicines may also have been imported into Iraq under the UN-administered 'oil-for-food' programme, which permitted the purchase of pharmaceuticals. This programme had been forged in the mid-1990s to alleviate the impact of the international sanctions regime on the suffering of ordinary Iraqis. These clandestine exports of medical supplies were bound for

Lebanon and the Gulf, where they were sold on at a considerable profit, to the benefit of the regime.[13]

As for the medicines remaining in Iraq, these were often distributed informally by Iraqi pharmacists. The formal regulatory system had eroded in the last few years of the Saddam regime, as the country's hardship grew. In turn, pharmacists were increasingly prepared to divert such substances to their friends and contacts, often for reciprocal benefits. For the rest, a 'self-provisioning' philosophy existed in the country's hospitals, that is to say a practice of bringing one's own medicines.[14] There is, therefore, no question that these prescription drugs were as illicit as any being bought and sold in the region, because of the steady erosion of the state and its official procedures.

In the absence of hard drugs, the main alternative to the abusive consumption of pharmaceuticals was the use of solvents. This included the likes of paint thinners, glue and 'liquid paper'. Compared to anti-depressants, this was the sordid, down-market end of drug abuse, favoured by default by the destitute and the socially marginal. As in other big regional cities such as Cairo and Istanbul, such forms of self-abuse were especially popular among street children and the self-protection gangs that they formed. In Baghdad the situation was comparable but worse. Some of these children were as young as five. Many of them were orphans, having lost strong male family figures in the conflicts between 1980 and the early 2000s. Children who had previously been housed in state orphanages found their way onto the streets as costly institutions were closed down and central authority began to break down in the run-up to the invasion. It was not just Iraqi jails that were thrown open during the last days of the regime, as selected media reporting at the time would have had us believe. These abusers quickly became known in Arabic as *kabsilun*, the 'capsule people', because of their favoured method of getting a 'high'.[15]

The arrival of psychotropic drugs had a big impact on Iraq's prisons. The drug of choice for Iraq's criminal classes during the late Saddamist era had been alcohol, with reports of heavy use.[16] However, in jails such as the notorious Abu Ghrayb, alcohol was difficult to access, not least because of its bulk, in contrast to the 'prescription drugs' that were in plentiful supply. These were brought to the prisons either by family members helping their relatives to manage the stress of incarceration or unscrupulous doctors, seeking to make a personal profit from such misfortune. For persistent offenders these substances were attractive, not least because their effect was to remove the inhibitions of the drug abuser and create an artificial sense of courage.

Petty criminals subsequently began to leave jail with a dependence on such substances, which promoted demand more widely. When the Saddamist regime decided to throw open the jails just before the US-led invasion, releasing somewhere between 40,000 and 75,000 inmates,[17] there was almost bound to be a big increase in criminal activity, especially in the absence of 'normal' economic or social activity. This impacted both the rising prescription-drug dependence itself and the nature and extent of the crimes committed when under the influence of such 'tablets'. With petty criminals swaggering under their influence, it was hardly surprising that there was a jump in such related crimes as violent robbery and assault.

Alcohol, meanwhile, was freely available, even in a context of the Faith Campaign. This was for two reasons. First, because of the presence of Iraq's important, but dwindling, Christian communities. No attempt was made to prevent Christians from distilling and consuming alcohol, as it was generally regarded as a component of Christian culture. Second, because of the weakness of some senior Ba'th party circles for the consumption of cigars and whisky as a sign of secular modernity and high political status. Occasionally, the two factors were present in one. Tariq Aziz, a former foreign, oil and deputy prime minister, was a Christian from the north, and a long-time Ba'th party member and confidant of Saddam Hussein. He was a man who took demonstrable pleasure in dismissing the impact of international sanctions by holding a large tumbler of Johnnie Walker Black Label whisky, while smoking a very large cigar.

Nevertheless, alcohol was subject to an anti-abuse campaign in the 1980s, apparently with some success.[18]

One prominent figure with whom the campaign was clearly unsuccessful was Saddam Hussein's elder son, Uday. His reckless forays into the Baghdad nightlife were regularly fuelled by alcohol binges.[19] At home he had a cellar containing top-of-the-range wines and spirits, the total stock of which was estimated to be worth some $1 million. Neither was Uday above keeping hard drugs in his home, in spite of the disapproving face of the regime. Upon the capture of his residence, following the US-led invasion in 2003, six bags of heroin of uncertain weight were seized.[20] Uday's increasingly erratic behaviour over the years preceding the final downfall of his father's regime was believed to stem from his mixing of anabolic steroids, used for body-building, with which he was increasingly fixated, with alcohol.

Some marijuana was smuggled into Iraq during this time, but it was little used, not least because of the relative expense of purchasing it.

Drugs and the Invasion of Iraq

The US-led invasion of Iraq began on 21 March 2003. By the beginning of May the initial bout of fighting was over, and the USA and its allies were in control of the country; the occupation had begun. The original invasion had been characterised by the USA's aerial bombing campaign, presented in US propaganda as one of 'shock and awe'. The aim was to intimidate Iraqis into abandoning the regime's residual structures of power. It certainly did a good job of intimidating Iraqis on an individual basis. Iraqi families stockpiled drugs, almost always by this point obtained through illicit means, as part of their essential survival kit—together with sugar, tea, playing cards, bandages and the like—in order to be able to remain calm under such a sustained onslaught.[21]

As the onslaught intensified, much of the Iraqi state simply melted away. A wave of attacks by Iraqis on state buildings went undeterred and unpunished. The US occupiers initially did not discourage these acts of political vandalism. Indeed, they often encouraged such spontaneous expressions of anger. This was because of the USA's association of regime institutions with a Ba'thism that was viewed as analogous to Nazism, rather than as an essential component of the maintenance of law and order. Most notoriously, one of the first acts of Paul Bremer, the head of the Coalition Provisional Authority (CPA), and the de facto American 'viceroy' in Iraq, who, like a latter-day Lord Cromer in Egypt, ruled Iraq in 2003/4, was to dissolve the Iraqi army. Bremer thereby left the country defenceless, while at the same time alienating the well-organised and professional officer corps, which had been a central coercive mainstay of power under Saddam Hussein.

The one exception was Iraqi Kurdistan, in north-eastern Iraq, which had been a separately self-administered area since 2001. It was no coincidence that the presence of centres of authority, the engagement of the Kurdish *peshmerga* militia, and a rigorous approach to internal security resulted in no reported illicit drugs-consumption problems in the predominantly Kurdish provinces.

The collapse of the state, and the disavowal of the army, meant that Iraq was literally lawless, except in those geographical and functional areas where the US military and its allies were specifically active. These latter reflected the USA's sense of its own interests in Iraq, rather than of the Iraqis themselves. These deployments tended to be directed towards such goals as securing the Sunni Arab periphery, given that this had been the primary confessional-cum-ethnic support base for the Saddamist regime, and in establishing military bases. The goal of reimposing law and order across the country was patchily pursued if it was pursued at all.

According to the Pentagon, the US military did not regard counter-narcotics as part of its mission in Iraq.[22] This meant that criminality, in such forms as trafficking, kidnapping and the extortion of businesses, quickly flourished. This included the area of illicit drugs, with hashish and opiates to the fore, in the south. It also meant that it was difficult to re-establish a robust national system for the approval and distribution of pharmaceutical drugs. As late as May 2007, for example, Iraq only had one functioning laboratory capable of analysing and certifying pharmaceutical products, either domestically produced or imported for safe use within the country.[23]

The Iraqi experience was, however, rather different in those areas where there was a strong sense of community. These included the strongly tribalised parts of the country. These areas were inhabited by both rural Arab Sunnis in the west and Arab Shias in the south. Informal, but strongly norm-based, tribal meetings were established to address a range of social misdemeanours, including substance abuse. Dealt with swiftly, transparently and hence effectively, this was a part of Iraqi society where drugs were much less likely to fester, resulting in significant levels of social damage.

Grassroots justice was not, however, as comprehensive as would have been desirable. Local religious courts were quickly established by Shia clerics in the destitute Shia working-class strongholds of places such as Saddam City, quickly re-named Sadr City, in eastern Baghdad. In spite of the consequent 'enforcement of morals' and the restriction on the distribution of alcohol that these courts enforced, reports of illicit drugs being sold openly in the street markets of Sadr City continued to persist. For such informal law enforcers, drugs were clearly not considered to be as theologically threatening as alcohol and pornography. Or perhaps it was more the case of drugs presenting local clerics with a baffling range of apparently unending varieties of pills and strips, while the likes of pornography was reassuringly Manichaean.

Both drugs activity and anti-drugs responses were strongly localised. Take, for instance, the affluent and well-integrated suburb of Karrada, located in an agreeable neighbourhood, next to the River Tigris. The senior officer in the Karrada police station, Colonel Thamir Sadoun Ali, lost 10 of his 200 men, killed as a result of trying to confront the new drugs gangs during the first four months of the American occupation of Iraq.[24] Evidence that drug trafficking and the associated violence was having a further impact on crime more generally during 2003 was evident from police testimonies. According to Colonel Ali, 80 per cent of criminal arrests showed signs of aggravation owing to narcotic intoxication.

Concerns about such a rapid spread of drug-fuelled behaviour were so acute that the Ministry of Justice took the decision early in the occupation to establish a specialist anti-drugs unit. Though a not unimportant organisational gesture, this move was more impressive in form than in substance. By the fourth quarter of 2004 only a handful of Iraqi policemen had received advanced counter-narcotics training. At the time, the US State Department had only five drugs experts based in Iraq, and their brief was only partially focused on trafficking.[25] The modest nature of the under-resourcing of the counter-narcotics effort can be seen in the presence of only one trained sniffer dog in the country in October 2005.[26] Even by 2011, Iraq only had eight dedicated anti-narcotics sniffer dogs, the main body of the formidable force of 302 canines being used to seek out explosives.[27]

The Insurgency

By the end of 2003 the anti-US insurgency was in full swing. It comprised Arab Sunni fighters, many of them of tribal origin, opposed to what they perceived to be the emergence of Shia majoritarianism. It also included their hardline fellow Sunnis of al-Qaeda in Mesopotamia, many of whom were more ideological in representation. The simple fact was that policemen and soldiers were too busy fighting the insurgency to devote significant capacity to such secondary issues as drugs. For the USA, which was trying to establish a 'hearts and minds' campaign to win over the trust of the civilian population in Iraq, there were other priorities, notably in the realm of the provision of essential civilian services. The CPA was at least honest in pointing to the provision of water and electricity as well as overall security, as the keys to ending the conflict, and in stating that drug issues were not at the top of their priorities.[28] As one Ministry of Interior official described it with brutal honesty: 'In the present circumstances we have to choose our priorities and the insurgency is killing more people than the drugs are'. One blogger in Iraq at the time put it more colourfully: 'People don't perceive them [illicit drugs] as a very immediate threat. It's like discovering you have cancer while you're fighting off a hungry alligator—you'll worry about the disease later.'[29]

What seemed to be happening during this initial period was a partial Iranianisation of the drug supply situation in Iraq. Police-generated research on the impact of drugs in post-invasion Iraq suggests that 'most' of the prescription drugs that entered Iraq came via the eastern border with Iran.[30] Certainly, Iraqi Shia living in as diverse a set of locations as the clerical city of

Najaf in the mid-south and the economic centre of Basra in the far south complained about Iranians smuggling and selling prescription drugs illicitly in their areas.[31]

Looters had also stolen drugs from hospitals, clinics and from the Ministry of Health itself during the early part of the period of chaos in Iraq,[32] in the aftermath of the invasion. These drugs were then sold openly in the various transient street markets that sprang up temporarily, especially in the greater Baghdad area. These markets were reported as 'teeming with illicit drugs'. The system for authorising medicine through prescriptions had largely broken down, not least for pure market reasons: drugs on the street often sold for one-third of the price for which they could be bought in licensed pharmacies. Those doing the selling had little knowledge of the drugs in which they were trading, and the ailments for which these pharmaceuticals had been developed. They included elderly women, who sell drugs under their black over-garment, the *abaya*.[33]

Some street vendors were reported as being semi-literate and hence unable even to read the simple directions for use included by the pharmaceutical manufacturers. Some of the medicines were being sold even though well past their official 'sell-by' date. Some market vendors had been selling drugs clearly labelled 'Not for Sale'.[34] In some cases children as young as ten years old had been left alone to look after the market stalls, raising the additional fear that such tablets were leaking into juvenile networks.

Children were already known to provide an expanding market. Illicit drugs were by now openly sold at or near school gates in Baghdad. In some cases children were persuaded to take drugs onto school premises in order to create new markets among their peers. They tended to be paid in drugs as well as cash by their suppliers. The overall atmosphere of insecurity in Iraq made it more difficult to try to rescue and rehabilitate such children, compared to other big cities in the region.[35] At least five NGOs working on children's problems had become involved in the tragic issue of children and drugs. According to one of the best known, Keeping Children Alive (KCA), the main reason for the big rise in child and youth consumption of illicit drugs was the psychological impact of the sustained political violence that had engulfed Iraq between 2004 and 2007. This was particularly acute if family members had been killed or maimed. In short, drugs had become a longer-term coping mechanism for young Iraqis brutalised by the experiences of their country during the mid-2000s.[36]

For those unfortunate enough to become dependent upon any of the problem drugs available in Iraq after the invasion there were meagre opportunities for detoxification, let alone rehabilitation. In the few cases where such facilities did exist, the cost of access was usually prohibitive. Meanwhile, demand increased for both sets of services, as the number of drug-abuse cases also increased.

The chaotic nature of the post-invasion Iraqi state makes it enormously difficult to hazard even a vague estimate of the number of users in the country. It has been estimated that there were more than 5,000 Iraqis consuming illicit drugs, especially heroin, in the south of the country in March 2006, compared to around 1,500 in 2004. Unconfirmed reports point to some 800 students being registered as in need of treatment in May 2010 alone. Overall, estimates for the country as a whole put the figure at about 10,000.[37]

Iraq as a Transit Route

It was not only as a major domestic market for illicit drugs that Iraq was becoming known immediately after the US-led invasion. It was acquiring importance as a transit space for narcotics mainly entering from Iran to the east. Iraq's size, its predominantly desert environment and the recent collapse of its capacity as a state had all contributed to giving a greater sense of fragility to the place than had existed under Saddam Hussein.

The head of the UNODC at the time, Antonio Costa, captured something of the predicament of Iraq. He pointed to the build-up of a 'vast network of smugglers' during the decade of sanctions in the 1990s, 'perhaps tens of thousands' in number.[38] Having lost their livelihoods with the downfall of the regime, such people were eager to find new sources of income, just like after the collapse of the Soviet Union. And they were well placed to redeploy their expertise to exploit these opportunities. During the first couple of years of the occupation the demand for the trafficking of goods was more likely to focus on the raw materials of the resistance to the US military presence, notably plastic explosive and weapons. Once the political situation began to settle down, the smugglers turned increasingly to banned goods, such as drugs.

The drugs entering Iraq were mainly opiates and cannabis. They came overwhelmingly from Iran. Maysan Province was the main conduit, at least at first. Initially, they came in small part for domestic use, but increasingly they were fulfilling the criteria of a commodity from which to extract value. If they arrived from predominantly one direction, they left from a choice of three: first, out through Iraqi Kurdistan in the north of the country; second, out through the south, via the commercial city of Basra; and third, westwards, across the desert, through Jordan. The opiates using the northern route tended to transit on towards Turkey, where they were further refined and then dispatched in the direction of Western Europe. Much of the contraband on the Basra route was shipped onwards to the borders with Kuwait and Saudi Arabia, much of the former being in the form of hemp drugs. The balance of the volume continued onwards to the southern Gulf. The authorities knew that the challenge of illegal drugs had grown well beyond anything else with which they were familiar when in 2005 security forces seized $10 million worth of contraband hashish in the southern Shia city of Najaf. Previously, a haul of this magnitude would have been unheard of. This shipment was believed to have come from Iran and to be en route across central, southern Iraq to Saudi Arabia.[39]

The westerly drugs exit route via Jordan, reflected the Kingdom's status as a drugs transit space *par excellence*. Not only had this function changed but the nature of the narcotics being trafficked across Iraqi territory had also changed. Rather than the prescription drugs that were bound for local use, it was hard drugs, notably heroin, that crossed beyond the country that was the latest risk. As we have seen, prior to the 2003 invasion, Jordan had been experiencing few problems of drugs smuggling from Iraq.[40] Most of the narcotics entering the kingdom did so from the north, and were bound for points to the south-west and south-east, rather than the east. The profile of drugs in movement were varied: hashish from Lebanon, bound for Palestine and Egypt; heroin still then refined in Turkish 'laboratories', zig-zagging back into the Middle East, and bound for Israel and Palestine; synthetic drugs such as Captagon, coming from Europe and moving towards markets in Saudi Arabia and the smaller Gulf states, where they were particularly popular. For sure, there had been a big smuggling trade from Jordan to Iraq, via the Syrian desert, in order to beat UN sanctions. But this had focused on a range of goods as varied as vehicle spare parts, guns and consumer durables. Narcotic drugs were not a serious component of this lucrative trade.

This experience changed significantly in 2004, signalled by a series of big drug finds on the Jordanian–Iraqi border, and to a lesser extent the Syrian–Iraqi and Saudi–Iraqi borders. The drug hauls included heroin, cannabis and even some cocaine (smuggled from Turkey), with the heroin widely assumed to have come from Afghanistan. There was also evidence that significant quantities of precursor chemicals used in the refining of morphine base into heroin were travelling in the other direction. These would have transited through Jordan and into Iraq (and probably from there either up to the labs in Turkey or further east into Afghanistan).

Both of these trends suggested the beginnings of an involvement by serious, established traffickers, rather than opportunist new entrants. The fact that such cargoes were being smuggled west out of Iraq (as well as south to the Gulf) suggested that established smugglers were testing possible alternatives to the principal Afghanistan–Iran–Turkey heroin route. Supporting this supposition about the involvement of established networks was the fact that the impounded heroin was hidden in long-distance lorries. TIR trucks had long been a favoured means of smuggling hard drugs for major traffickers, especially through Turkey and onto the Balkans Route.

Staring into the Abyss

By December 2005 the situation in Iraq with regard to dangerous drugs was so serious that it had prompted no less a personage than Hamid Ghodse, the then chair of the International Narcotics Control Board (INCB),[41] to raise the alarm on the subject. Interestingly, his comments were not made in response to the wave of prescription drugs that were sweeping over the Iraqi capital and its southern areas. He had been moved to speak out because of what he rightly saw as the dangers of Iraq emerging as a long-term conduit for the transit trafficking of illicit drugs. 'There is enough evidence of a problem there that we are alarmed,' he was quoted at the time as saying.[42] His concerns were apparently exacerbated by the broader alarm felt within the agency of the trafficking problem in Afghanistan becoming more severe.

In drawing attention to the vulnerability of Iraq as a porous transit space for the smuggling of hard drugs, Ghodse decided that he had to do two other things. First, he had to heap a politician's praise onto the Iraqi authorities for cooperating with the INCB and for trying to battle the drug-trafficking problem on the ground. He therefore stated that the 'political will is there', even though the Iraqi state needed assistance. In this, Ghodse was partially correct at best: Iraqis had much to grapple with, even before adding illegal drugs to the list.

Second, Ghodse wagged his finger at the international donor community for the inadequacy of their programme support. In arguing for greater resources to help Iraq in its ailing anti-narcotics strategy, Ghodse made a point of criticising those who had done relatively little to halt the drugs trade, citing insurgency and terrorism as higher priorities, a thinly veiled criticism of, among others, the USA. Ghodse stated that this was a false choice in terms of priorities. He pointed to the convergence of complementary criminal activities such as drug smuggling and terrorism, with the funds secured from the former help-ing to sustain the latter. Furthermore, he stated that the 'weakening of border controls and security infrastructure made countries into convenient logistic and transit points, not only for international terrorists and militants, but also drug traffickers'.[43] He urged Iraqi leaders and the international community to act together before the Iraq transit route became more entrenched.

Added concerns of a different sort emerged some eighteen months later, with tangible evidence that a significant part of Iraq had been planted with illicit drugs. Rice farmers of the Euphrates basin, from as far north as the central southern city of Diwaniyah to Nasiriyah at the approaches to Basra in the far south, were reported to have changed their crop-planting practices. A shortage of water had made the cultivation of rice less viable than in the past. Farmers had turned to cannabis because it uses less water, although question marks remained alongside issue of long-term sustainability.

By this stage the US authorities were sufficiently concerned to begin to revisit the issue of problem drugs in Iraq. The number of entry points into Iraq for drugs from Iran had expanded to include Nineveh and Anbar in the north and centre, and Wasit and Basra as well as Maysan in the south.[44] This diversi-fication of smuggler risk was prompted by the feeble attempts at border con-trol, borders being reported as being 'all-but [sic] wide open', and multiple agencies on the Iraqi side suffering from little or no communication. The actual policing of the border suffered from inter-agency competition, as well as low state capacity. This was largely the outcome of poor training, lack of manpower and old equipment. It was only the presence of large numbers of military personnel for more political purposes, especially in the vicinity of the border, that acted as a deterrent to the traffickers.

From 2009 the Iraq authorities began to seize significant quantities of methamphetamine precursors, ephedrine and pseudoephedrine. This sug-gested that attempts were now being taken to try to produce 'speed' locally.

By 2012 even the Iraqi police had become well known for 'pill popping'. In some of the regions of Iraq military and police officials estimate that as many as 50 per cent of their colleagues work under the influence of illicit sub-stances.[45] Though not illicit as such, steroids are the most widely abused sub-stances, as notoriously illustrated by Saddam Hussein's son Uday. Today, both insurgents and police resort frequently to such body-building drugs. An esti-mated 1,000 kilograms of steroids are manufactured improperly. Artane and alcohol too were also being used as an escape, especially from the anxieties of work, where car bombs and casual killings often singled out the police.[46]

The conflict in Syria, which began in 2011 and which is reported as having claimed some 250,000 lives, has emerged as yet another source of illicit drugs in Iraq. In the refugee camp in Domiz-Dohuk, 100,000 strong in May 2013, the impact of drugs once again appears to be moderate. Two or three camp residents are seized every day and accused of drugs-related offences. This is said to correspond to 0.5 per cent of the camp's population. However, this would appear to be a major underestimation of the scale of the problem. The Dohuk camp is regarded as being 'a ticking bomb', as far as the drugs threat is concerned. There is no reason to think that the other two main comparable Syrian camps in Iraq do not suffer from the same problems. As one would expect, levels of prostitution and crime more generally are taking place in Dohuk camp. With a large number of Syrian army deserters in the camp, a lot of mental illness has also been reported, with illicit drugs a trigger or a dependency.[47]

Conclusion

Under Saddam Hussein, Iraq's drug of choice was spirit alcohol, preferably taken in large glass tumblers; a real man's drink, in keeping with the prevailing image of Ba'thism, with its strutting, neo-fascist overtones. By contrast, drugs were regarded with suspicion or disdain, and were subject to tough penalties, especially during the 'Faith Campaign' of the 1990s. The reinvigorated circulation of problem drugs grew in the approach to the US-led invasion of Iraq. Faced with bombardment, occupation and the subsequent ravages of terrorism, ordinary Iraqis needed something to give them solace, albeit on a temporary basis.

The end of the war left Iraq defenceless and exposed. Its long land borders were prey to most forms of transnational movement. The Iranians were the first to exploit Iraq's location and their porous mutual border. With drugs to the fore, goods leaked westwards towards the European continent and southwards towards the Gulf. Soon enough, the Iraqis began to take advantage of such opportunities directly for themselves—only they did so even more successfully than the Iranians because of their experience of trafficking contraband over a fifteen-year period of international sanctions. By this time, Baghdad's moral opprobrium towards hard drugs had long since disappeared.

But Iraq's belated engagement with drugs has not been exclusively external and regional. In many parts of the country and for extended periods of time Iraq has been engulfed by drugs. The ramshackle way in which they have been consumed—from solvent sniffing to pill popping, its consumers often know not what—have had more than a little of the desperate about them, just like Iraq passing through its hell of the mid- to late 2000s. If some communities were spared its ravages that was at least in part owing to the modes of pre-modern authority present in such formations as religious communities and tribes. Whether Iraq has come out of its collective drugs overdose, or will once more have to face the effects of growing local cultivation, distribution and consumption, remains to be seen.

CONCLUSION

There is nothing particularly surprising about the relationship between drugs and the Middle East. Indeed, quite the opposite. The region has been an important area for the cultivation, consumption and distribution of such substances—predominantly hemp and opiate-based drugs—for hundreds of years, if not longer. During that time, and especially over the last couple of centuries, since Napoleon's rediscovery of the Middle East, drugs have fitted nicely into the exoticised image that Westerners have, both in the form of the direct experience of foreign visitors doing an Oriental version of the European 'Grand Tour' and the consumer fashion for all manner of things Egyptological in the nineteenth century. They have become firmly referential to other aspects of 'the East', from its sartorial tastes to its brothels to its opium dens.

Importantly, the pursuit of the East by the West has not been limited to the exotic. There has been a puritanical dimension to it as well. It is now a little over a century since the world's emerging international institutions began to develop a global regime to regulate some of the more salient aspects of the drugs sector. It certainly took some time to embed. This was partly because its proponents were starting from scratch and partly because of the slowness of the international communications of the day. Once the USA, the world's single drugs-policy superpower throughout this period, had thrown its weight behind strategies of regulation and proscription, they would prove to be very difficult to budge as the foundation of international public policy on the subject. The current generation of post-twentieth-century reformers, from Latin America and Europe too, have found it hard to roll back the policy, thereby adding to their frustration.

If regimenting drugs has emerged as a particularly Western vocation, for the rest of the world the experiences have been very different, the Middle East being no exception. There was no particular impetus or desire for radical reform on drugs, although consumption levels of cocaine and heroin were spasmodically alarming in some regional countries such as Egypt in the 1920s and 1930s. The Iranian blight has been opiates since the 1920s, with amphetamines increasingly problematic at present. Where such momentum potentially did exist, prospects of change were limited. The states that faced the drugs challenge were in their own ways ill-suited to the tasks.

Take, for instance, the critical issue of state capacity. By the time of the First World War the old dynastic regimes, the Ottoman Empire and the Qajars in Iran, were close to collapse, primarily for reasons of internal crisis; many of the other indigenous, independent regimes of the day, such as Egypt and Yemen, were experiencing eroding levels of capacity; and the newer states, mostly colonial creations such as Iraq and Lebanon, were hamstrung by the taint of illegitimacy. This helps to explain American exasperation with what Washington perceives as a lack of motivation in establishing a working partnership on the ground. Regional countries were seen as quite simply structurally inhibited and devoid of the necessary administrative culture. They were, in short, unable to play the complementary role that the USA expected because of the strides taken in the formal domain of institutional development.

Furthermore, the impact of geo-narcotics did not become any less important with the onset of the second half of the twentieth century. In Afghanistan, especially after the turmoil of successive regime collapses, this has been a key factor from the 1970s onwards.[1] This book has, however, deliberately not addressed the issue of Afghanistan, for fear that the topic would eclipse all else! Nevertheless, Afghanistan remains the 'elephant in the room' in that its location and its political economy help clearly to dictate the impact of hard and soft drugs on the Middle East proper.

Much less is known about how drugs originating in Afghanistan move from inside its borders into Europe. If more were known then global actors would quickly realise the importance of cross-border smuggling between Iran and Turkey,[2] key countries that provide a land bridge between the cultivator/refiner countries and the consumer countries. Moreover, they would then become more aware of how such drugs are transported from Istanbul in a westerly or north-westerly direction. Here, the infamous illegal staging posts, running into and through the 'Balkan Route', are crucial. It is these that deliver the heroin into the periphery of Europe. Such drugs are initially wholesaled in Eastern Europe. They are then broken up into more digestible packages, and distributed through the larger and more prosperous countries of the region with a greater mark-up.

The story of drugs in the Middle East is not, however, simply one of hard drugs. Of greater surprise, though arguably the cause of less harm to the individual (though not the environment) is the routine consumption of softer drugs as a pastime in, for example, Yemen. An estimated 30 per cent of the adult male population are believed to consume qat on a regular basis. While qat is not illegal in Yemen, it is fast being criminalised internationally,[3] along a demand trail that has taken it beyond the horn of Africa, its traditional domain, into Europe and North America. Somewhat improbably, Chinese visa offices around the world now routinely and rather soberly warn aspirant visitors that qat is considered to be as illegal as any other drug.[4]

Even the recreational use of softer drugs may also come as a surprise in relation to Israel, a country built on the idealism of clean living, moral rectitude and corporate solidarity, the realisation of which is only belatedly unravelling, most recently as a result of successive military forays into the Gaza Strip and south Lebanon. In Israel, hashish consumption is arguably more prevalent than beer drinking, especially among the Ashkenazi Jews. Peeling back the layers of the sociological onion, however, we learn that hard drugs are on the rise in Israel as well, but with Sephardi Jews, including Falashas, and Israeli Arabs more likely to be involved, as smugglers, criminals and users, than their Ashkenazi counterparts.

At the end of the nineteenth century the Middle East conformed by default to the 'open availability' model as far as the general accessibility of drugs was concerned.[5] That is to say, that there was no clear or effective international regime regulating the acquisition, use or onward supply of drugs in the region as a whole. This situation changed profoundly in the early twentieth century, when the open availability model was superseded. In its stead, two new models emerged in competition at the more global level, to vie for paradigmatic dominance: the 'penal control' model and the 'medical regulation' model.[6] Crucially, both approaches were developed rather rapidly within the Western world, notably the USA.

Neither approach made much of an impact as far as most of the developing world was concerned, as there was little indigenous impetus for change. Drug producers located in the region, notably Iran and Turkey, had no vested interest in reducing or eradicating drug production and therefore sought to avoid the reach of the penal control model, the most intrusive as far as the region was concerned. This was also clear in other regions lying more or less adjacent to the Middle East, such as India and Yugoslavia. In areas of high dependency, notably in Iran, there was a yearning for the ending of massive drug use. But, with state building still an ongoing activity, as the state capacity discussion above attests, there was little opportunity for practising the medical regulation approach.

Just because the Middle East managed to side-step drugs institution building through the first half of the twentieth century did not mean that its consolidation was not taking place. Its prospects were actually rather propitious. As McAllister notes, by 1925 the foundation had been built for an international drugs regime; by 1931 the edifice was complete.[7] Once the geo-strategic distractions—in the shape of the Second World War and the onset of the Cold War—had passed, Iran and Turkey were much more compliant than in the past. Nevertheless, it was not until the 1960s that an explosion in substance abuse began to take place in the region, within a context of growing libertarian values across the European continent.[8] The likes of Lebanon and Morocco, with their access points onto Europe, were now heavily affected, alongside Iran, Turkey and others. They would find that a multilateral framework for addressing the illicit drug problem was already in place. They would also discover that, in addition to the existing institutions, there was also a cadre of experienced global civil servants, familiar with its operation and ready to extend its practice. The ability of the region to avoid the intrusive nature of the globalising activities of the anti-drugs machinery had run out.

Further changes have taken place over the intervening six decades, since this breakthrough in the 1950s and 1960s. At least three things have changed during this broad historical trajectory. First, it has become easier to achieve a drugs 'high', a function of a range of different factors, from the proliferation of the number of illegal labs in or servicing the region, through the development of more sophisticated synthetic drugs, to the number of countries hosting them. In general, those drugs highs have become more intense and more difficult to control.

This is not the product of any one particular development. It is more a convergence of various factors. This is partly a result of the assimilation of new techniques for increasingly dangerous types of drugs, but also the more effective methods of marketing a growing range of products on behalf of the pharmaceutical sector. Wraps of cheap heroin in the poorer areas of south Tehran, associated with the emergence of an increasing culture of intravenous usage, has increased the likelihood of addiction, as well as the spread of disease. In Iraq the experience of invasion in 2003 and the subsequent civil conflict has subjected ordinary Iraqis to a level of drugs exposure that was totally absent prior to the Second Gulf War.

Second, drugs issues have become increasingly conflated with other serious intra-societal and inter-state political issues across the region. So, for example, the issue of drugs in Lebanon during the civil war became inextricably inter-connected with the presence of other social phenomena such as inter-communal violence in Lebanon, revolution in Iran and war in Iraq. Meanwhile, the so-called Arab Spring of 2011 and its aftermath have had serious consequences for the movement and consumption of illicit drugs. State borders have become more porous as a result of the political introspection of armies. Police forces in countries such as Egypt and Libya have been less evident than in the past, fearing retribution from populations that have previously suffered at the hands of a poorly trained, crudely run and unaccountable service.

Third, state responses to drugs-related challenges have become better organised and resourced than in the past. More crucially, states have begun to adopt a template for responses that have inevitably outstripped the needs of other areas of policy. This can lead to some surprising outcomes. In Saudi Arabia, the resources and profile adopted by the kingdom vis-à-vis illicit drugs was much greater than that relating to Islamist terrorism, in spite of the international shock triggered by the outrages of 9/11. In retrospect, this may be less of a surprise than expected. In the 1990s Turkish truck drivers were executed simply for trafficking Captagon pills into the kingdom, a clear case of the negative principle of disproportionality run riot in formal law, not to mention a lack of compassion towards the individuals concerned. At least in Riyadh, multiple branches of the state were mobilised in the service of drugs policy, including the Ministry of Health.

The same cannot be said for the Gulf emirate of Dubai,[9] where dedicated state responses to the drugs issue on the health side of government are virtually absent. Where the authorities have become more rigorously involved, the outcome has sometimes led to unexpected and even risible outcomes. Note, for instance, the punitive consequences for those who bring even nominal amounts of cannabis into the country. If the administration in Dubai has backed away from this rigorously zero tolerance approach, under pressure from its allies, it has found policy sanctuary in obscurity, with significant uncertainty as to what exactly is its policy.

Production

Drugs production in the Middle East has long been associated with hemp-related plants and opiates. The former tends to consist of hashish—the resinous discharge of the cannabis plant—and marijuana—the dried leaves and other parts of the plant. The two best-known examples of this marijuana-like plant are bango, which is grown in the Sinai Peninsula, eastern Egypt and Sudan, and Kif, which is located in the Rif Mountains of northern Morocco. There is a lively debate about whether bango is a drug of fashion or whether it could actually supersede hashish as the drug of choice in areas where it is cultivated. These are difficult judgements to make, as different drug-consuming constituencies have a preference for different drugs, with, for example, an eclectic social mix of intellectuals, parts of the working class and students displaying a significant preference for such drugs. In general, drug preferences have tended to undulate somewhat over time.

While some Kif is consumed locally, much of it is set aside for export. This in part reflects the impoverished nature of north Moroccan society, which tends to struggle for viability. Its fortunes have picked up over the last decade and a half, since the death of King Hasan II, as his successor, Muhammad VI, has attempted to promote other types of exports, and the north has no longer been cut off from the rest of the country in the way that it had been. Even here, Morocco has had its limitations. Much of its wealth has been built upon its illicit European market, with lines of supply crossing the Gibraltar Straits, traversing France and/or Spain, with distribution points reflecting Moroccan expatriate communities in the likes of Holland. Though production was squeezed out of the Moroccan economy in the first decade of the 2000s, a comprehensive choking off of meaningful levels of supply since the world recession of 2008 has proved to be unfeasible for reasons of social and political stability.

If Morocco has a rather sophisticated and embedded economy, illicit drugs included, much less can be said by way of describing the rest of the region. Though the Middle East was a highly significant producer of drugs in the 1960s and 1970s, its role in the economic chain has shifted away from initial, primary production to a more intermediate role since then. Consider the roll call: Iran no longer produces large amounts of opium for the export market; Turkey only produces opium under licence for the licit sector; the refining of morphine base for the heroin market and trafficked into Turkey has shifted upwards to reflect the re-emphasis of the value chain vertically in favour of Afghanistan; Lebanon only produces hashish or opium when a largely chaotic, fluctuating and weak centralised state allows it to.

Beyond hemp and opiates, only the production of speed-type drugs can be said to represent an expansion of illicit drug output. Across the region, it is in Iran where the fondness for such synthetic drugs are at their most intense. The impetus for such a trend originates from the absence of opportunities in revolutionary Iran, whether economic or political at home. Such drugs as crystal meth are popular amongst the urban young. Indeed, it is claimed that the Iranian market is the fifth largest in the world. A total of 145 crystal meth labs were closed down in one year in Tehran alone.[10]

Societal Perceptions

The consumption of dangerous drugs was at least as much a pursuit of the people as of the patrician classes, provided one had physical access to such substances and, more crucially, could afford to purchase them. This is a practice that has not differed so much from other regions. In India, for example, Portuguese observers in the eighteenth century noted that opium was consumed by the rich and the poor alike, straddling different sectarian groupings. During this time, intra-regional production and consumption elicited relatively little outside interference, in spite of the proximity and growing interest of Europe.

In Latin America, drugs, in this case coca, tended to be consumed in their raw or semi-raw state. Increasingly, drugs drew the penetration of such neighbouring powers, as did spices and tea and other exotic commodities on which Western merchants and seafarers tried to make their fortunes. The market in France for hashish from North Africa in general, and Algeria and Egypt in particular, was but one manifestation of this.

After all, there were no religiously specific invocations against the use of drugs, as there were in the Qur'an in relation to alcohol. Opium consumption in rural Iran, especially by older males, was strongly habitual, and embraced regularly and with gusto. Much if not most of the output of the cannabis from the Rif Mountains was consumed locally. It was only recently that transnational organised crime turned its aggressive attentions to the trafficking of the now commoditised substances, with big profits in view.

In these earlier, more innocent days, drugs were attractive partly because they were a source of pleasure, and partly because their consumption could be justified on the grounds of their medicinal properties, notably as a general analgesic. In this way, the consumption of drugs in the Middle East was probably not so dissimilar from such patterns in the principal European countries, especially in the mid- to late nineteenth century, when respectable laboratories were hard at work seeking to discover new and more ingenious ways of deadening the pain of humanity.

The chronology of the demonisation of drugs certainly impacted Europe well before its arrival in the Middle East. From the outset of the development and extension of a prohibition regime in 1909 and 1911, European countries such as Britain were supporting the globalisation of illegality. The situation was very different elsewhere in the world, where the colonisation process was often still in full swing, and such matters were hardly a priority when new states did emerge. As late as the 1980s, hashish was being sold openly on the streets of central Cairo, unhindered by the authorities. For Egyptians, a hashish 'joint' is the cultural equivalent of an Englishman's couple of pints of warm beer: a defining characteristic of national identity, with a discernible, though marginal, impact on health.

In the end, however, the leaders and bureaucracies of the Middle Eastern states have come to embrace the global anti-drugs regime, with a commitment comparable to or even surpassing those of the Atlantic countries half a century before. Clerics and religious establishments, like the Ministries of Awqaf, part of cabinet government more or less across the Arab world, have easily adopted the moralistic rhetoric of their counterparts in the West. They have been more willing to inveigh against illicit drugs. Often working at the behest of governments, religious figures have been more willing to transpose arguments against alcohol to all substances that are believed to addle the brain. The inexorable extension of a structure of criminality has largely squeezed out all room for ambiguity towards drugs. Within two decades the region went from the easy-going attitude of Egypt and Morocco towards the domestic consumption of cannabis to the draconian use of capital punishment for drug trafficking in countries such as Dubai and Saudi Arabia.

State Responses

Many of the states of the Middle East were unwilling to admit that their countries had a significant set of drug-related problems until the 1980s and beyond. When such an admission was eventually made, often tacitly, warily even, states were reluctant to act with authority and conviction. This was because of the secular opprobrium that often accompanied drug taking, which was identified as at best evidence of worthlessness and at worst of godlessness. There were practical problems as well; states tended not to have the necessary expertise and experience to address issues of addiction, such as detoxification and rehabilitation. By that time many of the most egregious hardships related to drugs had already established themselves. For instance, the size of the prison population that is drug-dependent is significant in the likes of Iran or Lebanon.

Over time, the actual experience of people on the ground has led increasingly to a bifurcated approach to drugs. States increasingly came to identify the drug-related agenda with aspects of applying law enforcement. This was hardly surprising, as states in most of the region had always tended to privilege coercive instruments in their establishment and operationalisation, stretching back to their very creation in the colonial period. Over time, law-enforcement specialisations based on drugs and associated criminality were introduced, both for reasons of status and to ensure that such resources went as far as possible. Bilateral agreements were concluded, notably with countries enjoying a reputation in the field, often facilitated through the likes of the US Drug Enforcement Administration, the infamous DEA. The local anti-narcotics police came over time to resemble their senior partners in the West, in their training, their SUV budgets, their uniforms, their manoeuvres, their swashbuckling style and so on.

As the senior echelons of the security state slowly and reluctantly embraced the familiar mechanism of a tough response, so ad hoc and less well-endowed responses began to manifest themselves from the health sector. This response was predicated primarily on need, and was based upon both public and private health strategies. The former was a function of the need for emergency medicine, and was based on the ability of the medical profession to turn their attention to drugs from a general background in addiction. Families turned increasingly to private medicine for reasons of reputation, to maintain the good standing of family and clan in the midst of addiction. Doctors quickly realised that there was good money to be made. This could accrue both from 'health tourism', in the case of those seeking treatment abroad, and from the assurance of discretion where families could only afford treatment at home.

As both health and interior institutions have established profiles in their respective countries, a public-policy tussle has emerged over which ministries should lead on the overall issue of drugs policy. Given the emotive nature of the subject, states have found compromise difficult over such matters. It is feared that privileging one side of the debate or the other will simply result in imbalanced policy.

One attempt to remedy this situation has been to look to a third policy participant to try to hold the ring. In Jordan, for instance, the Social Affairs Ministry was fleetingly promoted in order to take on this responsibility. This experiment has not tended to be a success. Social Affairs Ministries usually have much less capacity than their fellow bodies, especially strong and well-resourced organisations, such as Interior Ministries. They tend to be expected to address a gamut of residual social-defence-oriented issues, with small budgets and a host of special interests: a typical drugs policy conundrum, one might mischievously observe. They have tended to be poorly constituted and hence not well placed to take on one of the more powerful ministries such as Health or Interior. They simply end up getting pushed from policy pillar to policy post.

The weaknesses of other drugs-related agencies in the region has appeared to stimulate compassion on the part of Interior Ministries, rather than necessarily generating contempt. In Saudi Arabia it is the Police Ministry that runs the main, recently constituted residential rehabilitation centre in Dera. In Jordan, a similar regime applies. In Jabal Luwaibdah, one of the older, fashionable districts close to the centre of Amman, the main police station has been divided into two, with police functions situated on the ground floor and an ad hoc drug-treatment centre on the top floor. When pressed, local policemen speak in unassuming tones about not wanting to see drug abusers slip back into previous habits. With little alternate provision, there are few other places where they can be sent. At least, it is asserted, the police on duty can act as social filter to discourage local 'pushers' from trying to resume a buyer–seller relationship.

Regional Consumption

For all the difficulties of trying to establish and chart trends as far as drug consumption in the modern Middle East is concerned, one can begin to make some tentative and partially formed statements about the region that have validity. First, these relate to the types of drugs consumed. Cocaine has enjoyed periods when its profile has been significant in the region. A good example of this in practice would be the 'white drugs' epidemic of the 1920s and 1930s in Egypt, when something approximating a mass market for cocaine and heroin emerged fleetingly because of a surge in demand. However, this phenomenon also passed, perhaps over a period of twenty years or so, as the profile of soft- and hard-drug preferences returned to the traditional.

Since those days, cocaine abuse has been largely identified with the 'smart set', especially since the growth in indigenous drug consumption as a reflection of more materialist values. The lack of coca production and the attendant high prices for the cocaine that is sold in the region best explains higher prices for cocaine in the Middle East. One can still find cocaine in the region, but it tends to be the preserve of the very wealthy, including celebrities, in the night-clubs of Beirut, Casablanca or Istanbul. With the exception of the occasional 'rogue' delivery, cocaine is either brought in by individuals for personal use or is purchased from middlemen whose niche is to service the rich. Indeed, cocaine is often simply another commodity, albeit an edgier one, which is consumed in order to display extremes of wealth.

But drug consumption is not simply about conspicuous consumption. Patterns of use reflect other factors. One is a case of preference driven by geographical proximity and entrenched over time. In Iran the drug of choice is opium and its derivatives. This reflects the long period of familiarity and availability of the drug, born of local production and, more recently, location next to the super-opiates production space of central–southern Afghanistan.

In Egypt the drug of choice is hashish, reflecting proximity to the cannabis-growing areas of northern Morocco, and located on the west-to-east desert trading routes. Over time these have become well-entrenched consumption factors that have had a bearing on more subjective factors, such as taste. So for Iran there appears to be no strong demand for hashish or other hemp-related drugs. In Egypt heroin can be found on sale, but until the last decade there was no mass consumption of the drug, though this may be changing if the surge in heroin among university students is a benchmark for the future. Consequently, prices are relatively high, demonstrating that price does matter, as an incentive or disincentive to use in the region. As a result, one can say with confidence that, among drug abusers at least, there is such a thing as having a 'taste' for certain drugs, whether opiates in Iran, hashish in Egypt or marijuana in Morocco.

That is not to suggest that drugs consumers in the Middle East are rigid or static or ignorant, though there is in some places a recklessness displayed towards the consumption of drugs. This is best illustrated, not by the traditional, cultivable, narcotic drugs in the region, but in the area of synthetic, psychotropic drugs, often referred to by the colloquial shorthand of 'prescription' drugs. Arguably, it is these drugs, spanning the range of man-made 'downers' and 'uppers', that have seen the largest expansion in misuse. Some of these new trends have been recent, such as the use of Valium in Iraq in 2003 and afterwards, as part of a strategy pursued to manage anxiety stemming from the US-led invasion. A surge in demand for milder, artificial opiates has been more evident since the onset of the Egyptian 'revolution' in early 2011. This has been marketed predominantly under the commercial name of Tramadol. Increasingly, Egyptian youth (mostly males, but not exclusively so) are taking the likes of Tramadol because these are affordable drugs coming from new suppliers such as China and India.[11] They can be consumed together with other substances in a dangerous poly-drug cocktail. Locally based epidemiologists have been warning of an 'epidemic' of Tramadol sweeping the country.

Egypt and manufactured opioids are not the only illustration of such a new trend. It is stimulants that appear to be the drug of choice in the Arab Gulf states, due to boredom and the pursuit of contrived highs, such as 'dune rac-ing' in Saudi Arabia or revving up sports cars along the Shaikh Zayid Highway, the main thoroughfare out of Dubai. Captagon is the most recognisable of the commercial brands, literally enjoying a mass circulation. These pills are mainly manufactured in European countries, such as Belgium and Holland in the west, and Romania and Bulgaria in the east. Syria was another increasingly convenient source of cheap pills. Its future as a manufacturer in the context of that country's hot civil war appears uncertain. The spread of Captagon has created tremendous fear among the ruling generation in countries such as Saudi Arabia in particular, alarmed that the rising youth demographic will see its health decimated by such pill popping. Consumption concerns are also evident in some of the smaller Gulf states, drug abuse having formed a long-term problem in Kuwait.

In many ways the debates and concerns expressed by the Gulf states are reminiscent of that which took place in the Western countries in the 1970s and 1980s. Genuine fears existed that drugs would 'destroy a generation'. And there were some casualties; some people do die from consuming Ecstasy, though whether that number is, as a proportion, greater or lesser than the number that die in horse-riding accidents, equestrian events being much loved in the Arab world, especially in the Gulf, is not an issue for this work. Moreover, there is still much we do not know or understand about drugs, even in the West: their long-term impact on the brain and the nervous sys-tem; whether there is such a thing as 'an addictive personality'; whether it is helpful to speak of 'gateway drugs' in terms of the graduated nature of addic-tion; and so on.

What we do know is that for some drugs at least, use can cease. Many of the GIs who abused heroin in Vietnam ended such practices when they returned home. Young people tend to end or drastically reduce their consumption of drugs when they settle down to start a family, as the trend in Israel reveals, whatever the destructive strategy of Hizbollah. Hard-drug consumption does not simply and inexorably continue to rise; otherwise, after three or more generations of drug taking, virtually the whole world would be in some way dependent. Nevertheless, the cost of drugs is still enormous. Weaning those who are thoroughly dependent on hard drugs off them is expensive, time consuming and, like a comparable disease, alcoholism, contains no absolute endpoint of success.

Trafficking

The trend away from the local production of illicit drugs in the Middle East since the 1960s and early 1970s means that over time trafficking has become an increasingly important criminal activity when compared to intra-regional drugs production. This has occurred in two highly important ways. First, it has been an important method by which, for example, a raw drug such as Kif-style marijuana is smuggled from its production areas in the Rif Mountains northwards into Europe. Second, an increasing volume of drugs passing through the Middle East, such as heroin exiting Afghanistan for Iran, Turkey and the Balkans Route, has already been refined.

The growth of the Sahel as a transit route for coca from Latin America north and eastwards across the Atlantic, to North Africa and Europe has caused some feelings of foreboding as far as the future availability and impact of cocaine is concerned. The crime-driven nature of these flows, and their flexibility in choosing new and successful drugs routes, has certainly raised concerns that new and cheaper markets may emerge. Trafficking routes continue to be dynamic and generally responsive to changes on the ground. The latest changes appear to be taking place as far as the cocaine conduit into West Africa is concerned. Smugglers seem to have been quick to respond to new opportunities offered by political upheaval and possible state collapse, notably in Mali. They see it as a potentially softer route up into Europe. There is no apparent suggestion hitherto that the drug might be used to 'make a market' in Morocco, the purchasing power of the Moroccan economy being modest to say the least. The impact of such change can be unpredictable.

The best illustration of the trafficking of illicit drugs through the region is Dubai, in the Arab Gulf. Indeed, this is even more remarkable if one bears in mind the scale and capacity at the disposal of the emirate. With no drugs produced on the site of this 'city-state', hiding the smuggling of contraband produce clearly has its challenges. A large deep-sea dock, with a culture of criminality and impunity; a rapidly expanding airport hub, crucially with regular flights to and from Africa, Asia and Latin America; long desert borders; and an indifferent regulatory regime have all resulted in impenetrable external trading activities.

Finally, smuggling is not all one-way traffic. True, the vast majority of the inter-state flows of contraband opiate drugs move from the developing world to the developed world in a near-exclusively east-to-west direction. The one main exception in the Middle East is the precursor drug inputs that are used in the refining of the raw morphine base into heroin.[12] There is no discernible industrial need by the economy of Afghanistan to justify the importation of acetic anhydride, the transformatory input for heroin, which is manufactured in Ukraine and points west. Governments from regional countries identified as the sources of heroin are always quick to take issue with Western countries over drugs traversing from the east, while ignoring the substantial flows of drugs that emanate from the opposite direction.

NOTES

A NOTE ON TERMINOLOGY

1. Qat is 'a stimulant from the buds or leaves of *Catha Edulis*, that is chewed or drunk as tea'. The definitions of the drugs listed here, with slight modifications are taken from the CIA World Factbook, unless otherwise mentioned.
2. Heroin is 'a semisynthetic derivative of morphine'.
3. Cocaine is 'a stimulant derived from the leaves of the coca bush'.
4. Cannabis is 'the common hemp plant'.
5. Hashish is 'the resinous discharge of the cannabis or hemp plant'.

INTRODUCTION

1. Such was the vehemence with which Gaddafi propounded these ideas that they were still being debated in the Arab world some six months later. See Othman al-Mirghani in *Asharq Al-Awsat'*, 24 August 2011 reprinted in *Mideast Mirror*, 24 August 2011, in which he reminded his readers of Gaddafi's 'rats, scum and drug addicts' speeches.
2. 'Gaddafi blames Osama bin Laden, Al Qaeda and hallucinogenic drugs', *Global Post*, 24 February 2011.
3. 'Gadaffi says protestors are on hallucinatory drugs', Reuters, 24 February 2011, available at http://www.reuters.com/article/2011/02/24/us-libya-protests-gaddafi-idUSTRE71N4NI20110224, site visited 2 September 2015.
4. Author's visit to Libya, November 1980.
5. For the latest, authoritative commentary on the phenomenon, see 'Precursors', *INCB* (New York: UN, 2011).

CONTEXTUALISING DRUGS IN THE MIDDLE EAST

1. Sir Thomas Russell, *Egyptian Service, 1902–1946* (London: John Murray, 1949), p. 231.

2. Theophile Gautier, quoted in Richard Davenport-Hines, *The Pursuit of Oblivion: A Global History of Narcotics* (London: Weidenfeld & Nicolson, 2001), p. 61.

3. Nikki Keddie, *The Roots of Revolution: An Interpretive History of Modern Iran* (New Haven: Yale University Press, 1981), p. 28.

4. National Health Insurance Commission (England) Minute Paper, attached to Board of Trade correspondence, 29 May 1916, FO371/1533.

5. Report on the Traffic in Narcotic Drugs in Constantinople during the period 1919–1923, drawn up by Major H.G. Hobson, Sanitary Commissioner, 8 August 1923, FO371/9249.

6. W. B. McAllister, *Drug Diplomacy in the Twentieth Century* (London: Routledge, 2000), p. 4.

7. Memorandum, dated 26 August 1921. Drawn up and signed by Lt.-Col. H. Woods, British representative of the Commission of Economic Studies, British High Commission, Constantinople, 14 September 1921, FO371/6657.

8. 'Memorandum for Dr Refik Bey, the Minister of Health for the Republic of Turkey', supplied with suggestions of how the Turkish government might suppress drug trafficking, 18 July 1929, FO371/13973.

9. 'Traffic in Opium and Other Dangerous Drugs', note by Secretary-General of the League of Nations, Geneva, 12 November 1929, p. 1, FO7024.

10. See extract from draft of Lausanne Treaty, pp. 68, article 9, and 125, article 4, 1923, FO371/9243.

11. Anderson, Home Office–Foreign Office, 30 May 1930, FO371/14758.

12. Edmonds–Cushendun, 27 September 1928, FO371/13258.

13. Bango is a rough, hemp-like plant, the whole of which can be—and often is—consumed.

14. Lindsay, Constantinople–Chamberlain, London, 14 June 1926, FO371/11714.

15. Though with the Iranians apparently doing so more publicly and less discreetly than the Turks: Clerk–Lloyd, 28 January 1929, FO371/13969.

16. Paul B. Stares, *Global Habit: The Drug Problem in a Borderless World* (Washington: Brookings, 1996), p. 22.

17. Penny Green, *Drugs, Trafficking and Criminal Policy: The Scapegoat Strategy* (Winchester: Waterside Press, 1998), p. 134.

18. Not that this necessarily amounted to a winning combination. For example, Russell's attempts to bring about the institutional marriage of the Coastguards and the Frontiers Administration, responsible for policing the Suez Canal and the Sinai respectively, was unsuccessful, even though Syria and Palestine were the main routes for hashish entering Egypt. Though a patient man, steeped in the political and bureaucratic culture of Egypt, even Russell had his failures. See Russell, Cairo City Police–Delevingne, 5 February 1942, FO371/31048.

19. According to Russell Pasha, the CNIB had secured four areas of success: to combat narcotic trafficking and addiction in Egypt; to trace and discover the origin of

narcotics entering the country; to cooperate internationally to supress global illicit traffic; and to represent Egypt's broader obligations within the League of Nations. See Russell–Shone, British Embassy, 26 December 1943, FO371/39364.

20. Annual Report on Egypt, 1922, submitted 16 December 1922, by Lord Allenby, High Commissioner, Cairo, FO/846/29.

21. For an authoritative description of how hashish is trafficked into and distributed within Egypt, see 'Report on Hashish Traffic in Egypt', Compiled in the European Dept., Ministry of Interior, February 1924, FO/846/29.

22. Russell, *Egyptian Service*, p. 231.

23. Ibid., p. 223.

24. Egypt was a conduit for the supply of quinine in order to alleviate the effects of malaria during the Second World War. See, for example, a deal involving 10 million quinine tablets, eventually supplied on credit, against the expected supply of 30 tons of opium. Angora (Ankara)—Ministry of Economic Warfare, 5 July 1944, FO371/44095.

25. Russell was also concerned with the 'black drugs', hashish and opium, though the effects of such drugs were never as serious as in the case of the 'white drugs'.

26. Ronald Seth, *Russell Pasha* (London: Wm Kimber, 1966), p. 175.

27. These fines were deemed to be 'hopelessly inadequate' by foreign experts who knew the situation on the ground well. See, for example, letter to editor of *The Times* from a priest, Herbert Hayes, 5 October 1921.

28. Seth, *Russell Pasha*, pp. 180–1.

29. For nine successive years Russell attended the Advisory Committee on Opium and Other Dangerous Drugs at Geneva as the representative of Egypt.

30. Elgin Groseclose, *Introduction to Iran* (New York: Oxford University Press, 1947).

31. Foreign Office, 'Traffic in Opium and Other Dangerous Drugs', Annual Report for the Year, 1928/9, Persian Government–Secretary-General–League of Nations, 12 November 1929.

32. Groseclose, *Introduction*, p. 215.

33. Groseclose, *Introduction*, p. 214.

34. For a reflection on attempts to curb opium production during a critical period, from the mid- to late 1950s, see A. E. Wright, 'The struggle against the evil of narcotics up to 1960', *Bulletin on Narcotics*, 3 (1960).

35. W. H. Forbis, *The Fall of the Peacock Throne: The Story of Iran* (New York: Harper & Row, 1980) p. 179.

36. 'Turkey–Iran "opium war" escalates, Iran to resume production', *Daily News*, Ankara, 15 January 1969.

37. 'Iranian premier Hoveida arrives', *Daily News*, Ankara, 11 June 1969. The two dominant issues on which the Iranian government used its leverage were the possible construction of a pipeline through Turkey to carry Iranian oil and regional relations between Iran and the Arab world, especially over Iraq and the United Arab Republic.

38. Forbis, *The Fall of the Peacock Throne*, p. 180.

39. For an insight into President Nixon's own strong views on the subject of illicit drugs see retrospectively Richard Nixon, *In the Arena: A Memoir of Victory, Defeat and Renewal* (New York: Simon & Schuster, 1990), p. 134, and Nixon quoted in Richard Reeves, *President Nixon: Alone in the White House* (New York: Simon & Schuster, 2001), p. 245.

40. Feroz Ahmed, *The Turkish Experiment in Democracy, 1950–1975* (London: Hurst/ RIIA, 1977), p. 417.

41. There would be two further technocratic premiers, Ferit Melen and Naim Talu, though both administrations would suffer from the same structural weaknesses as that of Erim.

42. James W. Spain, 'The United States, Turkey and the poppy', *Middle East Journal*, 29 (3) (Summer 1975), pp. 295–309, p. 304.

43. Poppy straw is 'the entire cut and dried opium, poppy-plant material, other than the seeds'. Opium is extracted from the poppy straw.

1. MOROCCO: 'THE GREEN PETROL'

1. See YouTube footage of a William Shawcross documentary entitled *Queen and Country*, 2002.

2. It was told to me by a British diplomat at a dinner party in Rabat on 16 April 2012.

3. In Morocco, the Royal Gendarmerie tend to be relatively well organised and well paid, making them the most loyal branch of law enforcement, compared to both the army and the police. They enjoyed a reputation for being particularly loyal to King Hasan II.

4. Such 'drugs tourists' from the West who languish in Moroccan jails for drugs-related offences are widely known as being 'a sorry bunch'.

5. Ketterer, 'Networks of discontent in northern Morocco', pp. 30–4.

6. Pete Brady, 'Moroccan hashish journey', *Cannabis Culture Magazine*: see http://www.cannabisculture.com/v2/print/5618, site visited 23 February 2012.

7. C. R. Pennell, *Morocco* (Oxford: Oneworld, 2003), p. 146.

8. See Walter B. Harris, *France, Spain and the Rif* (London: Edward Arnold, 1927).

9. Unattributable interview, 17 April 2012.

10. Douglas E. Ashford, *Political Change in Morocco* (Princeton: Princeton University Press, 1961) p. 22.

11. Barry James, 'France's odd silence on Moroccan drug trade', *New York Times*, 20 November 1995, available at http://nytimes.com/1995/11/20/news/20iht-drugs.t _l.html?pagewanted=print, site visited 23 February 2012.

12. Observatoire geopolitique des drogues report in Tim Boekhout van Solinge, 'Drug use and drug trafficking in Europe', *CEDRO*, http://www.cedro-uva.org/lib/boek-hout.drug.html, site visited 23 February 2012.

13. Nick Pelham, 'Morocco's king shows tolerance as late rains bring record hashish crop', *The Independent*, 15 August 2000.

14. James, 'France's odd silence'.

15. Boekhout van Solinge, 'Drug use and drug trafficking in Europe'.

16. US Department of State, '1996 International Narcotics Control Strategy Report, March 1997', available at http://www.hri.org/docs/USSD-INCSR/96/AME/Morocco.html, site visited 23 February 2012.

17. See James, 'France's odd silence'; Nadelman, 'Commonsense drug policy', p. 123.

18. 'Cannabis in the Rif, Morocco', http://laniel.free.fr/INDEXES/GraphicsIndex/KIFIN_MOROCCO/Cannabis_Moroc., site visited 23 February 2012.

19. US Department of State, '1996 International Narcotics Control Strategy Report, March 1997', http://www.hri.org/docs/USSD-INCSR/96/AME/Morocco.html, site visited 23 February 2012.

20. 'Making a hash of it', *The Economist*, 13 July 2006.

21. Giles Tremlett, 'Ketama Gold puts Morocco top of Europe's cannabis league', *The Guardian*, 27 May 2003.

22. Susan Taylor Martin, 'Harboring hashish', *St Petersburg Times, Online*, 17 June 2002, http://www.sptimes.com/2002/06/17/news_pf/Worldandnation/Harboring_hashish.sht..., site visited 23 February 2012.

23. As described by one of the country's dissident singers of the day. See Steven Erlanger, 'Moroccan rap star hits political notes', *International Herald Tribune*, 22–23 August 2009.

24. 'DROGUE Malgre la "lutte sans merci" déclarée en 1992 par Hassan II: Les cultures de cannabis se sont encore etendues au Maroc', *Le Monde*, 25 May 1994.

25. 'Morocco: Country Profile, Drugs and Crime', p. 4.

26. 'Africa and the Middle East', at http://www.state.gov/j/inl/rls/nrcrpt/2006/vol1/html/62112.htm, site visited 11 May 2012.

27. On the Berbers of Morocco see Michael Brett and Elizabeth Fentress, *The Berbers: People of Africa* (Oxford: Blackwell, 1996).

28. Christopher Petkanas, 'The last casbah: with Marrakesh now Miami in a caftan, Tangier remains the destination du jour for romantic dropouts', available at NYTimes.com/tmagazine, p. 53.

29. Unattributable interview with official, Rabat, 21 April 2012.

30. Pelham, 'Morocco's king shows tolerance'.

31. Bureau of International Narcotics and Law Enforcement Affairs, '2008 International Narcotics Control Strategy Report for Morocco', 27 February 2009, available at http://morocco.usembassy.gov/policy/key-reports/2008-international-narcotics-control, site visited 14 August 2015.

32. Ibid.

33. Abdellatif El Azizi, 'Maroc Connexion', *Telquel*, no. 257, 20–26 (January 2007).

34. These remarks are drawn from the statement of then Foreign Minister Taieb Fassi

Fihri, during a visit to Spain in 2010. 'Morocco: drug trafficking rising', available at http://www.news24.com/printArticle.aspx?iframe&aid=Oe456e11–38be-48e6–83ac-83, site visited 23 February 2012.

35. Interview, Abdelkrim Bennani, Palace official, Rabat, 19 April 2012.

36. 'Morocco: fighting the drugs war', *HighBeam RESEARCH*, available at http://www.highbeam.com/doc/1G1–13886112.html/print, site visited 23 February 2012.

37. 'Agriculture in Morocco', Wikipedia, available at http://en.wikipedia.org/wiki/Agriculture_in_Morocco, site visited 23 February 2012.

38. 'Morocco: Drug trafficking rising'.

39. Unattributable interview with foreign official, Rabat, 20 April 2012.

40. 'Africa and the Middle East'.

41. Morocco supplies Melilla with perishable products, while about 35,000 Moroccans cross daily either to work or to shop. See 'Moroccans blockade Spanish enclave in North Africa' in Associated Press, 13 August 2010.

42. I am grateful to Laia Soto Bermont, a doctoral candidate at the University of Oxford, for drawing this concept to my attention. 12 June 2012.

43. Martin Elvins, *Anti-Drugs Policies of the European Union* (Basingstoke: Palgrave, 2003), pp. 72–92.

44. Raphael Minder, 'Spain's dangerous mix: drugs, unemployment and austerity', *International Herald Tribune*, 31 May 2012.

45. For Tangiers and its more flamboyant visitors see Iain Finlayman, *Tangier: City of Dreams* (London: Flamingo, 1993).

46. This is a description that the Moroccan state itself admits.

2. LEBANON: LOCAL FASHION, REGIONAL POLITICS

1. 'LEBANON: Fashion show highlights drugs problem amongst Lebanese youths', itnsource.com, 30 September 2010. Supplemented with assorted interview material.

2. Sultan Sleiman, 'Declining fortunes for Lebanon's agriculture', Reuters, 19 March 2001.

3. Jonathan Randal, *The Tragedy of Lebanon* (London: Hogarth Press, 1990), p. 137.

4. 'Lebanon: crop production', available at http://www.country-data.com/cgi-bin/query/r-8014.html, site visited 13 August 2010. Data as from December 1987.

5. Nicholas Blanford, 'Lebanon's green economy—the marijuana surge', *Ya Libnan*, 16 October 2007, available at http://yalibnan.com/site/archives/2007/10/lebanons_green.php, site visited 13 August 2010.

6. Avner Yaniv, *Dilemmas of Security* (Oxford: Oxford University Press, 1987), p. 81.

7. Randal, *The Tragedy of Lebanon*, p. 287.

8. Gary Gambill, 'Syria after Lebanon: Hooked on Lebanon', *Middle East Quarterly* (Fall 2005), pp. 35–42, p. 35.

9. For a detailed, unverifiable but eminently plausible description of how the interface between drugs and occupation worked in Lebanon see Jihad Rene Albani, 'History of the Drug Traffic in Lebanon and Syria', 2 February 2001, available at http://www.10452lccc.com/reports/rene/traficing.htm, site visited 19 August 2011.

10. Nick B. Williams, 'Syrians cash in on drug trade in Lebanon's notorious Bakaa Valley narcotics: some suggest that the money trail reaches all the way to Damascus', *Los Angeles Times*, 27 January 1992.

11. 'Lebanon: crop production'.

12. Sleiman, 'Declining fortunes for Lebanon's agriculture'.

13. Chastening, because upon his eventual return to Lebanon Michel Aoun switched sides, joining the Syrian-led alliance of its Lebanese allies. Indeed, Aoun's would be the faction's largest Christian component.

14. US Department of State, International Narcotics Control Strategy Report, March 1995, available at http://almashriq.hiof.no/lebanon/300/360/362/narco-leb-95.html, site visited 13 August 2010.

15. In March 1998 Beirut adopted an anti-narcotics law, but omitted to involve local banking and financial organisations in its measures, or coordinate closely with international institutions. See Rima Fahl, 'Dirty laundry', in *MEED, Special Report Banking*, 2 March 2001, p. 36.

16. UNODC, 'Country Profile: Lebanon', 2007, available at http://www.unodc.org/egypt/en/country_profile_lebanon.html, site visited 19 August 2011.

17. E. Aaraj and J. Hermez, 'The drug problem in the Middle East: strategies and results', Soins Infirmiers et Developpment Communitaire, June 1998, p. 6.

18. Donald Neff, 'No more heroin in the Beqaa?', *Middle East International*, 5 December 1997, p. 14.

19. Ibid.

20. Brian Whitaker, 'Green gold', *The Guardian*, 11 June 2001.

21. Neil MacFarquhar, 'Lebanese Farmers Miss the Good Old Days', *IHT*, 6 April 2001.

22. Hack, Christopher, 'World: Middle East Lebanon's growing drug worries', BBC, 11 October 1998, available at http://news.bbc.co.uk/1/hi/world/middle_east/191154.stm, site visited 19 July 2011.

23. US Department of State, 'International Narcotics Control Board Report, 1998', February 1999, available at http://www.clhrf.com/reports/narcoticslebanon.htm, site visited 13 August 2010.

24. Whitaker, 'Green gold'.

25. Blanford, 'Lebanon's green economy'.

26. This was an insurgency in the Palestinian camps in northern Lebanon. It proved stubbornly difficult to put down. In the end the Lebanese military succeeded, but only after sustaining significant casualties.

27. Interview, Michel Sukkour, former head of Drug Enforcement Bureau, Ministry of Interior, 27 September 2010.

28. Quoted in 'Illicit drugs in Lebanon: the current state of play US report outlines problems, action', *Lebanonwire*, 6 June 2003.

29. Nicholas Blanford, 'Lebanon's drug barons reap a bumper harvest as soldiers steer clear', *The Times*, 20 October 2008.

30. Interview, Michel Sukkour.

31. Arguably the ISF's capability has been growing as a result of the specialist training being rendered by the USA. See 'US assistant chief for narcotics says his country provides training to ISF', *NOW Lebanon*, 14 January 2010, available at www.nowlebanon.com.

32. One report referring to the 2001 planting in defiance of the cannabis ban stated that in one unnamed village in the Beqaa it was claimed that there were 460 adults and 400 guns: Whitaker, 'Green gold'.

33. Blanford, Ibid.

34. 'Meet Noah, one of Lebanon's drug barons', AFP, 4 October 2008.

35. Deirdre Collings describes Valium addiction as 'a problem for many women' in Lebanese society. See 'Peace for Lebanon? Reflections on a question', in Deirdre Collings, ed., *Peace for Lebanon? From War to Reconstruction* (Boulder: Lynne Rienner, 1994), p. 304.

36. There are labs in Lebanon attempting to make Ecstasy pills, but these are generally dismissed as being of poor quality, less powerful and of having a lesser status than their European-manufactured counterparts.

37. Elie G. Karam, Lillian A. Ghandour, Wadih E. Maalouf, Karim Yamout and Mariana M. Salamoun, 'A rapid situation assessment (RSA) study of alcohol and drug abuse in Lebanon', *J. Med. Liban* 58, 2 (2010), pp. 76–85, p. 76.

38. The ballpark figure used by Nadya Mikdashi, the executive director of SKOUN, one of Lebanon's most important handful of anti-drugs NGOs.

39. Karam et al., 'A rapid situation assessment', p. 76.

40. 'Ecstasy a growing rave in Lebanon's drug market', *Daily Star*, 3 July 2010.

41. That is to say $3,000 a month, with sales rapidly falling off in the chill of the winter months.

42. Mona Alami, 'Party drug nation', *NOW*, 15 August 2010, available at http://www.nowlebanon.com/Print.aspx?ID=194082, site visited 19 August 2011.

43. See 1,097 sample survey conducted jointly between the Ministry of Education and the Pompidou Group of the Council of Europe. See 'Cannabis most popular illegal drug among students', *Daily Star*, 10 October 2009.

44. Karam et al., 'A rapid situation assessment', p. 76.

45. Patrick Galey, 'Inadequate border control sees increased drug flow into Lebanon', *Daily Star*, 3 March 2010.

46. Rosemary Sayigh, 'Palestinians in Lebanon: uncertain future', in Collings, ed., *Peace for Lebanon?*, p. 104.

47. To quote a contemporary tourism minister.

48. Judith Palmer Harik, *Hezbollah* (London: I. B. Tauris, 2004), p. 108.

49. Hasan Nasrallah speech, quoted in 'Ecstasy a growing rave', *Daily Star*, 3 July 2010.

50. For example, a known Mexican trafficker of Lebanese descent, Salim Boughader Mucharrafille, was arrested in 2002 for smuggling 200 people across the border, said to include Hizbollah [sic] supporters. See 'WT exclusive: Hezbollah [*sic*] uses Mexican drug routes into US', *Ya Libnan*, 27 March 2009.

51. See, for example, the Bogatá-based Lebanese alleged money launderer, Shukri Mahmoud Harb, who apparently had links with both Colombian cocaine cartels and Hizbollah [sic]. See Annie Jacobsen, 'Hezbollah and drugs lords: a dangerous alliance', 17 November 2008, available at http://www.the aviationnation.com/2008/11/17/hezbollah-on-drugs, site visited 11 October 2010.

52. For example, see Tom Knowlton, 'Al Qaeda and Hezbollah plot a dangerous alliance', *Defence Watch*, 1 January 2003, in which the article said: 'Western analysts believe that Hezbollah [*sic*], which receives significant amounts of overt military and financial aid from Iran and Syria, is involved in drug trafficking predominantly for the purpose of the [*sic*] facilitating the fall of the West through drug addiction'. See http://www.freerepublic.com/focus/f-news/815186/posts, site visited 11 October 2010.

53. The original report was carried in *Der Spiegel*. See David Lev, 'Report: Hizbullah [sic] earning millions off European drugs trade', *Israel News*, 1 September 2010.

54. Dalila Mahdawi, 'Hizbullah [sic] denies profiting from German drugs trade', *Daily Star*, 11 January 2010.

55. Interview, Antoine Laham, 29 September, 2010.

56. Interview, Chantal Chedid, clinical psychologist, SKOUN, 23 September 2010.

57. Interview, Nadya Mikdashi, co-founder and executive director, SKOUN, 23 September 2010.

58. Most of this section is based on a visit to the Zouk Mikael headquarters of the NGO hosted by Nadi Sfeir, and featuring conversations with half a dozen of the charity's staff. Visit took place on 24 September 2010.

59. An approach to drugs rehabilitation now some forty-five years old, in which increasing levels of individual and social responsibility are practised within a drugs-free residential setting. See Oum el-Nour, *Annual Magazine, 2005*, issue 15, p. 17.

60. Oum el-Nour, *Annual Magazine, 2009* issue 18, p. 27.

61. Interview, Father Hadi Aya, Roumieh jail, 23 September 2010.

3. QAT IN YEMEN: JEOPARDISING DEVELOPMENT

1. In the UN human development index, Yemen is 153rd out of 177 countries.

2. It does so in two ways. First, because over time qat consumption 'tends to reduce the workers' motivation'. Second, because of the long lunch breaks, that for many

commence at midday. See Robert Draper III, 'Medical issues in Yemen—typhoid, qat and malaria are just a few', available at thesop.org, site visited 24 September 2006.

3. Shelagh Weir, 'Economic aspects of the qat industry in north-west Yemen', in B. R. Pridham, ed., *Economy, Society and Culture in Contemporary Yemen* (London: Croom Helm, 1985), pp. 64–82, p. 64.

4. Shelagh Weir, *A Tribal Order* (London: British Museum Press, 2007), p. 20.

5. Martha Mundy, *Domestic Government: Kinship, Community and Polity in North Yemen* (London: I. B. Tauris, 1995), p. 74.

6. For example, it had forbidden qat growing on state-owned land, and consumption was only permitted at the weekends. See Brian Whitaker, 'Weaning Yemen off qat', *Middle East International*, 18 June 1999. For a more detailed listing of the restrictions on the part of the PDRY see the 1977 Qat Laws.

7. It was widely assumed on the Arabian Peninsula, notably by Saudi Arabia, that the government of North Yemen had prior knowledge of the Iraqi invasion of Kuwait on 2 August 1990. Underlying the alleged conspiracy was a plan for the dismemberment of Saudi Arabia, with North Yemen receiving the Asir.

8. Tim Mackintosh-Smith, 'Yemen—travels in dictionary land', posted on the Qat page, available at http://www.al-bab.com/yemen/soc/qat.htm, site visited 15 June 2010.

9. Abdul Rahim al-Showthabi, 'As qat prices increase on occasions, people still continue to buy it', *Yemen Post*, 20 October 2008.

10. In Kuwait men and women operate parallel informal systems of visiting, based roughly on their position in the social hierarchy. During those visits, at which the use of stimulants is limited to tea and coffee, participants debate and discuss matters with one another, including issues of national importance.

11. Some claim that female participation in qat sessions has risen as high as 40 per cent of the population. The male rate is claimed to be over 80 per cent. Robert Fox, 'A national obsession', *Sanaa*, 16 March 2010. See http://www.travelblog. org/Middle-East/Yemen/Sanaa/blog-482776.html The figure for male consumption is also the one cited in Tim Marshall, 'Yemen: legal high Is "fueling extremism"', Sky News, 15 January 2010.

12. One author writing about contemporary Yemen has stated: 'Trying to do business in Yemen without chewing qat would be like trying to do business in Washington or London without doing lunch, dinner or drinks.' See Elisabeth Eaves, 'Dispatches From Yemen', *Slate*, 21 May 2004.

13. For an insight into mediation, including the use of qat, see Paul Dresch, *Tribes, Government and History in Yemen* (Oxford: Clarendon Press, 1989; Oxford: Clarendon Paperbacks 1993), p. 53.

14. Franco Grima, *Warriors of Arabia* (Malta: Franco Grima, 2009) p. 174.

15. Shelagh Weir, *Qat in Yemen: Consumption and Social Change* (London: British Museum Press, 1985), p. 40.

16. In the disparaging words of Hugh Scott, explorer and scientist, writing some seventy years ago. See Hugh Scott, *In the High Yemen* (London: John Murray, 1942), p. 95.

17. Claude Fayein, *A French Doctor in the Yemen* (London: Robert Hale Ltd, 1957), p. 37.

18. The unemployment rate, though frankly unknown, is estimated to be 40 per cent, and doubling every twenty-five years. Half the country is living on an income of less than $2 a day.

19. Michael Horton, 'Yemen's dangerous addiction to qat', *Jamestown Foundation Terrorism Monitor*, 17 April 2010.

20. World Food Programme figures cited in Hugh Macleod and John Vidal, 'Yemen threatens to chew itself to death over thirst for narcotic qat plant', available at http://www.theguardian.com/environment/2010/feb/26/yemen-qat-water-drought, site visited 26 February 2010.

21. Magda Abu-Fadil, 'Qat increasingly turns on Yemeni women groupies', *Huffington Post*, 7 February 2009.

22. 'Official authorities seek to eliminate qat trees', *Yemen Post*, 10 April 2010.

23. More recently this has been countered by a study by the Yemeni academic Fethi Sakkaf, who estimates that 20 million working hours are lost every day in Yemen through staff leaving work early to prepare for qat consumption. Study mentioned in Mohamed Hasni, 'War deprives Yemeni elite of drug of choice', available at http://www.telegraph.co.uk/expat/expatnews/6642189/War-deprives-Yemeni-elite-of-drug-of-choice.html, site visited 24 November 2009.

24. The author Kevin Rushby, for example, has eulogised the consumption of qat in his book *Eating the Flowers of Paradise*, in which he writes of there being 'no rush, just a silky transition, scarcely noticed, and then the room casts loose its moorings. "Capturing moments of eternity", someone once called the subtle tinkering with time that Qat effects.' Reprinted in Mohamed Elmasry, 'Yemen, coffee and qat', *MediaMonitors*, 20 April 2007.

25. See Dresch's criticism in *Tribes, Government and History in Yemen* (1993), p. 20.

26. Horton, Ibid.

27. Christopher Ward, 'Practical responses to extreme groundwater overdraft in Yemen', in Kamil A. Mahdi, Anna Wurth and Helen Lackner, eds., *Yemen into the Twenty-First Century* (Reading: Ithaca, 2007), pp. 155–181, p. 157.

28. Macleod and Vidal, 'Yemen threatens to chew itself to death'.

29. Horton, Ibid.

30. The World Bank reject this assertion, pointing out that 90 per cent of the crop is grown by small farmers. See Julie Valoria-Williams of the World Bank, quoted in Abigail Fielding-Smith, 'Yemen economy hooked on qat', *Financial Times*, 20 January 2010.

31. Sanaa has at least three qat markets in the central *souq*, and there is a more perma-

nent set of dealers on the city's northern rim, who operate from shops and small stalls. See Roger Gaess, 'Why Yemen is qat's cradle', *Globe and Mail*, 6 January 2010.

32. Horton, Ibid.
33. 'Water crisis threatens state's future', *Oxford Analytica*, 24 May 2010.
34. Tutwiler, 'Research agenda for sustainable agricultural growth', p. 229.
35. Gaess, 'Why Yemen is qat's cradle'.
36. Abdulsattar Hatitah, 'Tackling Yemen's qat epidemic', *Asharq al-Awsat*, 11 August 2009.
37. 'Yemen's qat habit soaks up water', *al-Motamar*, 12 April 2007.
38. Abdul Ghani et al., 'The influence of khat-chewing on birth-weight', pp. 1–3.
39. Jane Novak, 'Qat and babies', *Yemen Times*, 26 November 2007.
40. Yusuf al-Shiraif, 'Qat: the cursed plant in Yemen', originally published in *Weghat Naza* magazine, translated and reprinted in *Yemen Times*, 11 January 2010.
41. The joke is reproduced in Robert D. Burrowes, *The Yemen Arab Republic* (Boulder: Westview/Croom Helm, 1987), p. 93.
42. Hatitah, 'Tackling Yemen's qat epidemic'.
43. Al-Shiraif, 'Qat: the cursed plant in Yemen'.
44. Elmasry, 'Yemen, coffee and qat'.
45. Ibid.
46. Horton, 'Yemen's dangerous addition'.
47. Paul Dresch, *A History of Modern Yemen* (Cambridge: Cambridge University Press, 2000).
48. This should be viewed as more of a provincial and clan-related rebellion than a sectarian struggle, both the Houthis and former President Saleh coming from the Zaidi or Shia community in Yemen. The rebels have raised a set of demands that are political rather than primordial in nature, and which, if recognised, would confer upon them tangible political privileges.
49. 'Qat leaves bind troops and rebels alike', *Gulf News*, 7 November 2009.
50. Ibid.
51. Stephanie Hancock, 'Kicking Yemen's qat habit', BBC, 2 August 2008.
52. J. E. Peterson, *Yemen: The Search for a Modern State* (London: Croom Helm, 1982), p. 77.
53. Whitaker, 'Weaning Yemen off qat'.
54. Fayein, *A French Doctor in the Yemen*, p. 126.
55. 'Narcotic Leaf the Key to Yemeni Life in Britain', Reuters, 15 July 2001.
56. Ethiopian qat is reputed to be superior to the qat grown in Yemen.
57. For example, the likes of Germany, the Netherlands and Scandinavia all proscribe it.
58. 'Qat ban fails in US', Yemen Gateway's Qat Page, 25 November 2000.
59. Duraid al-Baik, 'Qat cripples Yemen', *Gulf News*, 26 October 2006.

4. EGYPT: THE LAND OF THE HASHISHEEN

1. See analysis of illicit drugs sector in Egypt during the age of Sir Thomas Russell, Sir Thomas Russell, *Egyptian Service, 1902–1946* (London: John Murray, 1949).

2. 'Egypt: drug trafficking', December 1990, available at http://www.country-data. com/cgi-bin/query/r-4190.html, site visited 15 March 2011.

3. Extended author visit to el-Batniyyeh, 18 November 2012.

4. The film starred a famous Egyptian actor, Ahmad Zaki.

5. Ashraf Khalil, 'Drug smokers in Egypt suffer hashish shortage after crackdown', *Times Online*, 5 May 2010.

6. 'Egypt: drug trafficking'.

7. According to the FCO travel advisory for Egypt: 'Possession, use or trafficking in illegal drugs is a serious offence and can, even for possession of small amounts, lead to lengthy prison sentences (25 years), life imprisonment or the death penalty. Those convicted to life imprisonment on drugs charges will normally spend the rest of their life in prison with no possibility of parole or pardon.' See http://www. fco.gov.uk/en/travel-and-living-abroad, updated 10 March 2011.

8. Adam Makary, 'Egypt needs to wage war on drugs', Al-Jazeera, 25 October 2008, available at http://www.aljazeera.com/focus/2009/10/200910203538491522. html, site visited 15 May 2014.

9. Interview, Professor Imad Hamdi, 16 April 2011.

10. Gabriel G. Nahas, 'Hashish in Islam 9th to 18th century', *Bulletin of the New York Academy*, pp. 814–31, p. 817.

11. Most of the next section is based on the data collection by Professor Imad Hamdi, head of the department of psychiatry, Cairo University, and his research team under the overall title of 'The National Addiction Research Program: Substance Use and Misuse in Cairo (2007–2008)'. Power point presentation of the headline figures given to the author by Prof. Hamdi.

12. The study was produced by the Fund for the Prevention and Treatment of Addiction and Abuse. See 'Abdel Salam, Mohamed, 'Egypt report links drugs to sexual exploitation of girls', *Bikyamasr*, 11 August 2010, available at http://bikya-masr.com/wordpress/?p=15528, site visited 17 March 2011.

13. For a recent paper focusing on the profile of females in the drugs problem in Egypt, see Dr Laila Abdul Jawad, 'Waraqa amal hul al-tafaalat al-asriya wa taalata al-mukhadarat lida al-inaath', Ministry of Housing, Cairo, 2009.

14. 'Hashish shortage in Egypt sparks plot theories', *Egypt News*, 6 April 2010 quotes one smoker who says: 'I prefer hashish. Bango drives me crazy—it's too strong.'

15. In a recent example, four unemployed labourers were apprehended following the killing of a young woman, when she resisted their attempts to sexually assault her. See 'Eye on crime', *Daily News*, 10 October 2008.

16. Yomna Kamel, 'The culture of bango', *Middle East Times*, 22 April 2008.

17. 'El Bango', lyrics by Islam Khalil, translated by Tahseen Alkoudsi, and available at http://www.shira.net/music/lyrics/el-bango.htm, site visited 10 May 2011.

18. Figures taken from a study by Egypt's National Council for Fighting and Treating Addiction and published in '6 million drug addicts in Egypt: study', AFP, 3 October 2007.

19. 'Egypt Drug Addiction', Narconon Egypt website, available at www.narconan.org/drug-rehab/Egypt, site visited 17 March 2011.

20. Interview, Ehab el-Kharrat, head of Freedom NGO, 11 April, 2011.

21. Reem Nafie, 'Drug empire falls', *al-Ahram Weekly*, no. 679, 4–10 March 2004.

22. 'Egypt: 120 bango farms discovered in Sinai', available at http://www.highbeam.com/doc/1G1-58309196.html, site visited 10 May 2011.

23. See Helen Miles, who corroborates the self-indulgence of the well to do in 'Drugs: Egypt takes on the traffickers', Free Online Library, available at http://www.thefreelibrary.com/Drugs+-+Egypt+takes+on+the+traffickers.-a016999836, site visited 15 May 2014.

24. In reality, Tramadol and its ilk are included in the category of pharmaceutical drugs, third on the list of most abused drugs in Egypt, rather than being included with the opiates, thereby effectively under-counting the impact of opiates.

25. Interview, Professor Imad Hamdi, 16 April 2011.

26. Makary, 'Egypt needs to wage war on drugs'.

27. According to a 2008 report from the General Direction to Fight Drugs [*sic*], approved by the International Drugs Committee during its fiftieth session held in Vienna in 2007, Egypt is ranked second after South Africa as an opium-poppy producer in the continent of Africa. See 'Exposing Egypt's drug trade', 18 February 2009, available at http://menassat.com, site visited 15 May 2014.

28. Interview, General Tareq Ismael, director-general of ANGA, 13 April 2011.

29. 'Egypt: drug trafficking'.

30. Hamdi et al., 'The National Addiction Research Program', p. 17.

31. Amr Osman estimates that as many as 52 per cent of 'addicts' live with their families. Interview, 11 April 2011.

32. The prison population of Egypt is estimated at around 60,000, excluding political prisoners and those incarceration centres run by the intelligence.

33. Interview with AIDS and social policy expert Sally Fikri, 10 April 2011.

34. In Egypt it is considered a bad omen for IV drug users to secure 'the tool' before obtaining the drugs. Hence, the cavalier attitude to the use of syringes that have already been used by multiple injectors. See 'EGYPT: Needle sharing rife among drug users', IRIN (a service of the UN Office for the Coordination of Humanitarian Affairs), 21 June 2009.

35. Ibid.

36. Citing WHO/EMRO research, 2005.

37. Interview with Essam Youssef, Montana Studios, Cairo, 10 April 2011.

38. Chip Rosseti, 'Junkies on the Nile: Egyptians addicted to drug-fuelled debut novel', available at http://publishingperspectives.com?p=11873, site visited 6 April 2010.
39. Alaa el-Eswany, *The Yacoubian Building* (London: Harper Perennial, 2002).
40. Tzvi Ben Gedalyahu, 'Bedouin terrorists attempt takeover of northern Sinai, 12 dead', available at Arutz Sheva, http://www.israelnationalnews.com/News/News.aspx/142018, site visited 30 January 2011.
41. Dina Kraft, 'Testimony tells of abuse by bedouin smugglers', *IHT*, 17 February 2011.
42. See 'Exposing Egypt's drug trade'.
43. In 1999 around 1,000 members of the Azazmeh tribe attempted to relocate across the border. Various motives from blood feuds to competition for coveted drug-smuggling routes to food shortages and lack of work in Egypt were all advanced by way of speculation over the precise motives. See Patrick Cockburn, 'Bedouin tribe cross Sinai to defect to Israel', *The Independent*, 17 March 1999.
44. Evidence for this was the dialogue that the Fund for Drug Control and Treatment of Addiction at the Ministry of State for Family and Population has established with script writers on the Ramadan soaps, with a view to negotiating a code of ethics. The portrayal of drugs and cigarettes in such dramas has been described as 'shocking' by the manager of the fund, Amr Osman. Interview, 11 April 2011.
45. Khallaf Rania, 'Out of control', *al-Ahram*, 9–22 July 2015.
46. I would like to thank my colleague Dr Walter Armbrust for sharing his extensive knowledge of Egyptian cinema with me.
47. The media lauded the Interior Ministry for its 'great efforts', as observed by Mohamad el-Far, 'Egypt: Shedding some light on drugs investigations process', 21 April 2010, available at http://talkingdrugs.org/egypt-shedding-some-light-on-drugs-investigations-process, site visited 8 November 2011.
48. Religious leaders issued a death threat to journalist Abu Baker al-Majed of *al-Badil* newspaper and threatened to kidnap his children if he did not rescind a report on the drugs trade. See 'Exposing Egypt's drug trade'.
49. Khalil, 'Drug smokers in Egypt suffer hashish shortage'.
50. See Johnny West, *Karama! Journeys through the Arab Spring* (London: Heron Books, 2012).
51. Muqallid, Diana, 'Tragedy and the power of the new media', *Asharq al-Awsa*t, reprinted in the *MidEast Mirror*, 18 June 2010.
52. 'Police in Egypt kill man', available at http://talkingdrugs.org/police-in-egypt-kill-man, site visited 15 March 2011.
53. 'Egyptian policemen charged over Khaled Said death', BBC, 1 July 2010.
54. Interview, Tareq Ismael, ANGA, 13 April 2011.
55. Ibid.
56. Major-General Mohsen Murad, the director of public security at the Ministry of Interior, identified the need to regain trust in the police as the basis of the restoration of security across Egypt. See *The Telegraph*, 5 April 2011.

57. David D. Kirkpatrick, 'Crime wave is terrifying Egypt, even its police', *IHT*, 13 May 2011.

58. Interview, journalists at Roz el-Yusef, 9 April 2011.

59. Interview, Sally Fikri, 10 April 2011.

60. Interview, Lieutenant-Colonel Raafat Sakr, ANGA, 13 April 2011.

61. 'Exposing Egypt's Drug Trade'.

5. ISRAEL: CRIME AND ETHNICITY

1. My thanks to Professor Derek Penslar of Toronto University for identifying the source of the quotation.

2. See Sammy Smooha, 'Arab–Jewish relations in Israel: a deeply divided society', in Anita Shapira, ed., *Israeli Identity in Transition* (London: Praeger, 2004), pp. 31–67.

3. Not that Ashkenazi 'tokers' are completely immune from the negative fallout from drugs use. The American spy Jonathan Jay Pollard, with a Jewish nationalist background, served a thirty-year prison sentence as a result of such behaviour. Pollard and his first wife took part in 'drug-fueled parties' and then got embroiled in debt as a consequence. See Ronen Bergman, 'Israelis just don't get America', *International New York Times*, 30 July 2015.

4. David Ginsburg and J. L. Kaufman, *Problems of Drug Addiction in Israel* (Geneva: UNODC, 1955).

5. Ibid.

6. Ibid.

7. UN, *2009 World Drug Report*, cited in 'UN: Israeli teens among world leaders in heroin use', *Haaretz*, 9 January 2009.

8. Overview of the drug situation in Israel in http://www.antidrugs.org.il/template/default_e.asp?maincat=42&catId=257&pageId=..., site visited 21 May 2010.

9. Judy Dempsey, 'Paradise lost in Israel', *Financial Times*, 3 June 2000.

10. 'Police seize 82 kilos of heroin, biggest drug bust ever', 15 November 2008, available at www.israelnationalnews.com/News/Flash.aspx/155866, site visited 30 April 2010.

11. 'Israel becomes major hub in the international cocaine trade, abuse rising', *Haaretz* digital edition, 19 October 2013, available at www.haaretz.com.news/national/11.553277, site visited 21 October 2013.

12. UN, *2009 World Drug Report*.

13. Sharp, *US Foreign Aid to Israel*.

14. Zvi Lavi, 'Police: 10% of youth use drugs', ynet news.com, 13 July 2009, site visited 31 March 2010.

15. 'Drug abuse in the global village', available at www.israelnationalnews.com/News/Flash.aspx/155866, site visited 30 April 2010.

16. IADA, *Annual Report*, 2005/2006, p. 37.

17. Report in Hebrew weekly *Yediot Tel Aviv*, reprinted as 'TA considers supplying

heroin to addicts', *Jerusalem Post*, 17 February 2008, and posted as 'Israeli City Considers Heroin Maintenance Program', access to web discussion available at info@csdp.org, site visited 30 April 2010.

18. Ken A., 'Smack in the middle of Israel', 2002, available at www.heroinhelper.com/bored/stories/israel.shtml, site visited 30 April 2010.

19. Ibid.

20. For more on the IIADA, see About Israel Anti-Drug Authority, http://www.anti-drugs.gov.il/template/default_e.asp?maincat=40&catid=248, site visited 21 May 2010.

21. UNODC, *Country Profile: Israel*, n.d., site visited 31 March 2010.

22. IADA, *17th Annual Report*, p. 3.

23. View expressed by Mohammad Barakeh, Chair of Knesset Committee on Drug Abuse, [and himself an Israeli Arab] at a special committee meeting to mark International Day against Drug Abuse and Trafficking, 26 June 2009, downloaded from www.knesset.gov.il.

24. Yaakov Lappin, 'The North's drug-busters pounce', *Jerusalem Post*, 20 May 2009.

25. 'IDF notes drug abuse problem in army; "tough" measures to be taken', *Yediot Aharanot*, 4 December 2000, published in BBC/SWB/ME, 6 December 2000.

26. Shama and Iris, *Immigration without Integration*, p. 123.

27. Menachem Amir, 'Organised crime in Israel', Transnational Organised Crime, vol. 2, no. 4 (Winter 1996), pp. 21–39, p. 35.

28. 'ISRAEL: organised crime', *Oxford Analytica*, 8 September 2003.

29. Ibid.

30. 'Israeli police crack drug smuggling ring', *Israel Line*, 2 August 2001, reprinted from the *Jerusalem Post*.

31. Ben Hartman, 'Two bodies found in car near Ramle in suspected double murder', *Israel News*, 25 December 2004.

32. Oxford Analytica, 'ISRAEL: organised crime'.

33. 'Israel ranks no. 32 least corrupt country in the world', *Haaretz*, 17 November 2009.

34. Danielle Haas, 'Israel battles illegal antiquities trade', Reuters, Jerusalem, 14 November 1999.

35. Amir, 'Organised crime in Israel', p. 35.

36. Ibid.

37. Isabel Kershner, 'Mobster rubbed out, public tunes in', *IHT*, 22–23 November 2008.

38. Michal Zebede, 'Traffickers target Israeli girls to replace foreign sex slaves', *Haaretz*, 17 August 2009.

39. Yuval Goren, 'Tel Aviv police hunt head of women trafficking ring', *Haaretz*, 3 September 2009.

40. As the editorial in *Haaretz* on 23 October 2003 described it. See the editorial

reprinted under the title 'The pity of Tannenbaum', in the *Jerusalem Post* on the same date. Available at www.mia.org.il/archive/031023jp.html, site visited 29 October 2010.

41. 'On Lebanon–Israel frontier, a quiet drug war', Associated Press, 12 April 2009.

42. 'Police conduct major drug bust', *Israel Line*, 24 August 2000.

43. 'Taibe crime wars: Lau missile fired at resident's house', Ynet news.com, Israel News, 17 August 2012.

44. 'A quiet drug war'.

45. Amir, 'Organised crime in Israel', p. 27.

46. For more on the party see its website www.aleyarok.org.il

6. SAUDI ARABIA: AN INEVITABLE PART OF MODERNISATION?

1. Interior Ministry spokesman, Mansour al-Turki, cited in 'Saudi cops seize drug-laden glider', Sapa-AFP, 28 September 2011, available at http://www.iol.co.za/news/world/saudi-cops-seize-drug-laden-glider-1.1146492, site visited 1 December 2011.

2. The MIKSA (Ministry of Interior, Kingdom of Saudi Arabia) programme consists of an ambitious and extensive series of projects that embody the latest technology in border surveillance. It began with a project to protect Saudi Arabia's border with Iraq, following Iraq's invasion of Kuwait in 1990. With the Iraq part of the border defence already adjudged a success, a new project, costing $2.8 billion, was awarded in 2009. This is to include: a system of secure border posts; surface and aerial monitoring of the border line; and surveillance of the kingdom's sea borders. See Habib Toumi, 'Saudi Arabia Building High-Tech Border Fence', *Gulf News*, 22 January 2015.

3. By the first Gulf War is meant the invasion of Kuwait by Iraq in 1990, followed by the war to oust its forces in 1991, as opposed to the Iran–Iraq War of 1980–8 and the later second Gulf War and the US-led invasion of Iraq in 2003.

4. Turki al-Saheil, 'Saudi Arabia cracks down on drug smuggling', *Asharq al-Awsat*, 12 October 2011.

5. My visit to the Ministry of Interior in Riyadh took place on 7 December 2011.

6. For the document regulating the activities of the NCNC, aka NCCD, see Articles 1–26 in 'Regulation of National Committee for Combating Drugs', available at http://ncnc.sa

7. For further protestations of inter-agency coordination see Ali Bluwi, 'Major breakthrough in war against drugs', available at http://www.arabnews.com/print/445895, site visited 25 March 2013.

8. Matthew Murphy, 'Dealing drugs in Saudi Arabia is a very stressful business', in VICE United States, available at http://www.vice.com/print/drug-dealing-in-saudi-arabia-sounds-like-a-very-stressful-, site visited 19 May 2014.

9. Visit to Customs department in Riyadh, 12 December 2011.

10. Khalid Sharani, 'Concerted efforts to check drug trafficking in kingdom', *Saudi Gazette*, 26 June 1999.

11. Manal Quota, 'Suicide a Growing Problem among Women', *Arab News*, 15 September 2005.

12. In spite of this functional responsibility, the role of the Majlis remained nominal. There was, for instance, no dedicated commission focusing on illicit drugs. The anti-drugs issue had to share itself institutionally with the Security Commission and the Family and Social Commission. The uncertain nature of the Majlis's future also worked against the building up of settled expertise. Interview, Dr Fayez Shahri, Office of NCNC, 14 December 2011.

13. Faiza Saleh Ambah, 'Those smuggling drugs into Saudi Arabia risk certain death if caught', *Seattle Times*, 18 May 1997.

14. Visit to Half-Way House, associated with al-Amal Hospital in Riyadh, 10 December 2011 and extensive interview with three recovering heroin abusers.

15. Interview with Yusef AlHuzim, Al-Anood Foundation headquarters, 11 December 2011.

16. Such dialogues also addressed women and the Shia.

17. Interview with Dr Yusef AlHuzim.

18. There are no accurate statistics available on HIV. Tentative recent attempts have been made to try to address the HIV issue in a non-emotive way. See, for example, '86 Saudi women with HIV marry; 79 deliver healthy babies: charity', *Saudi Gazette*, 9 December 2011 (no byline). Given the unreliability of previous studies published in the Saudi press, one must take with a pinch of salt the claims that: since figures were first kept in 1984, only 16,334 people have contracted full-blown AIDS in Saudi Arabia, of whom 4,458 were Saudi citizens; only 1,175 new cases of AIDS were detected in 2011, of which just 493 were Saudi citizens.

19. Interview, Saeed al-Sriha, 8 December 2011.

20. Nawaf Afit, '140,000 drug users in KSA, says study', *Crossroads Arabia*, 5 May 2009, available at http://xrdarabia.org/2009/05/05/the-saudi-drug-problem/, site visited 1 December 2011.

21. 'Smugglers and the Saudi drug policy', carried on the Sand Gets in my Eyes blog, 6 July 2009, available at http://sandgetsinmyeyes.blogspot.com/2009/07/smugglers-and-saudi-drug-policy.html, site visited 3 September 2011.

22. Mohit Joshi, 'Saudi customs agents boast of biggest drug haul in history', 7 April 2009, available at http://topnews.in/saudi-customs-agents-boast-biggest-drug-haul-history-2185943, site visited 1 December 2011.

23. Interview, Dr Fayez Alshehri, secretary-general, NCNC, 6 December 2011.

24. Telephone interview with Dr Maha al-Mazrou', director of the drug-testing laboratory in Dammam, 11 December 2011.

25. The reason for a certain tentativeness in identifying countries of origin is explained

by the fact that there is no database for Saudi Arabia as a whole, while the use of brand marks, such as the 'Lexus' luxury car trade mark on poor-quality drugs in the kingdom may well be explained by local or new entrant producers attempting to give credibility to their versions of the drug.

26. Department of Anti-Smuggling and Organized Crime, Turkish Police (KOM) Annual Report, 2007, p. 20.

27. KOM Annual Report, 2008, p. 18.

28. KOM Annual Report, 2010, p. 21.

29. Respected Arab drugs expert Elie Araj, cited in Aryn Baker, 'Conservative Saudi Arabia is becoming a hotbed for amphetamines', available at http://world.time.com/2013/10/29/conservative-saudi-arabia-is-becoming-a-hotbed-fo, site visited 19 May 2014.

30. Presentation by senior figure (rank of colonel) in Border Guard, 6 December 2011.

31. 'Saudi in huge drugs crackdown', *Maktoob News*, 16 August 2009.

32. Interview with Dr Alshehri.

33. An armed revolt from among Yemen's Zaidi, Shia population in the northern most part of Yemen, around the city of Saadah, has been led by the Houthi clan. Political frustrations resulted in a civil war in 2004, with the Houthis backed by Yemen's former leader, Ali Abdullah Saleh. Violent resistance has been punctuated by attempts at third-party mediation, all efforts at which have so far been fruitless. The violent chaos on the border has left Saudi Arabia feeling vulnerable, including with regard to illegal drugs. A sign of mounting frustration on the Saudi side has been clear in the aerial bombardment that Riyadh and its allies have unleashed on the Houthi-controlled area, more or less continuously since March 2015.

34. For more on terrorism in Saudi Arabia see Awadh Asseri, *Combating Terrorism*.

35. In Riyadh: primary school hours, covering the six-to-twelve age group, run from 7 a.m. to 12.30 p.m.; secondary school hours, covering the twelve-to-fourteen age group, run from 7 a.m. to 1 p.m.; high school hours, covering the fifteen-to-seventeen/eighteen age group, run from 7 a.m. to 2 p.m. These timings may change, notably with the alterations in the observance of Ramadan around the year.

36. Princess al-Anood was one of only two of King Fahd's wives whom he did not subsequently divorce, the other being a member of al-Ibrahim family.

37. Interview with Dr Yusef AlHuzim.

38. Author's predicament, al-Anood Foundation, 11 December 2011.

7. IRAN: GRAPPLING WITH ADDICTION

1. For a general discussion of 'harm reduction' within the context of wider social mores see Amir Arsalan Afkhami, 'From punishment to harm reduction: resecularization of addiction in contemporary Iran', in Gheissari, ed., *Contemporary Iran*.

2. Meysam Aqakhanlu, 'Iran's war on drugs: three decades of failure', *Mianeh*, Tehran, 14 January 2008.

3. 'Afyun', in *Encyclopedia Iranica*, available at http://www.iranicaonline.org/art-ciles/afyun-opium, last updated 15 December 1984.

4. Hashem Kalantari and Fredrik Dahl, 'Iran has 130,000 new drug addicts each year: report', Reuters, 15 November 2009, available at http://www.reuters.com/article/2009/11/15/us-iran—drugs-idUSTRE5AEOZ020091115, site visited 7 August 2015.

5. UN Common Country Assessment, 2003, p. 37.

6. Dr Mohammed Mehdi Gooya, chief of the Health Ministry's disease-management centre, cited in *Mardom Salan*, 18 April 2006 in Bill Samii, 'World: narcotics supply reduced, but Iran and Afghanistan still suffering', in RFE/RL 26 June 2006, available at http://www.rferl.org/content/article/1069462.html, site visited 14 May 2010.

7. Kaveh L. Afrasiabi, 'US, Iran to stop Afghan narco-traffic', Asia Times Online, 9 March 2009.

8. This is not to suggest that there is not a problem with alcohol abuse in contemporary Iran, especially in the poorer suburbs of south Tehran. See http://www.bbc.co.uk/news/world-middleeast-18504268 and http://www.rferl.org/content/iran-alcohol-abuse-on-the-rise/24617070.html

9. Karl Vick, 'Opiates of the Iranian people', *Washington Post*, 23 September 2005.

10. Payvand's Iran News, 'International Narcotics Control Strategy Report: Iran', US Department of State, 3 March 2004.

11. Recent study referred to in 'Drug supply reduction: an overview of drug supply and trafficking in Iran', unpublished report, n.d.

12. Andrew North, 'Iran's drugs war', *The Middle East*, November 2000.

13. By 2000, an estimated $600 million had been spent on static border defences alone. See 'Iran's anti-narcotics effort faces obstacles', *RFE/RL Iran Report*, vol. 3, no. 21, 29 May 2000.

14. Farmani, Hiedeh, 'Iran vows to win war on drugs', AFP, 22 May 2009.

15. 'Iran: Four Afghan bandits killed in Khorasan', IRNA, 21 January 2001.

16. FNA, 'Police seize tons of narcotics in western Iran', n.d., available at http://english.farsnews.com/newstext.php?nn=8812261019, site visited 14 May 2010.

17. Kim Sengupta, 'West seizes £800m-worth of drugs from Iranian ports', *The Independent*, 13 July 2008.

18. US Department of State in Payvand's Iran News, 'International Narcotics Control Strategy Report: Iran', 3 March 2004, available at http://www.payvand.com/news/04/mar/1012.html, site visited 14 May 2010.

19. Kamin Mohammadi, 'As the young party hard in Iran, the country experiences a severe drugs epidemic', Mail Online, 24 March 2007.

20. Tomas Muzik, 'Country factsheets, Eurasian narcotics, Iran 2004', *Central Asia-Caucasus Institute & Silk Road Studies Program*, Washington DC: Johns Hopkins–SAIS.

21. Max Chamka, '3 grams of opium for 1 dollar', 6 June 2005, *Caucaz Europenews*, Zahedan, Baluchistan.

22. 'Iran tops world drug addiction-rate list report', Iran Focus, 24 September 2005.

23. Aqakhanlu, 'Iran's war on drugs'.

24. This accusation was made by a former member of Iraq's military industries organisation in London to *al-Zaman*, 26 June 2000. Reproduced in 'Smuggling and the "black economy"', *RFE/RL Iran Report*, vol. 3, no. 36.

25. The smuggling of Iranian-produced petrol into Afghanistan for use by the Taliban government was routine at the time. Interview with former deputy minister, Tehran, 30 September 1998.

26. Statement of the National Council of Resistance in Iran, 'Iranian Resistance calls on UN General Assembly's special session on drugs to condemn mullahs' regime', 8 June 1998, available at http:/iran-e-azad.org/english/ncr/980608.html, site visited 14 May 2010.

27. 'Iran: drugs and decay', *The Economist*, 31 March 2001.

28. William Samii, 'Iran's war on drugs: potential for US–Iranian cooperation?', *WINEP Special Policy Forum Report*, 21 November 2000, Washington DC.

29. United Nations Common Country Assessment for the Islamic Republic of Iran, n.d., p. 37.

30. 'Jundollah, Iran's Sunni Muslim rebels', Reuters FACTBOX, 16 July 2010.

31. The Pakistani ambassador to Tehran was quoted as saying that his country had helped Iran in the capture of the Jundollah leader. See 'Rigi arrest may show easing Afghan regional tensions', Reuters ANALYSIS, 25 February 2010.

32. 'Iran executes Jundollah member', http://www.aljazeera.com/news/middleeast/2010/05/2010524102054273572.html, 24 May 2010.

33. Najmeh Bozorgmehr, 'Militant separatist executed in Iran', *Financial Times*, Tehran, 25 May 2010.

34. 'Jundollah, Iran's Sunni Muslim rebels'.

35. 'Official says EU help in fight against drugs "inadequate"', IRNA, 30 November 1999; reprinted in BBC/SWB/ME/3707 MED/3, 2 December 1999.

36. 'Iran's anti-narcotics effort faces obstacles'.

37. Confidential interview with FCO official, London, 17 November 1998.

38. For a commentary on the specialist workshop held in Tehran see Mike Trace, 'Iranian and British Workshop on Drug Demand Reduction', Tehran, 25–27 February 2001. Supplied to author on 11 April 2001.

39. Interview with a member of the Office of the UK Coordinator on illegal drugs, London, 4 May 2001.

40. Interview, 12 July 2010.

41. This initiative brings together Afghanistan's six neighbours, as well as Russia and the USA. In April 2004 Iran signed the Berlin Declaration on Counter-Narcotics, providing for a security belt to be applied around Afghanistan to limit narcotics exports.

42. Payvand's Iran News, 'US Narcotics Report: Iran', 3 March 2004.

43. Samii, 'Iran's war on drugs'.

44. Janne Bjerre Christensen, *Drugs, Deviancy and Democracy in Iran: The Interaction of State and Civil Society* (London: I. B. Tauris, 2011), p. 66.

45. Philip Robins, 'Join forces with Iran in the global war against drugs', *Christian Science Monitor*, 4 January 1999.

46. UN, 'Afghanistan, Iran and Pakistan agree to strengthen counter-narcotics efforts', SOP Newsire, 12 June 2007.

47. UNODC, 'Counter-narcotics operation on the border between Iran, Pakistan and Afghanistan', n.d., available at http://www.unodc.org/unodc/en/frontpage/counter-narcotics-operation-on-the-border-between-Iran,-Pakistan-and-Afghanistan, site visited 14 May 2010.

48. Some of the EU–Iran cooperation takes place through the ECO, a multilateral organisation, thereby avoiding the need for direct and exclusive contact with the government of Iran. Interview with European Commission officials, Brussels, 21 March 2011.

49. Thomas Erdbrink, 'On frontier, Iran wages unheralded battle against drugs', *IHT*, 12 October 2012.

50. Farmani, 'Iran vows to win war on drugs'.

51. DCHQ Annual Report 2011.

52. 'Iran says losing fight against drug traffickers', Reuters, 16 August 2001.

53. 'Drug control chief criticizes official approach', *RFE/RL, Iran Report*, vol. 4, no. 25, 29 June 2001.

54. Samii, 'Iran's war on drugs'.

55. A. Mokri, 'Substance abuse treatment and HIV in Iran', 2005, available at www.uclaisap.org/dssat2005/presentations/Mokri.htm.

56. Jim Muir, 'Iran's battle with heroin', BBC, 7 June 2002, available at http:/news.bbc.co.uk/1/hi/world/middle_east/2031624.stm, site visited 14 May 2010.

57. Examples of DCHQ roadside poster campaign include: a spider's web with the slogan 'Drug Addiction is the Cause of Desperation'; a bird's nest with the eggs smashed with the slogan 'Drug Addiction Breaks Families'; the slogan 'Drug Addiction Destroys Everything', outside the DCHQ building itself. Author observations, 3 October 1998.

58. Yassaman Taqibeigi, 'Health-Iran: drug addiction spreading HIV/AIDS', Inter Press Service, 6 March 2001.

59. Payvand's Iran News, 'Iran has 1.2 million hooked drug addicts: official', 29 June 2003.

60. DCHQ Annual Report, 2011, p. 43.

61. Muir, 'Iran's battle with heroin'.

62. Ibid.

63. Kamin Mohammadi, 'The hero and the heroin', an abridged version of an article

that appeared in the *Financial Times*, 16 July 2005; full article available at http://www.kamin.co.uk/Pages/Hero_Heroin.htm, site visited 18 May 2010.

64. Interview with new head of DCHQ and Iranian police chief, Esmail Ahmadi-Moqaddam, 'Iran seeks world cooperation in war on drugs', Press TV, 9 March 2010.

65. Robert Tait, 'Iran tries a little tenderness in fighting addiction', *The Guardian*, 12 November 2005.

66. Anthony Lloyd, 'Land of three million heroin addicts', *The Times*, 16 June 2005.

67. Mohammadi, 'The hero and the heroin'.

68. Samii, 'World: narcotics supply reduced'.

69. Bill Samii, 'Iran: government reverses course in war on drugs', *RFE/RL*, 29 September 2005.

70. For more on this see Christensen, *Drugs, Deviancy and Democracy in Iran*, chaps. 3 and 5.

8. TURKEY: FROM CULTIVATOR TO CONDUIT

1. 'Turkish pop star Tarkan held in drugs raid', CNN, Istanbul, 26 February 2010.

2. 'Turkish Singer Tarkan may get two years in jail for drugs', *RIA Novosti*, cited in *Vestnik Kavkaza*.

3. Even such bulky goods as livestock, for example, are trafficked across the Iran–Turkey border. See Anatolia News Agency, 'Turkey: agriculture minister announces measures to curb livestock smuggling', Ankara, 12 September 1999, in BBC/SWB, 16 September 1999.

4. Anonymous interview, 26 July 2011.

5. As a result of the reorganisation, the Gendarmerie acquired a specialist counter-narcotics force of 700, spread across the 81 provinces of the Turkish republic. Confidential briefing of the author by senior Gendarmerie officers, Ankara, 26 September 2001.

6. The governor of the province of Van made this point during an interview with the Turkish daily newspaper *Yeni Safak*. Quotation cited in Rainsford, Sarah, 'Turkey at the drugs crossroads', BBC, Istanbul, 6 October 2005.

7. Anonymous interview, 30 July 2011.

8. Anam, 'PKK's Trafficking in Europe', Independent Media Centre Ireland, France, 26 July 2002.

9. The outstanding academic commentator on the Kurds, Martin van Bruinessen, supports this contention with his conclusion that 'There is a small elite of expert border-crossers, but most smuggling (and, without exception, all large-scale smuggling) is carried on through the bribing of border officials'. See his *Agha, Shaikh and State: The Social and Political Structures of Kurdistan* (London: Zed Books, 1992), p. 190.

10. Michael Jonsson and Svante Cornell, 'Kurds and pay: examining PKK financing', *Jane's Intelligence Review*, 13 March 2008.

11. Of the six-city survey included in the study, more than a quarter of the respondents had used heroin in their lifetime, rising to more than 40 per cent in the cases of Diyarbakir and Istanbul. See UN, 'Health Services, Education and Community Action: Preventing Drug Abuse in Turkey', UNODC annual report, Ankara, 2003, p. 24.

12. Department of Anti-Smuggling and Organized Crime, Turkish National Police, Ministry of Interior, *Turkish Drug Report, 2005*, Ankara, 2006, p. 18.

13. Every year this route is taken by around 1.5 million trucks, 250,000 coaches and 4 million cars, making the route extremely difficult to police without excellent intelligence. In 1998 Tim Boekhout van Solinge estimated that 75 per cent of the heroin smuggled into Europe used the Balkans Route. See Ioannis Michaletos, 'Turkish organized crime', Worldpress, Athens, 12 November 2007.

14. The Turkish authorities now accept that 'Turkish nationals' play an important role in criminal activity in Europe, especially with regard to drugs. Anonymous interview, 26 July 2011.

15. John Doxey, 'Losing the battle and the war against drugs', *The Free Library*, Istanbul, 1 October 1997.

16. Law 4208 on the Prevention of Money Laundering, and the Regulation on Fundamentals and Means of Controlled Delivery, published in the *Official Gazette*, No. 23111, 15 September 1997.

17. For a more detailed narrative of the challenge to the Turkish state in the 1990s see Philip Robins, 'Back from the brink: Turkey's ambivalent approaches to the hard drugs issue', *Middle East Journal*, vol. 62, no. 4 (Autumn 2008), pp. 630–50.

18. Abdullah Çatlı alone was reported as having thirteen passports, all issued with the approval of senior officials, in spite of the existence of warrants for his arrest by Interpol and the Turkish National Police. Stephen Kinzer, 'Turkish panel links killings to authorities', *New York Times*, Istanbul, 8 April 1997.

19. According to a prominent pro-Kurdish politician, Güven Özata, there were an estimated 3,500 unsolved killings in the south-east over the decade to 1996. See Stephen Kinzer, 'Scandal links Turkish aides to deaths, drugs and terror', *New York Times*, Istanbul, 10 December 1996.

20. This was done formally by the Turkish state, which created a 'super governorate' in the south-east, which was no longer to be covered by a range of liberal freedoms, but where the law of the gun would rule.

21. For a discussion of the emergence of an anti-narcotics policy in Turkey, see Philip Robins, 'Public policy making in Turkey: faltering attempts to generate a national drugs policy', *Policy and Politics*, vol. 37, no. 2 (April 2009), pp. 289–306.

22. '1998: the year that was', *Turkish Probe*, 3 January 1999.

23. *Turkish Daily News*, 15 August 1998.

24. An Islamist-led coalition government had been brought down in July 1997, as a result of actions by an alliance of the Kemalist state, building on a political strength

galvanised during what came to be called the 28 February (1997) process. The Islamist government was the forerunner of the Justice and Development Party (AKP), which came to power in November 2002, and which ultimately undermined the Kemalist state as an independent political actor. To designate criminal gangs as being even more of a threat than Islamic fundamentalism was a statement indeed.

25. It is not intended here to lump Turkish Alevis into the same confessional category as Shiites in, say, Iran and Iraq, simply to establish the broad doctrinal fact that all such groups share the same reverence for the Prophet Muhammad's cousin and son-in-law, Ali. The periodic persecution of Turkish Alevis by Turkish Sunnis reflects the experience of Shias in modern-day Iraq.

26. KOM, Annual Report, 2010, March 2011, Ankara, p. 16.

27. Anatolia News Agency, 'Adana police carry out huge drug bust', *Hurriyet Daily News*, Adana, 21 April 2010.

28. Daily News with Wires, 'Doubts grow over Kuşadası shooting', *Hürriyet Daily News*, Kuşadası, 16 April 2010.

29. For more on this genre of film see Arslan, *Cinema in Turkey*.

30. Starring Şener Şen as Ali Osman, the *kabadayı*, the neighbourhood 'big man', who looks after the poor and the young where the state is unable or unwilling to do so.

31. *Can* was also released in 2008.

32. For a biography of Hüseyin Baybaşin see Mahmut Baksi, *Teyre Baz ya da bir Kürt İşadami Hüseyin Baybaşin*, Istanbul: Peri Yayınları, 1999.

33. Brian G. Carlson, 'Huseyin Baybasin: Europe's Pablo Escobar', *SAIS Review*, vol. 25, no. 1 (Winter–Spring 2005), pp. 69–70.

34. 'Keeping tabs on the Turkish connection', BBC, 14 November 2002.

35. Hüseyin Baybaşin, interview with Cüneyt Arkın, Show Television, 'Facts revealed about state gang in Turkey', in *Cyprus PIO*, Amsterdam, 27 January 1997.

36. Ian Cobain, 'Feared clan who made themselves at home in Britain', *The Guardian*, 28 March 2006.

37. Tony Thompson, 'Heroin "emperor" brings terror to UK streets', *The Observer*, 17 November 2002.

9. DUBAI: THE DRUGS HUB

1. 'Radio One DJ Grooverider sentenced to four years' jail in Dubai for drug possession', *Mail Online*, 19 February 2008.

2. Duncan Campbell, 'Drug laws make Dubai the riskiest destination for unwary travellers', available at http://www.theguardian.com/travel/2008/jun/09/unitedarabemirates.travelnews, 9 June 2008.

3. 'Tourists warned of UAE drug laws', BBC News, 8 February 2008.

4. Hani M. Baathish, 'Prosecutors set up in Dubai airport', *The National*, 26 October 2008.

5. Sarah Turner, 'Drug laws threatens Dubai's clubbing dream', *The Observer*, 24 February 2008.

6. There are no definitive figures on the breakdown of Dubai's demography, owing to the sensitivity of a country where its 'citizens' are such a minority of the total. Most such figures should therefore be regarded as indicative.

7. Dubai's Iranian population, overwhelmingly merchants in occupation, came to settle in the country a century ago at the prompting of the ruler, who shrewdly spotted an opportunity to expand the economy. Insulated from the tax levels they had faced before migrating to Dubai, these Iranians stayed permanently and later acquired citizenship.

8. Dubai has oft been referred to as the gold-smuggling centre of the world. See Rosemarie Said Zahlan, *The Origins of the United Arab Emirates* (London: Macmillan, 1978), p. 150.

9. Peter Lienhardt, *Shaikhdoms of Eastern Arabia* (Basingstoke: Palgrave, 2001), p. 122.

10. Said Zahlan, *The Origins of the United Arab Emirates*, p. 154.

11. Lienhardt, *Shaikhdoms of Eastern Arabia*, p. 172.

12. Hashim Abdullah Sulaiman Sarhan, 'Drugs Abuse in the United Arab Emirates', Ph.D. thesis, Department of Social Policy, Newcastle University, 1995, p. 270.

13. Ibid., pp. 4, 110.

14. Though this action was taken at a federal level, the level of decision making in which Abu Dhabi takes precedence, Dubai ranks second in seniority in the federation. It is unlikely that Dubai would have agreed to such an institutional step unless it had been in broad agreement. Dubai has refused to implement federal policy in the past. In general, the UAE should be understood as a loose organisation, which does not impose the will of the largest emirate from the centre.

15. Interview, Simeon Kerr, *Financial Times*, 15 December 2010.

16. Sarhan, 'Drugs Abuse in the United Arab Emirates', p. 258.

17. For example, there are estimated to be 26,000 CCTV cameras located across Dubai. Confidential interview, Dubai, 16 December 2010. For comparative purposes there are around 10,000 such cameras in London.

18. Anonymous interview, Dubai, 12 December 2010.

19. See Awad Mustafa, Melanie Swan and Hassan Hassan, 'UAE death sentence for Briton and Syrian to face significant checks', *The National*, 27 June 2012.

20. For more information on the matter see the charity Detained in Dubai, run by the attorney Radha Stirling, at www.detainedindubai.org

21. Rasha Abu Baker, 'Drugs cases dominate Dubai courts', *The National*, 23 April 2009.

22. That does not mean to say that Dubai has the most lax regulatory framework within the UAE. The free zone in Ras al-Khaimah, for example, is notorious for being considerably more lax.

23. Interview with Mohammad Matar al-Marri, the executive director of the cargo operations division at Dubai Customs, quoted in James Reinl, 'UN raises concern over Dubai port', *The National*, 17 July 2009.

24. Saudi Arabia has sunk considerable investment into its container-searching systems, notably at the Batha crossing. Nevertheless, its machines are only able to process around 900 trucks a day out of the 2,000 seeking cross-border passage. Briefing from Saudi Customs, Riyadh, 12 December 2011.

25. Interview with deputy director-general, General Mostafa Bader, ANGA HQ, 3 November 2011.

26. KOM, Annual Report, 2010 pp. 15/16.

27. Awad Mustafa, 'Dubai "being used as hub for drug traffic" say police', *The National*, 30 January 2010.

28. See 'The Emirates Story' at www.emirates.com

29. Paloma Minter, 'Airports: The race to increase capacity', in *MEED Special Report UAE*, 14–20 March 2008, p. 53.

30. Awad Mustafa, 'Airport cocaine seizure is the largest this year', *The National*, 22 June 2010.

31. Gillian Duncan and Neil Parmar, 'Free zones flourish in Emirates', *The National*, 31 December 2011.

32. Reinl, 'UN raises concern over Dubai port'.

33. Christopher Davidson, 'Dubai labours under money-laundering image', *New York Times*, 2 December 2010.

34. Christopher Davidson, 'Dubai's double game?', *Money Jihad*, 2 July 2010.

35. Confidential interview, Dubai, 12 December 2010.

36. Report by Federation of American Scientists, referred to by Kenneth Rijock, himself a former money launderer, in Davidson, 'Dubai labours under money-laundering image'.

37. Nick Mathiason, 'Dubai's dark side targeted by international finance police', *The Observer*, 24 January 2010.

38. Davidson, 'Dubai labours under money-laundering image'.

39. Mohammad Matar al-Marri, the executive director of the Cargo Division, Dubai Customs, quoted in Salam Hafez, 'Taking the fight to the drug lords', *The National*, 15 November 2008.

40. For more on Kabul Bank's relationship with Dubai see Dexter Filkins, 'Troubles at Afghan bank jolt financial system', *New York Times*, 31 August 2010.

41. Jonathan Steele and Jon Boone, 'Wikileaks: Afghan vice-president "landed in Dubai with $52 m in cash"', http://www.theguardian.com/world/2010/dec/02/wikileaks-elite-afghans-millions-cash, 2 December 2010.

42. Mathiason, 'Dubai's dark side'.

43. Steele and Boone, 'Wikileaks'.

44. Ibid.

45. Ibid.

46. Elizabeth A. Kennedy, 'Wikileaks: bribery, graft rampant in Afghanistan', Associated Press, 3 December 2010.

47. Deb Riechamann, 'US Sanctions target Afghan money laundering', Associated Press, 18 February 2011.

48. Joe Bennett, *Hello Dubai* (London: Simon & Schuster, 2010), p. 230.

10. IRAQ: INSURGENCY AND STATE COLLAPSE

1. Paul Rexton Kan, 'Drugging Babylon: the illegal narcotics trade and nation-building in Iraq', *Small Wars and Insurgencies*, vol. 18, no. 2 (June 2007), pp. 216–30, p. 218.

2. Roland Watson et al., 'Saddam sells medicines and aid for life's little luxuries', *The Times*, 4 October 2000.

3. Briefing by British Defence Intelligence Staff (DIS), London, 8 June 2000.

4. Rana Sabbagh, 'Border with Iraq moved to curb smuggling', Reuters, 6 May 1991.

5. On this occasion arms from Iraq were transported through Jordan to the Dead Sea, where they were handed over to Jewish Israeli criminals, who sold the guns at a large mark-up in the West Bank. The arms-smuggling ring was broken up by the Jordanian state. Interview with retired army general and military adviser to the GID, Amman, 1 October 2000.

6. The only evidence I have been able to find says that 'Saddam Hussein's security apparatus in Basra was reportedly heavily involved in the illicit trade'. See Patrick Cockburn, 'Opium: Iraq's deadly new export', *The Independent*, 23 May 2007.

7. 'Iraq to commute sentences of convicts volunteering for army', Iraqi TV, 18 February 1999, BBC/SWB/ME/3464 MED/5, 20 February 1999.

8. Reuters, 'IRAQ: cabinet meeting views intifadah, oil market, drug trafficking', Iraqi TV, 21 January 2001.

9. Jonathan Finer, 'Iraq used for transit of drugs, officials say', *Washington Post Foreign Service*, Baghdad, 15 June 2005.

10. The president of the INCB, Hamid Ghodse, quoted in 'UN: Iraq becoming transit point for drugs', Associated Press, 12 May 2005. Ghodse also interviewed by the BBC on that day: see 'Iraq and Afghanistan have become major drug trafficking countries', available at http:.bbc.co.uk/1/h/world/middle_east/4541387.stm

11. US State Department report, 2008, available at http://www.state.gov/j/inl/rls/nrcrpr/2008/voll/html/100782.htm.

12. To quote the head of the Iraqi police's anti-drugs squad, Omar Zahed. See 'Drug crisis grips Baghdad', BBC News, 4 October 2003.

13. Watson et al., 'Saddam sells medicines and aid'.

14. Presentation by Loulouwa al-Rashid, French academic, St Antony's College, Oxford, 21 May 1999.

15. Peter Beaumont, 'Drug craze is fuelling murder on streets of Iraqi capital', *The Observer*, 14 September 2003.

16. Ibid.

17. Ibid.

18. Health official cited in Nizar Latif, 'Basra becomes hub of drug abuse', *The National*, Baghdad, 23 May 2010.

19. See a variety of reports, such as: Robert Fisk, 'Details emerge of Uday's notorious parties', *The Independent*, 7 June 2003; Rebecca Leung, 'Hussein home movies', *60 Minutes*, CBS, 11 February 2009; Suzanne Goldenberg, 'Uday: career of rape, torture and murder', *The Guardian*, 23 July 2003.

20. Cognac, tequila, and vodka appeared to be Uday's favourite spirits. He also had large stashes of beer, French wines and Dom Perignon champagne. See 'Inside Uday's mansion: drugs, booze and porn', *Yorkshire Post*, 15 April 2003.

21. Baghdad Burning blog, 'Of drugs and Iraq', distributed through www.countercurrents.org, 13 October 2004.

22. Unnamed source cited in T. Christian Miller, 'AFGHAN OPIUM: Iraq drug trade grows', 11 October 2004, available at Bellaciao.org

23. Iraqi Ministry of Health/WHO, 'Press release: assuring quality medicines for the people of Iraq', 8 May 2007.

24. Beaumont, 'Drug craze is fuelling murder'.

25. Miller, 'AFGHAN OPIUM'.

26. 'Drug use soars in Iraq', 12 October 2005, available at www.jointogether.org

27. Andrew E. Kramer, 'US troops leave, but dogs stay', *IHT*, 6 December 2011.

28. 'Drug use in Iraq growing', *Boston Globe*, 28 August 2007.

29. Baghdad Burning, 'Of drugs and Iraq'.

30. Amal Hamdan, 'Iraq drug market explodes', Al-Jazeera, Baghdad, 17 February 2004.

31. Baghdad Burning, 'Of drugs and Iraq'.

32. Hamdan, 'Iraq drug market explodes'.

33. See http://www.tclondon.org.uk/pages/news/drug-and-alcohol-abuse-growing-in-iraqi-forces.php, n.d., site visited 18 March 2014.

34. Hamdan, 'Iraq drug market explodes'.

35. 'Iraq's children drug addicts, dealers', 25 December 2008, available at www.heyyetnet.org

36. This hypothesis was presented by Ali Mussawi, the president of KCA, as a result of a survey conducted by his NGO among children and their families in the centre and south of the country. He also found increasing evidence of substance dependency among middle-class as well as working-class children through the first few months of 2007. See 'IRAQ: drug abuse among children on the rise', IRIN, 9 May 2007.

37. 'IRAQ: officials note rise in drug trafficking, consumption,' IRIN, 27 March 2006.

38. Cited in Baghdad Burning, 'Of drugs and Iraq'.

39. Nizar Latif, 'Drugs a draw for smugglers', *The National*, 28 May 2010.

40. According to the experienced head of the anti-narcotics department of the Jordanian police, Tayel Majali. See Jon Leyne, 'Drug smugglers exploit Iraq chaos', BBC News, Amman, 18 October 2004.

41. The INCB is a Vienna-based international organisation that monitors the implementation of the UN drug conventions.

42. Ghodse quoted in 'UN: Iraq becoming transit point for drugs', Associated Press, 5 December 2005.

43. Ghodse in ibid.

44. '2011 International Narcotics Control Strategy Report' (INCSR), Iraq', available at http://www.state.gov/j/inl/rls/nrcrpt/2011/vol1/156361.htm, site visited 28 August 2012.

45. http://www.tclondon.org.uk/pages/news/drug-and-alcohol-abuse-growing-in-iraqi-forces.php, site visited 18 March 2014.

46. '2012 International Narcotics Control Strategy Report (INSCR)', available at http://www.state.gov/j/inl/rls/nrcrpt/2012/vol1/184100.htm, site visited 28 August 2012.

47. 'Drugs, prostitution and official corruption: Syrian refugee camp in Iraqi Kurdistan', 11 May 2013, available at http://www.ekurd.net/mismas/articles/misc2013/5/state7073.htm, site visited 18 March 2014.

CONCLUSION

1. Some studies suggest that the development of indigenous heroin refining in Afghanistan took place as early as the mid-1990s. See Paul B. Stares, *Global Habit: The Drug Problem in a Borderless World* (Washington: Brookings, 1996).

2. See Elvins, *Anti-Drugs Policies of the European Union*. There is no mention of Turkey in the index of the book, in spite of the fact that Turkey is a key entry-point into the EU from the drug trafficking belt. It also ignores Turkey as having a semi-formal relationship with the EU.

3. The latest manifestation of this came on 24 June 2014, when Britain banned the sale of qat, for fear that it would become a distribution point for the drug, banned in most other favoured destinations. See 'Khat and mouse', *The Economist*, 28 June 2014.

4. See Chinese visa section, Old Jewry, London for evidence in the British capital.

5. That is not to assert that drugs have never been proscribed in the Middle East. In 1623, for instance, tobacco was banned in the Ottoman Empire because smokers were falling asleep over their pipes and had become a fire hazard. The ban was rescinded in 1655, with the country going on to be one of the world's leading suppliers. Martin H. Levinson, *The Drug Problem: A New View Using the General Semantics Approach* (Westport: Praeger, 2002).

6. Draft of undelivered speech by Pino Arlacchi, then executive director of UNDCP. Sent on 11 July 2000 by Sandeep Chawla, author of speech.

7. McAllister, *Drug Diplomacy*.

8. In trying to determine a socially acceptable level of drug abuse government experts have leant in the direction of the 1960s as a benchmark. Lecture by senior UK anti-drugs official, now retired, 7 March 2000, Oxford.

9. For a companion analysis of Dubai see Philip Robins, 'Narcotic drugs in Dubai: lurking in the shadows', *British Journal of Middle Eastern Studies*, vol. 41, no. 2 (2014), pp. 151–66.

10. Ramita Navai, *City of Lies: Love, Sex, Death and the Search for Truth in Tehran* (London: Weidenfeld & Nicolson, 2014), pp. 138–9.

11. 'Chemical highs', *The Economist*, 26 July 2014, p. 50.

12. Precursor traffic is also an issue in Latin America, where it originated as an 'international issue' in the 1990s, having been subject to domestic control since the early 1980s. See Nicholas Dorn, Jorgen Jepsen and Ernesto Savona, *European Drugs Policies and Enforcement* (Basingstoke: Macmillan, 1996).

SELECT BIBLIOGRAPHY

General

Buxton, Julia, *The Political Economy of Narcotics: Production, Consumption and Global Markets*. London: Zed Books, 2006.

Berdal, Mats and Monica Serrano, eds., *Transnational Organized Crime and International Security: Business as Usual?* Boulder: Lynne Rienner, 2002.

Carrier, Neil and Gernot Klantschnig, *Africa and the War on Drugs*. London: Zed Books, 2012.

Davenport-Hines, Richard, *The Pursuit of Oblivion: A Global History of Narcotics*. London: Weidenfeld & Nicolson, 2001.

Edwards, Adam and Peter Gill, eds., *Transnational Organised Crime: Perspectives on Global Security*. London: Routledge, 2003.

Governing the Global Drug Wars. Special Report, London: LSE Ideas, October 2012.

Jordan, David C., *Drug Politics: Dirty Money and Democracies*. Norman: University of Oklahoma Press, 1999.

Kleiman, Mark A. R., Jonathan P. Caulkins and Angela Hawken, *Drugs and Drug Policy: What Everyone Needs to Know*. Oxford: Oxford University Press, 2011.

Mares, David R., *Drug Wars and Coffee Houses: The Political Economy of the International Drug Trade*. Washington DC: CQ Press, 2006.

McAllister, W. B., *Drug Diplomacy in the Twentieth Century*. London: Routledge, 2000.

McCoy, Alfred W., *The Politics of Heroin in South-East Asia: CIA Complicity in the Global Drugs Trade*. Chicago: Lawrence Hill Books, 1972.

Mercille, Julien, *Cruel Harvest: US Intervention in the Afghan Drug Trade*. London: Pluto Press, 2013.

Nadelmann, Ethan A., 'Commonsense Drug Policy', *Foreign Affairs*, vol. 77, no. 1 (January–February 1998), pp. 111–126.

Pan American Health Organisation/WHO, *Drug Policy and the Public Good*. Oxford: Oxford University Press, 2010.

Paoli, Letizia, Victoria A. Greenfield and Peter Reuter, *The World Heroin Market: Can it be Cut?* Oxford: Oxford University Press, 2009.

Pryce, Sue, *Fixing Drugs: The Politics of Drug Prohibition*. Basingstoke: Palgrave Macmillan, 2012.

Robson, Philip, *Forbidden Drugs*, 3rd edn. Oxford: Oxford University Press, 2009.

Room, Robin et al., *Cannabis Policy: Moving Beyond Stalemate*. Oxford: Oxford University Press/Beckley Foundation Press, 2010.

South, Nigel, ed. *Drugs: Cultures, Controls and Everyday Life*. London: Sage, 1999.

Thachuk, Kimberley L., ed., *Transnational Threats: Smuggling and Trafficking in Arms, Drugs and Human Life*. Westport: Praeger, 2007.

Dubai

Bennett, Joe, *Hello Dubai*. London: Simon & Schuster, 2010.

Davidson, Christopher M., *Dubai: The Vulnerability of Success*. London: Hurst, 2008.

Lienhardt, Peter, *Shaikhdoms of Eastern Arabia*. Basingstoke: Palgrave, 2001.

MEED Special Report UAE, 14–20 March 2008.

Robins, Philip, 'Narcotic drugs in Dubai: lurking in the shadows', *British Journal of Middle Eastern Studies*, vol. 41, no. 2 (2014), pp. 151–66.

Sarhan, Hashim Abdullah Sulaiman, 'Drugs Abuse in the United Arab Emirates', Ph.D. thesis, Department of Social Policy, Newcastle University, 1995.

Said Zahlan, Rosemarie, *The Origins of the United Arab Emirates*. London: Macmillan, 1978.

Egypt

Nahas, Gabriel G., 'Hashish in Islam 9th to 18th century', *Bulletin of the New York Academy*, pp. 814–31.

Russell, Sir Thomas, *Egyptian Service, 1902–1946*. London: John Murray, 1949.

Saad el Din and John Cromer, *Under Egypt's Spell: The Influence of Egypt on Writers in English from the Eighteenth Century*. London: Bellew, 1991.

Seth, Ronald, *Russell Pasha*. London: Wm Kimber, 1966.

Iran

Christensen, Janne Bjerre, *Drugs, Deviancy and Democracy in Iran: The Interaction of State and Civil Society*. London: I. B. Tauris, 2011.

Drug Control Headquarters, *Drug Control in 2011*. Tehran, March 2012.

Gheissari, Ali, ed., *Contemporary Iran: Economy, Society, Politics*. Oxford: Oxford University Press, 2009.

Hooglund, Eric and Leif Stenberg, eds., *Navigating Contemporary Iran: Challenging Economic, Social and Political Perceptions*. London: Routledge, 2012.

Keddie, Nikki, *The Roots of Revolution: An Interpretive History of Modern Iran*. New Haven: Yale University Press, 1981.

Navai, Ramita, *City of Lies: Love, Sex, Death and the Search for Truth in Tehran.* London: Weidenfeld & Nicolson, 2014.

Iraq

Kan, Paul Rexton, 'Drugging Babylon: the illegal narcotics trade and nation-building in Iraq', *Small Wars and Insurgencies*, vol. 18, no. 2 (June 2007), pp. 216–30.
Makiya, Kanan, *Cruelty and Silence: War, Tyranny, Uprising and the Arab World.* London: Penguin, 1993.
Metz, Helen Chapin, ed., *Iraq: A Country Study.* Washington DC: Library of Congress, 1990.
Miller, Judith, 'Terrorism, money, and drugs', available at http://w3.newsmax.com/a/jan11/terrorism/, site visited 18 March 2014.

Israel

Amir, Menachem, 'Organised crime in Israel', *Transnational Organised Crime*, vol. 2, no. 4 (Winter 1996), pp. 21–39.
Ginsburg, David and J. L. Kaufman, *Problems of Drug Addiction in Israel.* Geneva: UNODC, 1955.
Lavie, Smadar, *The Poetics of Military Occupation.* Berkeley: University of California Press, 1990.
Miller, Louis, and Stanley Einstein, *Drugs and Society: Contemporary Social Issues.* Jerusalem: Jerusalem Academic Press, 1976.
Shama, Avraham and Mark Iris, *Immigration without Integration.* Cambridge, MA: Schenkman Publishing Co., 1977.
Sharp, Jeremy M., *US Foreign Aid to Israel.* Washington DC: Congressional Research Service, 2012.
Smooha, Sammy, 'Arab–Jewish relations in Israel: a deeply divided society', in Anita Shapira, ed., *Israeli Identity in Transition.* London: Praeger, 2004, pp. 31–67.

Lebanon

Aaraj, Elie, *Assessment of Situation and Response of Drug Use and its Harms [sic] in the Middle East and North Africa.* Beirut: MENAHRA, 2012.
Gambill, Gary, 'Syria after Lebanon: Hooked on Lebanon', *Middle East Quarterly* (Fall 2005), pp. 35–42.
Karam, Elie G., Lillian A. Ghandour, Wadih E. Maalouf, Karim Yamout and Mariana M. Salamoun, 'A rapid situation assessment (RSA) study of alcohol and drug abuse in Lebanon', *J. Med. Liban* 58, 2 (2010), pp. 76–85.
MEED, Special Report Banking, 2 March 2001.
Palmer Harik, Judith, *Hezbollah.* London: I. B. Tauris, 2004.
Randal, Jonathan, *The Tragedy of Lebanon.* London: Hogarth Press, 1990.

UNODC, 'Country Profile: Lebanon', 2007, available at http://www.unodc.org/ egypt/en/country_profile_lebanon.html.

Yaniv, Avner, *Dilemmas of Security*, Oxford: Oxford University Press, 1987.

Morocco

Ashford, Douglas E., *Political Change in Morocco*. Princeton: Princeton University Press, 1961.

El Azizi, Abdellatif, 'Maroc connexion', *Telquel*, no. 257, 20–26 (January 2007).

Elvins, Martin, *Anti-Drugs Policies of the European Union*. Basingstoke: Palgrave, 2003.

Harris, Walter B., *France, Spain and the Rif*. London: Edward Arnold, 1927.

Ketterer, James, 'Networks of discontent in northern Morocco: drugs, opposition and urban unrest', *MERIP* no. 218, vol. 31, no. 1 (Spring 2001), pp. 30–33.

'Morocco: Country Profile, Drugs and Crime', UNODC 2003.

Pennell, C. R., *Morocco*. Oxford: Oneworld, 2003.

Saudi Arabia

Aburish, Said K., *The House of Saud*, London: Bloomsbury, 1994.

Awadh Asseri, Ali S., *Combating Terrorism: Saudi Arabia's Role in the War on Terror*. Oxford: Oxford University Press, 2009.

Menoret, Pascal, *Joyriding in Riyadh: Oil, Urbanism, and Road Revolt*. Cambridge: Cambridge University Press, 2014.

Al-Rasheed, Madawi, *A History of Saudi Arabia*. Cambridge: Cambridge University Press, 2002.

Toumi, Habib, 'Saudi Arabia Building High-Tech Border Fence', *Gulf News*, 22 January 2015.

Wardak, Ali, 'Crime and social control in Saudi Arabia', in James Sheptycki and Ali Wardak, eds., *Transnational and Comparative Criminology*. Abingdon: GlassHouse Press, 2005.

Turkey

Arslan, Savas, *Cinema in Turkey: A New Critical History*. Oxford: Oxford University Press, 2011.

Carlson, Brian G., 'Huseyin Baybasin: Europe's Pablo Escobar', *SAIS Review*, vol. 25, no. 1 (Winter–Spring 2005), pp. 69–70.

Erdinc, Cengiz, *Overdose Turkiye: Turkiye'de Eroin Kacakciligi* [Overdose Turkey: heroin smuggling, addiction and politics in Turkey]. n.p.: Iletisim, 2004.

Gingeras, Ryan, *Heroin, Organised Crime, and the Making of Modern Turkey*. Oxford: Oxford University Press, 2014.

Robins, Philip, 'Public policy making in Turkey: faltering attempts to generate a national drugs policy', *Policy and Politics*, vol. 37, no. 2 (April 2009), pp. 289–306.

——— 'Back from the brink: Turkey's ambivalent approaches to the hard drugs issue', *Middle East Journal*, vol. 62, no. 4 (Autumn 2008), pp. 630–50.

Spain, James W. 'The United States, Turkey and the poppy', *Middle East Journal*, 29 (3) (Summer 1975), pp. 295–309.

Stavrou, Nikolaos A., 'The politics of opium in Turkey', in *Drugs, Politics and Diplomacy: The International Connection*. Beverly Hills and London: Sage, 1974, pp. 214–28.

van Bruinessen, Martin, *Agha, Shaikh and State: The Social and Political Structures of Kurdistan*. London: Zed Books, 1992.

Yemen

Abdul Ghani, N., M. Eriksson, B. Kristiansson and A. Qirbi, 'The influence of khat-chewing on birth-weight in full-term infants', *Society of Scientific Medicine* (1987), pp. 625–627.

Burrowes, Robert D., *The Yemen Arab Republic*. Boulder: Westview/Croom Helm, 1987.

Carapico, Sheila, *Civil Society in Yemen: The Political Economy of Activism in Modern Arabia*. Cambridge: Cambridge University Press, 1998.

Dresch, Paul, *A History of Modern Yemen*. Cambridge: Cambridge University Press, 2000.

——— *Tribes, Government and History in Yemen*. Oxford: Clarendon Press, 1989; Oxford: Clarendon Paperbacks 1993.

Fayein, Claudie, *A French Doctor in the Yemen*. London: Robert Hale Ltd, 1957.

Grima, Franco, *Warriors of Arabia*. Malta: Franco Grima, 2009.

Mundy, Martha, *Domestic Government: Kinship, Community and Polity in North Yemen*. London: I. B. Tauris, 1995.

Peterson, J. E., *Yemen: The Search for a Modern State*. London: Croom Helm, 1982.

Scott, Hugh, *In the High Yemen*. London: John Murray, 1942.

Tutwiler, Richard N., 'Research agenda for sustainable agricultural growth and natural resources management in Yemen', in Kamil A. Mahdi, Anna Wurth and Helen Lackner, eds., *Yemen into the Twenty-First Century*. Reading: Ithaca, 2007, pp. 221–247.

Ward, Christopher, 'Practical responses to extreme groundwater overdraft in Yemen', in Kamil A.Mahdi, Anna Wurth and Helen Lackner, eds., *Yemen into the Twenty-First Century*. Reading: Ithaca, 2007, pp. 155–181.

Weir, Shelagh, 'Economic aspects of the qat industry in north-west Yemen', in B. R. Pridham, ed., *Economy, Society and Culture in Contemporary Yemen*. London: Croom Helm, 1985, pp. 64–82.

——— *Qat in Yemen: Consumption and Social Change*. London: British Museum Press, 1985.

——— *A Tribal Order*. London: British Museum Press, 2007.

INDEX